# Russia, the Soviet Union, and Eastern Europe

# Russia, the Soviet Union,

## and Eastern Europe

*A Survey of Holdings at the*
*Hoover Institution*
*on War, Revolution and Peace*

*edited by* JOSEPH D. DWYER

Hoover Institution Press
Stanford University Stanford, California

Hoover Press Survey 6

© 1980 by the Board of Trustees of the
    Leland Stanford Junior University
All rights reserved
International Standard Book Number: 0-8179-5011-7
Library of Congress Catalog Card Number: 78-70888
Printed in the United States of America

*Designed by Elizabeth Gehman*

*This work is dedicated to the memory of*
WITOLD S. SWORAKOWSKI;
*whose inspiration and years of service to*
*the Hoover Institution and the building of its*
*East European Collection have made this survey possible.*

# CONTENTS

# FOREWORD

The Russian and East European collection at the Hoover Institution is one of the world's greatest scholarly resources. It includes approximately 400,000 books and 6,876 periodical and 1,622 newspaper titles. No survey of these holdings has been published since Prof. Witold Sworakowski produced one on Russia in 1954; no work covering the East European materials has ever been published. It is hoped that this comprehensive description of the entire collection will increase its utility for students interested in Russian and East European political, social, and economic change.

The largest part of the collection deals with Russia and the USSR in general. Important holdings on the Baltic States and the Ukraine also exist. This survey includes materials on other East European countries—Albania, Bulgaria, Czechoslovakia, Hungary, Poland, Romania, and Yugoslavia—as well as one that is not ruled by a communist party, Greece. Materials relating to East Germany are part of the West European collection at the Hoover Institution. Traditionally the Russian and East European curator has been responsible for gathering materials about the international communist movement, and hence, a section of the Russian survey is devoted to that subject. The emphasis of the collection is on the twentieth century or, in the case of the East European countries, from the time of their independence, that is, around the First World War. But background material from the late nineteenth century and, in the case of Russia, from the mid-nineteenth century also forms part of the collection.

In accordance with the Hoover Institution's dedication to the study of war, revolution, and peace, the collection is concerned primarily with history, ideology, politics, and international relations of the various countries. As far as possible, coverage of economics, law, geography, and the humanities has been attempted.

The numerical results (in round numbers) of these collection efforts are as follows:

| Country | Volumes | Periodicals | Newspapers |
|---|---|---|---|
| Albania | 1,200 | 21 | 14 |
| Baltic States | 5,000 | 500 | 100 |
| Bulgaria | 9,000 | 100 | 41 |
| Czechoslovakia | 24,000 | 300 | 150 |
| Greece | 3,000 | 115 | 45 |
| Hungary | 13,000 | 200 | 42 |
| Poland | 35,000 | 1,500 | 270 |
| Romania | 12,000 | 60 | 50 |
| Russia | 263,000 | 3,500 | 650 |
| Ukraine | 6,000 | 230 | 80 |
| Yugoslavia | 18,000 | 350 | 180 |
| TOTALS | 389,200 | 6,876 | 1,622 |

This magnificent accomplishment is due to the work of the many scholars who have directed acquisition efforts. Apart from Professors Frank Golder, E. D. Adams, Ralph H. Lutz, and Harold H. Fisher—who laid the foundations toward the end of and immediately after the First World War—the following individuals have been in charge of the collection: Dimitri Krassovsky (1925–1947), Witold S. Sworakowski (1947–1964), Karol Maichel (1964–1974), Wayne S. Vucinich (1974–1977), Robert G. Wesson (1977–1978), and Joseph D. Dwyer (1978– ).

This publication has been made possible by the dedicated efforts of many staff members and part-time assistants at the Hoover Institution: William Boreysza (Poland), Wendy Bracewell (Albania and Bulgaria), Milorad M. Drachkovitch (Yugoslavia), Adorjan de Galffy and Laszlo Horvath (Hungary), Joseph Kladko (Ukraine), Hilja Kukk (Baltic States and Russia), Karol Maichel (Czechoslovakia), Nicholas Pappas (Albania and Greece), as well as Professors Sworakowski, Vucinich, and Wesson.

This survey of the Russian and East European collection is the final publication in a series that includes *African and Middle East Collections* by Peter Duignan, Karen Fung, George Rentz, and Michel Nabti; *East Asia* by John T. Ma; *International and English-Language Collections* by Kenneth M. Glazier and James R. Hobson; *Latin America* by Joseph W. Bingaman; and *Western Europe* by Agnes F. Peterson. In due course, these will be updated.

RICHARD F. STAAR
Associate Director

# EDITOR'S NOTE

This survey is the result of much background work on the part of present and past staff members of the Hoover East European collection. In addition to those persons mentioned in the Foreword, I would like to thank Rimma Bogert, Cleo Burns, and Amy Desai for their efforts in proofreading, checking, and typing, as well as all others who facilitated this publication.

A survey of the Hoover Institution's rapidly expanding and developing East European collection necessarily becomes out of date almost as soon as it is published. This work is meant to be selectively descriptive and should not in any way be considered all-inclusive or exhaustive. More detailed listings of the contents of the collection may be found in the Hoover printed catalog, *Catalog of Western Languages Collection of the Hoover Institution*, 63v., plus supplements (Boston: G. K. Hall, 1969– ); the new catalog of the archives, *Guide to the Hoover Institution Archives*, by Charles G. Palm and Dale Reed (Stanford: Hoover Institution, 1979); Karol Maichel's *Soviet and Russian Newspapers at the Hoover Institution: A Catalog* (Stanford: Hoover Institution, 1966); and numerous other specialized guides to Hoover holdings in specific subject areas, published mostly by the Hoover Institution Press.

JOSEPH D. DWYER

# ALBANIA

The Albanian Collection, the smallest of the East European collections at the Hoover Institution, contains approximately 1,200 books and pamphlets, as well as 21 periodicals dealing partially with Albanian affairs and fourteen newspapers and journals devoted exclusively to Albania. These figures do not include such publications on international affairs as the 47-volume records of the 1919 Paris Peace Conference, which dealt with Albanian problems among others. Holdings predating 1918 are limited. Pre-1945 holdings consist largely of secondary sources, and only about 20 percent are actually in the Albanian language or of official origin. Most official Albanian publications in the collection date from after 1945.

The relatively weak position of the Albanian holdings may be attributed to several factors. A common Latin alphabet was established for Albania only in 1908, and few American scholars could use Albanian-language material. The pre-1945 history of modern Albania is one of virtually unbroken foreign domination. Thus, the few works published on Albania before 1945 were commonly in Turkish, Greek, Serbian, French, Italian, German, or English. Finally, obtaining publications directly from Albania is still somewhat difficult because of the absence of diplomatic relations and cultural contacts between the United States and Albania. However, all twentieth-century historical events pertaining to Albania are covered in the collection.

Up to 1944, approximately 2,000 books had been published in Albanian or about Albania. Besides standard Western aids on the Balkans and Southeast Europe, bibliographical sources include the national bibliographies of Albania for monographs and serial articles: *Bibliografia Kombëtare e Republikës Popullore të Shqipërisë: Artikujt e periodikut shqip* (Tirana, 1969–1971; 1973) and *Libri shqip* (Tirana, 1969–1971; 1973–).

## THE MOVEMENT FOR INDEPENDENCE, PRE-1912

A number of general histories cover Albania from about 1877, the year of the defeat of Turkey by Russia and the start of the Albanian independence movement. Among the better studies of this period are C. A. Chekrezi's *Albanian Past and Present* (New York, 1919) and the most current American version of Albanian history, S. Skendi's *The Albanian National Awakening, 1878–1912* (Princeton, N.J., 1967). André Simonard's study, *Essai sur l'indépendance albanaise* (Paris, 1942), contains a useful bibliography. For Marxist interpretations of early Albanian history, see I. G. Senkevich's *Albaniû v period vostochnogo krizisa, 1875–1881 gg.* (Moscow, 1965) and his *Osvoboditel 'noe dvizhenie albanskogo naroda v 1905–1912 gg.* (Moscow, 1959).

## WORLD WAR I, 1912–1920

From its inception as an independent state in 1912 to the beginning of the Second World War, Albania experienced constant occupation or changes of political leaders. This variety of rulers makes the multilingual collections on Albania quite important. The period between 1912 and 1920 is covered by such works as:

> Bertotti, Emilio. *La nostra spedizione in Albania, 1915–1916* (Milan, 1926).
>
> Bourcart, Jacques. *L'Albanie et les Albanais* (Paris, 1921). Also useful is G. Collona di Cesaro's work, *L'Italia nella Albania meridionale: Note e documenti, 1917–1918* (Foligno, 1922), which includes some source material. To this can be added J. Godar's *L'Albanie en 1921* and *L'Albanie en 1922* (Paris, 1922), which are descriptions of conditions in Albania by a French observer.
>
> Cami, Muin. *La Lutte anti-impérialiste de libération nationale du peuple albanais, 1918–1920* (Tirana, 1973).
>
> Chung, Il-Yung. *Legal Problems Involved in the Corfu Channel Incident* (Geneva, 1959).
>
> Ferrero, Giacinto. *L'opera dei soldati italiani in Albania durante la guerra* (Florence, 1912).
>
> Giannini, Amedeo. *La formazione dell'Albania* (Rome, 1930).
>
> Mousset, Albert. *L'Albanie devant l'Europe, 1912–1929* (Paris, 1930).
>
> Peacock, Wadham. *Albania, the Foundling State of Europe* (London and New York, 1914).
>
> Stickney, Edith P. *Southern Albania or Northern Epirus in European International Affairs, 1912–1923* (Stanford, 1926).

Also to this period belong the documentary materials from the Paris Peace Conference. Memorials from representatives of the Albanian government include:

Paris. Peace Conference, 1919. Albania. *Exposé des revendications albanaises devant le Conseil des Dix* (Paris (?), 1919).

————. ————. ————. *Mémoire sur l'Albanie du Nord* (Paris (?), 1919).

————. ————. ————. *Notes additionelles relatives aux revendications albanaises* (Paris (?), 1919).

————. ————. ————. *Revendications de l'Albanie* (n.p., 1919).

To this period also belongs the publication by the Comité Unis des Albanais Irredents, *Les Droits de l'Albanie a ses frontières naturelles: Appel aux nations du monde civilisé* (Valona, 1921).

## THE INTERWAR PERIOD, 1920–1939

After three years of parliamentary instability, followed in 1924 by revolution and the countercoup of Ahmad Zogu, Albania was proclaimed a republic in 1925. Zogu made himself president and in 1928 took the title of King Zog. Besides the general histories mentioned above, the Institution possesses two Albanian works published by the communist government after 1945: Veizi, Fane. *Kongresi i Lushnjës* (Tirana, 1959), an account of the Albanian National Congress held in Lushnjë in 1920; and Moisiu, Vangjel. *Lufta për krijimin e Partisë Komuniste të Shqipërisë, 1917 –1941* (Tirana, 1957), a brief history of the origins of the Albanian Communist Party. It, along with Stilian Adhami's *Kronike e levizjes punëtore e sindikale në Shqipëri* (Tirana, 1969), covers the influence of the October Revolution in Russia on the Albanian revolutionary movement, socioeconomic conditions under King Zog, the Albanian labor movement, and the formation of the first communist groups in Albania. A. Calmes's study, *Rapport sur la situation économique et financière de l'Albanie* (Geneva, 1922) covers the period before 1921.

Among the small collection of Western European sources, one of the most important is Gustavo Traglia's *L'Albania di re Zog* (Rome, 1930), still the most detailed study of the subject. Amedeo Giannini's *L'Albania dall'independenza all'unione con l'Italia, 1913–1939* (Milan, 1940) is a short diplomatic history of Albania especially useful for its inclusion of numerous documents. Antonio Baldacci's *Studi speciali albanesi* 3v. (Rome, 1932–1933, 1938) contains historical, political, diplomatic, economic, and geographical descriptions of Albania, as does Roberto Almagia's historical study, *L'Albania* (Rome, 1930). Stavro Skendi's *The Political Evolution of Albania, 1912–1944* (New

York, 1959) reviews political developments in Albania from independence to the end of World War II. This period is probably best described in English by Joseph Swire in his *Albania: The Rise of a Kingdom* (London, 1929) and his *King Zog's Albania* (London, 1937). Another important work is the Federal Writers Project's *The Albanian Struggle in the Old World and the New* (Boston, 1939). The most detailed and scholarly study of Albania between 1918 and 1939 is Richard Busch-Zanter's *Albanien, neues Land im Imperium* (Leipzig, 1939). A more specialized work is Leon Maccas's *La Question gréco-albanaise* (Paris, 1921).

Unable to survive without outside assistance, Albania entered into close relations with Italy. The Hoover Institution holds various editions of bilateral treaties concerning these arrangements.

Of pre-1945 official documentary materials, the most important for research are the circulars of the Ministry of the Interior for the years 1920–1921, *Qarkaret e. Min. së P. të Mbrendshme të vjetit*, 2v. (Skutari, 1922). Other governmental publications containing economic data include:

> Albania. Laws, Statutes, etc. Ministry of Finance. Department of Customs. *Tarifa e tagrave doganore e shtetit shqypëtar* (Tirana, 1922).
>
> ———. Ministry of Finance. General Accountability Department. *Statistika doganore mbi importation-exportation* (Tirana, 1923).
>
> ———. Laws, Statutes, etc. *Ligja e tarifa doganore e shtetit shqypëtar* (Tirana, 1923), published by the Ministry of Justice.
>
> ———. Ministry of Interior. *Statistike mbi mënyrëu e sistemet industriale, tregtare e levizjet e popullit dhe sistemi ushtrues i zyrave të ndryshme qeveritare* (Tirana, 1923).

The collection also has works on laws and regulations pertaining to the army.

## WORLD WAR II

On April 7, 1939, Italian armies under Mussolini occupied Albania and held it until 1943. This period is described from the Italian point of view in the publications *Albania fascista* (Florence, 1940) and *Legislazione fascista e del lavoro in Albania* (Naples, 1942). The fascist regime was followed by the nazi occupation, 1943–1944. The period of the Second World War, with its communist-led guerrilla movement under Enver Hoxha, is described in numerous studies in various languages: *La Participation de l'Albanie à la guerre mondiale, 1939–1945* (Tirana, 1946) and *La Lutte antifasciste de libération nationale du peuple albanaise: Documents principaux, 1941–1944* (Tirana, 1975), which consist of many documents and texts, are complimented by such Italian works as Franco Benati's *La guerra più lunga: Albania, 1943–1948* (Milan, 1966) and Francesco Jacomoni di San Savino's *La politica dell'Italia in Albania nelle testi-*

*montianze del luoghotenente* (Cappelli, 1965). The Soviet viewpoint can be found in Nina Smirnova's *Obrazovanie Narodnoǐ Respubliki Albanii, 1939−1946* (Moscow, 1960). An important multiauthor work in Albanian, *Konferenca Kombëtare e Studimeve për Luften Antifashiste Nacionalçlirimtare të popullit shqiptar* (Tirana, 1975) was acquired recently. An abridged English version is also available: *The National Conference of Studies on the Anti-Fascist National-Liberation War of the Albanian People* (Tirana, 1975).

Yugoslav-Albanian relations during the war are summarized from the Yugoslav point of view in two books by Vladimir Dedijer: *Jugoslovensko-albanski odnosi, 1939−1948* (Belgrade, 1949) and *Il sangue tradito: Relazioni jugoslavo-albanesi 1938−49. Documenti ufficiali, lettere, fotografie, memoriali, coordinati ed elaborati* (Varese, 1949). Brief analyses of Serbian-Albanian relations are contained in D. Tucović's *Srbija, Albanija: Jedan prilog kratici zavojevačke politike srpske buržoazije* (Belgrade and Zagreb, 1946). An extensive Serbian émigré study on the same topic is Djoko Slijepcević's *Srpsko-Albanski odnosi kroz vekove sa posebnim osvrtom na novije vreme* (Munich, 1974).

Greco-Albanian relations during and after World War II are discussed in such works as *The Resistance Movement of the Northern Epirotes, 1941−1945* (Athens, 1947) and Pyrrhus Ruches's *Albania's Captives* (Chicago, 1965).

English studies include Edmond F. Davies's *Illyrian Venture: The Story of the British Military Mission to Enemy-Occupied Albania, 1943−1944* (London, 1952). The Hoover Institution also possesses an incomplete set of the journal *Mundimi*, which was dropped by Allied forces into Albania during World War II. (It was written in Albanian with an English translation.) Most of the leaflets are from 1944. An Albanian critique of British wartime policy toward Albania, Arben Puto's *Neper analet et diplomacise angleze* (Tirana, 1976), was recently added to the Hoover Institution collection.


## ALBANIA UNDER COMMUNIST RULE


Documentation from 1945 to the present far exceeds that of earlier periods. The Albanian government, recognizing the relatively low level of knowledge of Albania in other countries, has started printing books not only in Albanian, but also in Russian, English, Italian, French, and German. In addition, many Albanian-language publications have been issued in Yugoslavia, primarily in Priština. Although the Hoover Institution has a number of publications in the original Albanian, it has tried, whenever possible, to secure Western-language editions of a particular publication. General works in English dealing with this period of Albanian history include Nicholas C. Pano's *The People's Republic of Albania* (Baltimore, 1968), Ramadan Marmullaku's *Albania and the Albanians*

(London, 1975), and Anton Logoreci's *The Albanians, Europe's Forgotten Survivors* (London, 1977).

The transition to communism is described in a study by Jani I. Dilo, *The Communist Party Leadership in Albania* (Washington, D.C., 1961), and in a book by Glenn A. McLain, *Albanian Exposé: Communism Versus Liberalism for Albania* (Quincy, Mass., 1952), both strongly anticommunist, and in Skendi's *Albania* (New York, 1957). The Soviet viewpoint can be found in Petr Manchkha's work, *Albaniia na puti k sotsializmu* (Moscow, 1951).

Communist infighting, which led to a purge of pro-Yugoslav party members, is documented by Vladimir Dedijer, then a member of the Yugoslav cabinet, in his *Jugoslovensko-albanski odnosi* (Belgrade, 1949) and in his *Il sangue tradito* (see above).

Material on the Albanian constitution and legislative acts can be found in the Soviet publications *Konstitutsiia i osnovnye zakonodatel'nye akty Narodnoi Respubliki Albanii* (Moscow, 1951), *Konstitutsii evropeiskikh stran narodnoi demokratii* (Moscow, 1954), and *Konstitutsii zarubezhnykh sotsialisticheskikh gospodarstv* (Moscow, 1956) and in the Polish publication *Nowe konstytucje państw europejskich* (Warsaw, 1949). Laws, statutes, and land tenure are covered in *Narodnaia Respublika Albaniia* (Moscow, 1958) and *Narodnaia Respublika Albaniia: Tekst zakonov, perevel s albanskogo iazyka* (Moscow, 1961). In addition, copies of the constitution of the People's Republic of Albania are available in the Hoover collection in Albanian and English, as are commentaries in Albanian, for examples, *Konferenca shkencore për probleme të kushtetutes* (Tirana, 1976).

Weaknesses in the Institution's collection of Albanian official publications are partly compensated for by strong Communist party holdings. Party directives are published in the main organ of the Albanian Party of Labor, the monthly *Rruga e partisë*, issued since 1954. The Institution's holdings are incomplete, however. An important source for party decrees and correspondence is Tirana. Instituti i Studimeve Marksiste-Leniniste. *Dokumenta kryesore të Partisë së Punës të Shqipërisë*, 5v. (Tirana, 1960–1974), a collection of party documents from 1941 to 1970.

Laws passed by the People's Assembly are published in Albania. Constitution. *Kodifikimi i pergjitheshem i legjislacionit në fuqi të Republikës Popullore të Shqipërisë* (Tirana, 1958–). The first three volumes, published in 1958, contain the laws enacted between 1947 and 1957. Supplements are published annually. The Institution has the three basic volumes and the 1958 annual supplement. Albanian constitutional law is included in the Soviet publication, *Gosudarstvennoe pravo stran narodnoi demokratii* (Moscow, 1949). An interesting study of mountain law in northern Albania is Margaret M. Hasluck's study, *The Unwritten Law in Albania* (Cambridge, Eng., 1954).

The basic statistical source is the *Anuari statistikor i R.P.Sh.* (published in

Tirana under the title *Vjetari statistikor i Republikës Popullore të Shqipërisë* since 1965), an annual compilation first published in 1958, containing data on many aspects of the economy and society: territorial divisions, population, industry, agriculture, and education. The Albanian economy is also covered in three other works: Shpati, Ramazan. *Les Aspects de l'économie albanese* (Etienne, 1945), which has a useful bibliography; Silaev, A. *Albaniîa: Ekonomiko-geograficheskaîa kharakteristika* (Moscow, 1953); and Bardhosi, Besim. *The Economic and Social Development of the People's Republic of Albania* (Tirana, 1975).

## COMMUNIST PARTY HISTORY

The Hoover Institution has a good collection of the writings of First Secretary Enver Hoxha, including the multivolume collection of his works to date (*Vepra*). Books on Communist party history in languages other than Albanian include *Albanskiĭ narod za mir i sotsializm* (Moscow, 1956), *Report on the Role and Tasks of the Democratic Front for the Complete Triumph of Socialism in Albania submitted at the 4th Congress of the Democratic Front of Albania September 14, 1967* (Tirana, 1967), and Hoxha, Enver. *Selected Works I* (Tirana, 1974).

The work of Vangjel Moisiu (cited above), *Lufta e krijimin e Partisë Kommuniste të Shqipërisë, 1917–1941*, also contains material on this subject. A pamphlet by Ndreci Plasari, *Krijimi i Partisë Komuniste të Shqipërisë, 1939–1941*, gives a brief history of certain organizations of the Communist party in Albania during the Italian occupation and discusses strategy and tactics in the National Liberation War.

The standard history of the Albanian Party of Labor is given in *Historia e Partisë së Punës të Shqipërisë* (Tirana, 1968). The previously mentioned five-volume collection, *Dokumenta kryesore të Partisë së Punës të Shqipërisë*, contains documents and other material relating to the history of this movement between 1941 and 1970. V. Dedi's *Dokumenta e materiale historike nga lufta e popullit shqiptar për liri e demokraci, 1917–1941* (Tirana, 1959) is a selective collection of 574 documents and papers, for the most part in Albanian. An English edition of the official party history, *History of the Albanian Party of Labor* (Tirana, 1971), is also available. These works were published by the Historical Institute of the Albanian Party of Labor.

The position of Albania in the Sino-Soviet split has concerned scholars in recent years, and the Hoover Institution has a good collection of studies on this problem, including:

Griffith, William. *Albania and the Sino-Soviet Rift* (Cambridge, Mass., 1963).

Tang, Peter S. *The Twenty-Second Congress of the Communist Party of* the *Soviet Union and Moscow-Tirana-Peking Relations* (Washington, D.C., 1962).

Prifti, Peter. *Albania Since the Fall of Khrushchev* (Cambridge, Mass., 1970).

Hamm, Harry. *Rebellion gegen Moskau: Albanien-Pekings Brückenkopf in Europa* (Cologne, 1962).

Dodić, Lazar. *Historischer Rückblick auf die Stellung Albaniens in Welt-kommunismus, 1941–1968* (Trittau, Ger., 1970).

Kessel, Patrick. *Les Communistes albanaise contre le revisionnisme: De Tito à Khrouchtchev, 1942–1961* (Paris, 1974).

In addition, the Hoover Library possesses a sizable pamphlet file of Albanian propaganda in several languages on this subject.

On intraparty struggles and other trials and purges, little has been released from Albania. For one early purge, the Hoover does have stenographic records: Albania. Ministry of Justice. *Le Procès des éspions/Item Cako, Llukman Lutfiu, et Kasem Zhupa: Parachutés en Albanie. Compte rendu sténographique des débats du procès de Tirana, 24 mai–6 juin 1950, devant la Haute Cour Militaire de la République Populaire d'Albanie* (Paris, 1950).

Reports on the congresses of the Communist Party of Albania are represented in the Institution beginning with the Third Congress in 1956. Most are Russian, Polish, or English translations—sometimes all three languages.

The Institution holds a complete file on microfilm of the Albanian Party of Labor's daily organ, *Zëri i popullit*, as well as copies of the original since 1962. Holdings of the party monthly, *Rruga e partisë*, both originals and on microfilm, date from 1969. The Hoover Institution also receives three other Albanian newspapers published in Tirana: *Bashkimi*, the daily organ of the Democratic Front, with issues on file from 1948 to the present; *Puna*, biweekly publication of the Albanian Trade Unions, with issues from 1969 to 1973; and *Zëri i rinisë*, biweekly organ of the Union of Albanian Labor Youth, from 1968 to the present; as well as the official gazette, *Gazeta zyrtare*. These publications are supplemented by one Western-language Albanian periodical, *Albania Today*. In addition to these official Albanian periodicals, the Hoover Institution receives two émigré periodicals: *Albanian Resistance*, published irregularly in French, English, and Albanian in Paris by the National Democratic Committee for a Free Albania; and *Flamuri*, published monthly in Rome by the Albanian Agrarian Democratic Party "Balli Kombëtar," with articles in Albanian, English, French, and Italian. The Hoover Institution also holds issues for 1918–1919 of *L'Albanie* (Lausanne); *Adriatic Review* (Boston), for 1918–1919, with articles in Albanian and English; one issue (1954) of *Shqiperia* (New York), published by the National Committee of Free Albania; issues from 1970 to the present of *Albania Report* (New York), published by the Albanian Affairs Studies Group; and issues from 1966 of *Radio Free Europe: Albanian Monitoring*.

# BALTIC STATES

The foundation of the Baltic Collection was laid in the 1920s by Professors Frank A. Golder and Harold H. Fisher of the Stanford University Department of History while they were in the Baltic States as representatives of the American Relief Administration. In the 1930s, valuable materials, notably government documents from Estonia and Latvia, were added to the collection through the earlier exchanges set up by these professors with the universities of Riga and Tartu. Later, Prof. Malbone W. Graham of the University of California at Los Angeles added considerably to the collection by depositing his papers with the archives. In more recent years, the efforts of the Hoover Institution's late associate director, Witold S. Sworakowski, and Prof. Edgar Anderson of San Jose State University are noteworthy. Professor Sworakowski, formerly a Polish diplomat stationed in the Baltic States, knew many exiled Baltic statesmen and secured several important archival collections from them. Professor Anderson has made available for microfilming numerous rare Latvian and Lithuanian publications and has been influential in securing Latvian archival materials. The Baltic Collection now includes 5,000 volumes, some 500 periodicals, and 100 newspapers.

At present, relevant materials in the principal Western languages, particularly English, are added to the collection. Official publications from the three Baltic republics in the USSR are also currently received. The library still has a small residue of retrospective uncatalogued material in Baltic languages (available to users on request through the reference librarians). Although this survey lists only a small number of representative materials in the Hoover Library's Baltic Collection, a comprehensive view of the library's holdings can be gained from the Hoover Institution's card catalog or its printed equivalent: Stanford University. Hoover Institution. *Catalog of the Western Language Collections,* 63v. (Boston: G. K. Hall, 1969).

Baltic materials at the Hoover Institution may be divided into six categories: pre−World War I, World War I and the struggle for independence, independence, World War II, post−World War II period, and reference tools.

## PRE—WORLD WAR I

Coverage of the period preceding World War I is sparse for all three countries. The major share of holdings have been transferred from the Hoover Institution to the Stanford University Library (Green Library). This material, mainly in German, covers pre—twentieth-century history, archeology, commerce, economic conditions, navigation, and a few other subjects. There are a few serials, such as the publications of universities and learned societies, but the holdings are incomplete. The Hoover Institution has the records of the first general census of the population in the Baltic provinces in 1897: Russia. Tsentral'nyĭ Statisticheskiĭ Komitet. *Pervaiȃ vseobshchaiȃ perepis' naseleniiȃ Rossiĭskoĭ Imperii 1897 g.: v. 17, Kovenskaiȃ guberniiȃ; v. 21, Liflȃndskaiȃ guberniiȃ; v. 49, Estlȃndskaiȃ guberniiȃ.* The material classified under "Russia—History—Revolution of 1905" in both libraries contains considerable information about revolutionary movements in the Baltic provinces. Documentation on Latvian socialist revolutionaries dates from the end of the nineteenth century. A primary source on this subject is the *Okhrana Archive (1883—1919),* which contains documents about early revolutionary activity in all three Baltic provinces, particularly Latvia.

## WORLD WAR I
## AND THE STRUGGLE FOR INDEPENDENCE

For the next period, World War I and the struggle for independence, the material is more diverse. The library has the official gazettes of the German occupation of Estonia, Latvia, and Lithuania: *Verordnungsblatt für Livland und Estland* (Tartu, 1917—1918), *Verordnungsblatt der Provinzialverwaltung Livland* (Riga, October-November 1918), *Verordnungsblatt der deutschen Verwaltung für Kurland* (Mitau, December 28, 1915—February 21, 1916), and *Verordnungsblatt für die baltischen Länder* (Riga, September-November 1918). Only a few issues of the extremely rare official bulletin of the Latvian Socialist Republic, 1918—1919, *Latwijas sozialistiskas padomju waldibas sinotaja* (Riga, February 20—May 19, 1919), are missing from the collection. (This bulletin was printed in both Latvian and Russian.) The Institution also holds a collection of decrees issued by this government pertaining to sabotage, profiteering, and other subjects. Other rare items in the collection are the files of the first issues of the Lithuanian newspaper *Lietuvos Aidas* (Vilnius, 1917—1918) and the organ of the Central Committee of the Latvian Communist Party, *Die Rote Fahne* (Riga, January-May 22, 1919). There are a few German-language newspapers from Latvia and Lithuania, *Rigaer Tageblatt* (1914—1915), *Rigasche Zeitung* (1915—

1919), and *Die neue Zeit* (Kaunas, 1918–1919), and the Lithuanian-language newspaper *Dabartis* (Tilže, 1915–1918).
Of the historical monographs, the following works are useful:

Alisauskas, Kazys. *Kovos dėl Lietuvos nepriklausomybės, 1918–1920* (Chicago, 1972).
Anderson, Edgar. *Latvijas vēsture, 1914–1920* (Stockholm, 1967).
Bilmanis, Alfreds. *Latvia as an Independent State* (Washington, D.C., 1947).
Ezergailis, Andrew. *The 1917 Revolt in Latvia* (New York, 1974).
Ģērmanis, Uldis. *Oberst Vācietis und die lettischen Schützen im Weltkrieg und in der Oktoberrevolution* (Stockholm, 1974).
Graham, Malbone. *The Diplomatic Recognition of the Border States*, 3v. (Berkeley, 1935–1941).
Hehn, Jürgen von. *Von den baltischen Provinzen zu den baltischen Staaten* (Marburg, 1971).
*Istoriĩā latyshskikh strelkov, 1915–1920* (Riga, 1972).
Laaman, Eduard. *Eesti iseseisvuse sünd* (Tartu, 1936).
*Lietuvos kariuomenė: Išleido Sąjunga ginkluotomas krašto pajėjoms remti* (Kaunas, 1938).
Oiderman, M. "Estonian Independence," manuscript (covering the period of the Russian revolution and the establishment of an independent Estonia, 1917–1921).
Pitka, Johannes. *Minu mälestused suure ilmasõja algusest Eesti vabadussõja lõpuni* (Tallinn, 1921).
Senn, Alfred E. *The Emergence of Modern Lithuania* (New York, 1959).

Several archival collections contain materials on this period: the Joseph J. Hertmanowicz Collection (1916–1941), the Felikss Cielēns papers (1931–1945), the Wisłowski Collection (1914–1919), and the papers of Aleksander Keskül (1915–1963), an Estonian revolutionary who served as an intermediary between Lenin and the Germans during World War I. His file is not extensive, but it contains material about him and his exile activities. The archives of Gen. Nikolai N. Yudenich and his chief of staff, Gen. Boris V. Heroys, both contain documents on the political and military situation in Estonia and Latvia in 1919–1920. The unpublished memoirs of Oskars Ozels, a Latvian eyewitness, describe his experiences in Riga during Count Bermondt-Avalov's campaign in October and November 1919. The archive of Michel de Giers, a career diplomat in the imperial Russian government, contains documents on Estonia, Latvia, and Lithuania, 1919–1926. The records of the Baltic commissions and committees at the Paris Peace Conference, 1919–1920, are included in the rare unpublished document collection of the conference, *Recueil des actes de la conférence*, 8v. (Paris, 1922–1934), and in David Hunter Miller's *My Diary at the Conference in Paris*, 21v. (New York, 1924), with additional documents and correspondence on the subject in the archive of Ambassador Kaarel R. Pusta, 1918–1964 (see below). Documents on the admission of the Baltic States into the League of Nations, as well as information about economic conditions, banking and currency reform, state loans, armaments, public health, taxation, and border disputes in the newly founded Baltic States, can be found in the League's *Official Journal* and in document collections. The archives of Nicolai Koestner, Estonian consul in New York, and Anton Piip, Estonian statesman, contain memorandums relating to diplomatic recognition and admission of Estonia to the League of Nations.

## INDEPENDENCE

The coverage of the third period, that of independence, is excellent. Government documents, especially from Estonia and Latvia, are well represented and include the constitutions, laws and statutes, parliamentary debates, treaties, statistical studies, reports by ministries, and budgets. The most noteworthy are the minutes of the Estonian Constituent Assembly and the State Assembly: *Asutava Kogu protokollid* (Tallinn, 1919–1920), *Riigikogu protokollid* (Tallinn, 1921–1929), and *Riigikogu täielikud protokollid* (Tallinn, 1928–1934); the minutes of the Latvian Constituent Assembly: *Latwijas satwersmes sapulzes: Stenogramas, 1920–1922*; the Latvian government's rare official newspaper, *Valdibas vēstnesis* (Riga, 1920–1923, 1936–1939); the acts of the Lithuanian Constitutent Assembly: *Steigiamojo seimo darbai* (Kaunas, 1920–1922); and the minutes of the Lithuanian parliament: *Seimo stenogramas* (Kaunas, 1922–1925). Although serial holdings for this period are limited, the library has a few valuable titles, including a nearly complete set of *Bulletin de l'Esthonie* (Paris, 1919–1923). The file of the *Baltic Times* (Tallinn) covers the years 1938–1940 only, and the file of the *Riga Times* from March 7–April 25, 1925. There are no holdings of daily newspapers. The German government maintained a press-summaries service treating the larger daily papers in the three Baltic countries. The Hoover Library's collection of the summaries, classified as Germany. Publikationstelle. Berlin-Dahlem. *Presseauszüge*, covers the years 1934–1941. The summaries deal with a wide range of topics and serve as substitutes for the newspapers.

The monographs of this period include works by (and about) the national leaders and historians of Baltic and non-Baltic origin. Especially noteworthy are the following:

> Anderson, Edgar. *Die militärische Situation der baltischen Staaten* (Königstein, Ger., 1969).
> Bilmanis, Alfreds. *A History of Latvia* (Princeton, N.J., 1951).

Cielēns, Felikss. *Laikmetu maiņā* (Lidingö, Sweden, 1961–1963).

Dunsdorfs, Edgars. *Kārļa Ulmana dzīve: Celinieks, polītiķis, diktātors, moceklis* (Tumba, Sweden, 1978).

Hellman, Manfred. *Grundzüge der Geschichte Litauens und des litauischen Volkes* (Darmstadt, Ger., 1966).

Ojamaa, M. *Eesti ajalugu* (Stockholm, 1946).

Pusta, Kaarel. *Saadiku päevik* (Geislingen, Ger., 1964).

Pusta, Kaarel. *Kehra metsast maailma: Mälestusi* (Stockholm, 1960).

Rastikis, Stasys. *Kovose dėl Lietuvos,* 2v. (Los Angeles, 1956–1957).

Rauch, Georg von. *The Baltic States: The Years of Independence. Estonia, Latvia, Lithuania, 1917–1940* (Berkeley, 1974).

Rodgers, Hugh. *Search for Security: A study of Baltic Diplomacy, 1920–1934* (Hamden, Conn., 1975).

Sabaliunas, Leonas. *Lithuania in Crisis: Nationalism to Communism, 1939–1940* (Bloomington, Ind., 1972).

Uustalu, Evald. *The History of the Estonian People* (London, 1952).

The records of the American Red Cross Commission, 1919–1921, and the American Relief Administration to the Baltic States, 1920–1922, illuminate the economic, cultural, and political life of the three new republics. The diary of Thomas Orbison, chief of Latvian mission, 1919–1920, is part of the American Relief Administration archive. The archive of Kaarel R. Pusta, Estonian diplomat and statesman, covers the period 1918–1964 and includes a wealth of material that he collected throughout his career. Unfortunately, the archive is not yet indexed, but it can be used with the aid of its inventory list. The documents in the archive of the Latvian embassy in Stockholm cover the years 1917–1939. The papers of three Latvian statesmen and diplomats, Alfreds Berziņš, Jules Feldmans, and Mikelis Valters, contain material from 1918 to 1976. The manuscript of Berziņš's unpublished memoirs, 1934–1940, is one of two surviving copies. Noteworthy in the Valters's file are copies of secret dispatches to Gen. Jānis Balodis, Latvian deputy prime minister and minister of war, 1918–1940, and the minutes and records of the First and Second Conferences of Latvian Envoys Abroad, at Riga in 1923 and 1935. The correspondence, memorandums, photographs, and other materials in the file of Eduardas Turauskas, Lithuanian diplomat, journalist, and statesman, cover the years 1934–1958. His materials also include documents concerning the Soviet occupation of Lithuania in 1940–1941. The Jules Feldmans file includes data on the Russian occupation of the Baltic States in 1940. The diary of Frederick W. B. Coleman, American ambassador to the Baltic States, 1922–1931, contains short entries concerning his activities, particularly in Riga. A collection of photo enlargements from microfilms of the German Foreign Ministry deals primarily with Lithuanian affairs, but has references to Estonia and Latvia as well. The file covers the years 1920–1945 and includes information about relations between

Germany and the Baltic States and between the Soviet Union and the Baltic States toward the end of their independence.

## WORLD WAR II

A primary source of information about the World War II period is the microfilm collection of captured German documents. The documents are described in printed guides. Two sets are concerned with the Baltic States: the files of the offices of Reichskommisar für das Ostland and Reichsministerium für die besetzten Ostgebiete. These documents contain statistical data, economic legislation, and administrative directives. The library also has the official bulletins of the occupation governments, *Amtsblatt des Generalkommisars in Reval*, 1942–1943, and *Amtsblatt des Generalkommissars in Riga*, 1942–1943, as well as the semiofficial monthly journal *Ostland*, 1943–1944, published in Riga. The rarest items from this period are fifteen Lithuanian underground serials that appeared from 1940 to 1945: *Apžvalga* (1943–1944); *Atžalynas* (1943); *Frontas* (1943); *Kovojas lietuvis* (1943); *Į laisvė* (1943–1944); *Laisvas žodis* (1944); *Laisvės kovotojas* (1942–1944); *Lietuva* (1943); *Lietuvos kelias* (1944); *Lietuvos kovotojų frontas* (1943); *Lietuvos kovotojų sąjunga* (1943); *Lietuvos laisvės trimitas* (1943); *Nepriklausoma Lietuva* (1943–1944); *Progrindžio kuntaplis* (1944); and *Vieninga kova* (1943–1944).

Newsletters of consulates and various committees and publications of learned societies and individual authors constitute the basic collection. The holdings include very few serials, mainly those published by the Baltic legations and national councils, many of which were started in refugee camps. Among others, the Hoover Library has the *Latvian Information Bulletin* (Washington, D.C., 1937–) and the *Lithuanian Bulletin* (New York, 1943–1951).

The following monographs are noteworthy:

> *Eesti riik ja rahvas Teises Maailmasõjas*, 10v. (Stockholm, 1954–1957).
> Kaslas, Bronis. *The USSR-German Aggression Against Lithuania* (New York, 1973).
> Myllyniemi, Seppo. *Die Neuordnung der baltischen Länder, 1941–1944* (Helsinki, 1973).
> Oras, Ants. *Baltic Eclipse* (London, 1948).

See also the general histories mentioned in the preceding sections.

The extensive archive of the Latvian Central Committee covers the years 1918–1948. The Hoover Institution also has the archive of the Latvian Legion (1941–1945) and the papers of Jone Deveike, a Lithuanian historian and journalist (1930–1963); Jānis Lejiņš, a leader of the Latvian Agrarian party (1943–1971); Ona Šimaitė, a Lithuanian journalist (1941–1944); and Eduards

Kraucs, a Latvian-American photographer and television cameraman (1943–1977). All contain documents relating to the World War II period.

## POST–WORLD WAR II

The post–World War II period is represented by official materials received from the three Soviet republics, Western publications, and the underground documents (''samizdat'') from the Soviet Union.

Through purchase and exchange, the library receives the official publications of the governments and the Communist parties of the three republics, including stenographic reports of party congresses, proceedings of the republics' supreme soviets, statistical yearbooks, law codes, constitutions, and economic studies. The library subscribes to the official journals of the governments: *Kommunist Estonii* (Tallinn, 1957–); *Kommunist Sovetskoĭ Latvii* (Riga, 1956–); and *Kommunist: Zhurnal Tsentral' nogo Komiteta Kommunisticheskoĭ Partii Litvy* (Vilnius, 1947– with some issues missing). Publications of the academies of science relevant to Hoover Library's collection are also received. Historical works are emphasized; the following general histories are particularly useful: Eesti NSV Teaduste Akadeemia. Ajaloo Institut. *Istoriiâ Estonskoĭ SSR*, 3v. (Tallinn, 1961–1974); Latvijas Padomju Socialistikās Republikas Zinātņu Akademija. Vēstures Instituts. *Istoriiâ Latviĭskoĭ SSR* (Riga, 1971); and Lietuvos TSR Mokslų Akademija. Istorijos Institutas. *Lietuvos TSR istorija. 3. tomas: Nuo 1914 iki 1940 metų* (Vilnius, 1965). The Estonian cultural weekly *Sirp ja vasar* (Tallinn) has been received as a gift since 1970.

Western-language publications include monographs by individual authors and monographs and serials by Baltic professional societies, scientific institutions, and universities. The library has the quarterly journal of the Association for the Advancement of Baltic Studies (New York, 1970–); the summaries of proceedings of the conferences of the same association (1968–), and those of its serial publications within the scope of the Hoover Institution's collection. Others include the annual *Acta Baltica* (1960–) from the Institutum Balticum at Königstein-in-Taunus, Germany; *Latvian Information Bulletin* (Washington, D.C., 1937–1974 and 1976–); *Baltic Events* (Irvine, Calif., 1967–1975); *Eesti Hääl* (London, 1947–); and the bulletin, *ELTA Information Service* (New York 1956, 1965–).

The following monographs are noteworthy:

> *Eesti saatusaastad, 1945–1960*, 6v. (Stockholm, 1963–72).
> Dunsdorfs, Edgars. *The Baltic Dilemma: The Case of the De Jure Recognition by Australia of the Incorporation of the Baltic States into the Soviet Union* (New York, 1975).
> King, Gundar J. *Economic Policies in Occupied Latvia* (Tacoma, Wash., 1965).

Lejiņš, Jānis. *Mana dzimtene* (Västerås, Sweden, 1971).
Manning, Clarence A. *The Forgotten Republics* (New York, 1952).
Rei, August. *The Drama of the Baltic Peoples* (Stockholm, 1970).
Vardys, Vytas S. *Lithuania Under the Soviets* (New York, 1965).

The Hoover Institution is a depository for Soviet underground publications (samizdat), which began circulating in the free world in 1968 during the Moscow dissident trials. Links were established with the dissidents of the various nationalities, and by 1970 the samizdat publications network extended into the Baltic republics. These documents, first collected and distributed by Radio Liberty and presently by the Samizdat Archive Association, include information about civil rights and other opposition movements. The documents consist of letters and petitions to Soviet and Western government officials, trial reports, programs and statements of the various democratic movements, forbidden literary works, and other materials. Religious dissent, especially in Lithuania and Latvia, is well represented. There are a number of underground serials from Lithuania, beginning in the mid-1970s, of which the following titles are in the Hoover Library: *Alma mater* (1979−); *Aušra* (1975−); *Aušrelė* (1978−); *Dievas ir tėvynė* (1976−); *Lietuvos Katalikų Bažnyčios Kronika* (1975−); *Tiesos kelias* (1977−); and *Varpas* (n.d.). The library also holds an interesting hand-typed serial from Tartu, Estonia, *Poolpäevaleht* (1978). This journal claimed to be a dissident publication when published. In fact, however, it was a Soviet police decoy aimed at entrapping would-be dissidents.


## REFERENCE TOOLS

Bibliographies and encyclopedias form the nucleus of the reference collection. Readers will find the following bibliographies particularly useful:

Aav, Yrjö. *Estonian Periodicals and Books in Finnish Libraries,* 2v. (Zug, Switz., 1970).
*Baltic Material in the University of Toronto Library* (Toronto, 1972).
Balys, Jonas. *Lithuania and Lithuanians: A Selected Bibliography* (New York, 1961).
Ekmanis, Rolfs. *Latvian Literature Under the Soviets, 1940−1975* (Belmont, Mass., 1978).
Hanover. Niedersachsische Landesbibliothek. *Katalog des Schrifttums über die baltischen Länder* (Hanover, 1971).
Harvard University. Library. *Finnish and Baltic History and Literatures* (Cambridge, Mass., 1972).
Jēgers, Benjamiņš. *Latviešu trimdas izdevumu bibliografija, 1940−1970,* 3v. (Stockholm, 1968−1977).

Kantautas, Adam. *A Lithuanian Bibliography: A Checklist of Books and Articles Held by the Major Libraries of Canada and the United States* (Edmonton, Alberta, 1975).

Königsberg. Universität. Ostpreusseninstitut. *Der Osten im Buch: Besprechungen der wichtigsten Ostliteratur 1936* (Königsberg, Ger., 1937).

Lietuvos TSR Spauda. *Valstybinė suvestinė bibliografija, 1940—1955*, 2v. (Vilnius, 1962—1964).

Ozols, Selma. *Latvia, a Selected Bibliography* (Washington, D.C., 1963).

Parming, Marju Rink, and Parming, Tönu. *A Bibliography of English-Language Sources on Estonia: Periodicals, Bibliographies, Pamphlets, and Books* (New York, 1974).

Ränk, Aino. *A Bibliography of Works Published by Estonian Historians in Exile, 1945—1969* (Stockholm, 1969).

Riga. Valsts Bibliotēka. Bibliogrāfijas un Metodiska Darba Nodula. *Latvijas PSR, 1940—1960: Literatūras radītāja* (Riga, 1961—).

Salasoo, Hugo. *Foreign Language Publications in Estonian Archives in Australia* (Sydney, 1969).

Thomson, Erik. *Baltische Bibliographie, 1945—1956* (Würzburg, 1957).

———. *Baltische Bibliographie 1957—1961, und Nachträge 1945—1956* (Würzburg, 1962).

U.S. Library of Congress. Slavic and Central European Division. *Estonia: A Selected Bibliography*, compiled by Salme Kuri (Washington, D.C., 1958).

In addition to the bibliographies in the Hoover Library, two important ones in the Green Library should be mentioned: Winkelmann, Eduard A. *Biblioteca Livoniae historica* (Berlin, 1878); and *Livländische Geschichtsliteratur* (Riga, 1878—1913).

The Hoover Library has the prewar *Eesti entsüklopeedia*, 8v. (Tartu, 1932—1937) and *Eesti nõukogude entsüklopeedia*, 9v. (Tallinn, 1968—1978). The Latvian Collection has only one small encyclopedia: *Latvijas PSR mazā enciklopedija*, 3v. (Riga, 1968—1970). The Lithuanian Collection includes four encyclopedias: the large work *Lietuvių enciklopedija*, 36v. (South Boston, Mass., 1953—1969); *Mažoji lietuviškoji tarybinė enciklopedija*, 3v. (Vilnius, 1966—1971); *Encyclopedia Lituanica*, 6v. (Boston, 1970—1978); and one still in the process of being published, *Lietuviškoji tarybinė enciklopedija* (Vilnius, 1976—).

The Green Library holds a rare prewar biographical dictionary, *Eesti biograafiline leksikon* (Tartu, 1926—1929) and its supplement, *Eesti biograafilise leksikoni täiendusköide* (Tartu, 1940). The Hoover Library has the following Baltic biographical directories:

Arnis, Ernests. *Latvju tautas politiska atmoda* (Lincoln, Neb., 1971).

*Deutschbaltisches biographisches Lexikon, 1710—1960* (Cologne, 1970).

Doveika, K. *Lietuvių rašytojai didžiajme tévynės kare* (Vilnius, 1967).
Harrison, Ernest. *Lithuania, 1928* (London, 1929).
Latvijas Padomju Socialistikās Republikas Zinātņu Akademija. Valodas un
Literatūras Instituts. *Latviešu literatūras darbinieki* (Riga, 1965).
Nirk, Endel. *Eesti kirjanduse biograafiline leksikon* (Tallinn, 1975).

The current biographical dictionaries of the Soviet Union, pre—World War II
editions of *International Who's Who* (London, 1937—), *Who's Who in Central
and East Europe* (Zurich, 1935—), and other reference sources in the collection
that include biographical information on persons from the Baltic region yield
additional data.

# BULGARIA

Although the scope of the Bulgarian Collection officially begins with the Balkan Wars in 1912, the collection includes some background materials for earlier periods. The Bulgarian holdings at the Hoover Institution consist of approximately 9,000 volumes (books and pamphlets), over 100 periodical titles (36 currently received), and 41 newspapers (10 currently received). Taken as a whole, the collection constitutes an excellent reference source.

## REFERENCE WORKS

Among Bulgarian reference and bibliographic works held by the Hoover Library, the most important are:

Bŭlgarska Akademiiâ na Naukite. *Kratka bŭlgarska entsiklopediiâ*, 5v. (Sofia, 1963–1969).

Bulgaria. Glavna Direktsiiâ na Statistikata. *Statisticheski godishnik na Tsarstvo Bŭlgariiâ* (Sofia, 1909–1942).

————. Tsentralno Statistichesko Upravlenie. *Statisticheski godishnik na Narodna Republika Bŭlgariiâ, 1959–1960* (Sofia, 1962–1977).

Akademiiâ Nauk SSSR. *Bolgariiâ: Istoricheskaiâ bibliografiiâ* (Moscow, 1954–).

*Bŭlgariiâ v chuzhdata literatura: Bibliografski ukazatel*, 5v. (Sofia, 1944–1967).

Bŭlgarski Bibliografski Institut. *Godishnik*, 9v. (Sofia, 1945–1962).

Pundeff, Marin V. *Bulgaria: A Bibliographic Guide* (Washington, D.C., 1965).

*Bŭlgarski periodichen pechat, 1844–1944*, 3v. (Sofia, 1962–1969).

*Bŭlgarski periodichen pechat, 1944–1969: Bibliografski ukazatel*, 3v. (Sofia, 1975–1976).

Dellin, L. A. D. *Bulgaria* (New York, 1957).
Ognianoff, Christo. *Bulgarien* (Nürnberg, 1967).

In addition to these bibliographical and reference monographs, the Hoover Library regularly receives the *Bŭlgarski knigopis: Knigi i novi periodichni izdaniiâ* (Sofia), *Bŭlgarski knigopis. Sluzhebni izdaniiâ i disertatsii* (Sofia), *Letopis na statiite ot bŭlgarskite spisaniiâ i sbarnitsi* (Sofia), and *Letopis na statiite ot bŭlgarskite vestnitsi* (Sofia) for ongoing bibliographic reference.

## PRE-1912 HISTORY

This period is covered by basic monographic works in Bulgarian and other languages, such as:

Akademiiâ Nauk SSSR. Institut Slavîanovedeniiâ. *Istoriiâ Bolgarii*, 2v. (Moscow, 1954–1955).

Bŭlgarska Akademiiâ na Naukite. Institut za Bŭlgarska Istoriiâ. *Istoriiâ na Bŭlgariiâ*, 2d ed., 3v. (Sofia, 1961–1964).

Pastukhov, Ivan. *Bŭlgarska istoriiâ*, 2v. (Sofia, 1942–1943).

Two of the most valuable works are the Soviet collection edited by P. Pavlovich, *Avantiûry russkogo tsarizma v Bolgarii: Sbornik dokumentov* (Moscow, 1935) and B. D. Kesiakov's *Prinos kŭm diplomaticheskata istoriiâ na Bŭlgariiâ, 1878–1925*, 3v. (Sofia, 1925–1926), which contains texts of treaties, conventions, accords, and protocols signed up to 1925. An important work on this period is Alois Hajek's *Bulgarien unter der Türkenherrschaft* (Stuttgart, 1925). Also useful is Georgi P. Genov's collection of major Bulgarian treaties from 1774 to 1938, *Actes et traités internationaux concernant la Bulgarie* (in *Godishnik na Sofiiskiiâ Universitet*, v. 34) (Sofia, 1938–1939). A valuable Russian-language collection concerned with Bulgaria after the Turkish wars is Bŭlgarska Akademiiâ na Naukite. *Osvobozhdenie Bolgarii ot turetskogo iga: Dokumenty*, 3v. (Sofia, 1961–1967). Its companion volume, *Osvobozhdenie Bolgarii ot turetskogo iga: Sbornik statei* (Sofia, 1953), is also informative. Equally valuable is *Dokumenti za osvoboditelnata voĭna, 1877–1878* (Sofia, 1937) a small collection of documents on the liberation of Bulgaria. .

Foreign diplomatic documentation of this period is well represented at the Hoover Institution. (A survey can be found in the annual volumes of the *Godishnik* of the Bŭlgarski Bibliografski Institut [Sofia, 1945–1955].) The struggles of the Bulgarian people against the Turks are chronicled in the military historian Ivan Kinov's *Vŭzorŭzhenata borba na bŭlgarskiiâ narod sreshtu osmanskoto gospodstvo* (Sofia, 1961). Much material can also be found in memoir literature of the period. The Hoover Institution has both the Bulgarian and English versions of the autobiography of Zakhari Stoîanov, a classic work on the Bulgarian uprising of 1876: *Pages from the Autobiography of a Bulgarian Insurgent* (London, 1913). Other such works include I. Andonov's *Iz spomenite mi ot tursko vreme* (Plovdiv, 1927), Arthur Hyde's A *Diplomatic History of Bulgaria, 1870−1886* (Urbana, Ill., 1931), and Khristo Siliânov's *Pisma i izpovedi na edin chetnik 1902g.* (Sofia, 1967). A Western diplomat's view of Bulgaria in this period is provided by Sir George W. Buchanan's *My Mission to Russia and Other Diplomatic Memoirs*, 2v. (New York, 1923). The impressions of English travelers in Bulgaria have been collected and edited by Michel Leo in *La Bulgarie et son peuple sous la domination ottomane, tels que les ont vus les voyageurs anglo-saxons, 1586−1878* (Sofia, 1949). The Czech scholar Constantine Jiřeček's *Bŭlgarski dnevnik, 1879−1884* (Sofia, 1930−1932) is also a valuable memoir. The lives of Bulgaria's early revolutionaries are covered in M. P. Arnaudov's *G. S. Rakovski: Zhivot, proizvedeniiâ, idei* (Sofia, 1922), G. Bakalov's *Nashite revoliûtsioneri: Rakovski, Levski, Botev* (Sofia, 1924), and in a number of other works.

On the occasion of the one hundredth anniversary of the April 1876 uprisings, Bulgarian scholars prepared many important source books and studies; those in the Hoover Library include:

> *April 1876: Spomeni. Sbornikŭt e posveten na 100-godishninata ot April-skoto vŭstanie* (Sofia, 1976).
>
> Gandev, Khristo N. *Aprilskoto vŭstanie 1876* (Sofia, 1974).
>
> Khristov, Khristo. *Agrarniiât vŭpros v bŭlgarskata natsionalna revoliû-tsiiâ* (Sofia, 1976).
>
> Kosev, Konstantin, et al. *Istoriiâ na Aprilskoto vŭstanie 1876* (Sofia, 1976).
>
> *Otrazhenie na Aprilskoto vŭstanie v chuzhbina* (Sofia, 1976).
>
> *Voenna podgotovka i provezhdane na Aprilskoto vŭstanie 1876* (Sofia, 1976).
>
> *Vŭzpomenatelen sbornik po sluchaĭ stogodishninata ot Aprilskoto vŭstanie i Botevata cheta*, 2v. (Sofia, 1976).

The Bulgarian uprisings of 1875−1876 and the reaction to them in Britain is the subject of David Harris's exhaustive study, *Britain and the Bulgarian Horrors of 1876* (Chicago, 1939). The same field of study is explored in R. Shannon's *Gladstone and the Bulgarian Agitation of 1876* (London, 1963).

The immediate postliberation period is covered by Nikola Stanev's *Naĭ-nova istoriiâ na Bŭlgariiâ, 1878−1920* (Sofia, 1925). The same period, treated more narrowly, is covered in such monographic works as:

> Jelavich, Charles. *Tsarist Russia and Balkan Nationalism* (Berkeley, 1958).

Madzharov, M. I. *Istochna Rumeliĭa: Istoricheski pregled* (Sofia, 1925). Krachunov, K. *Velikite dŭrzhavi i Bŭlgariĭa, 1886—1887* (Sofia, 1928). Panaĭotov, Ivan. *Russiĭa, velikite sili, i bŭlgarskiĭat vŭpros, 1888—1896* (Sofia, 1941). Kozhukharov, K. D. *Istochniĭat vŭpros i Bŭlgariĭa, 1875—1890* (Sofia, 1929).

The internal revolution following the unification of Bulgaria and the events of 1878—1885 are covered in C. E. Black's *The Establishment of Constitutional Government in Bulgaria* (Princeton, N.J. 1943). This valuable work contains English translations of the 1879 Bulgarian constitution and the 1883 amendments. S. Radev's *Stroitelite na sŭvremenna Bŭlgariĭa* (Sofia, 1911) is a detailed history of the same period (1879—1886) from the viewpoint of a Bulgarian diplomat. Bulgaria's victorious war with Serbia in 1885 is well documented at the Hoover Institution in the official histories, I. Mitev's *Istoriĭa na Srŭbsko-Bŭlgarskata voĭna, 1885* (Sofia, 1971), Kristin Krachunov's *Diplomaticheska istoriĭa na Srŭbsko-Bŭlgarskata voĭna, 1885—1886* (Sofia, 1921), and Ivan Vednedikov's *Istoriĭa na Srŭbsko-Bŭlgarskata voĭna 1885 godina* (Sofia, 1910).

Other sources include biographies of the first two rulers of modern Bulgaria, such as E. C. Corti's *Alexander von Battenburg* (Vienna, 1954), and those on Ferdinand I, including E. Daudet's *Ferdinand I, tsar de Bulgarie* (Paris, 1917) and Josef Knodt's *Ferdinand der Bulgare* (Bielefeld, Ger., 1947). Statesmen of this period are discussed in Dimitŭr I. Marinov's *Stefan Stambolov i noveĭshata ni istoriĭa: Letopisni spomeni i ocherki* (Sofia, 1909).

## THE BALKAN WARS AND WORLD WAR I, 1912—1918

The holdings for this period constitute a good research collection, and the events are documented by a variety of sources. To these belong such official publications as the records of the proceedings of the National Assembly, *Stenografski dnevnitsi*, and the reports of parliamentary committees. There are also numerous contemporary and interwar publications concerning these events issued by various ministries, for example, the seven-volume documentary collection on the Balkan wars, Bulgaria. Armiĭa. Shtab na Voĭskata. *Voĭnata mezhdu Bŭlgariĭa i Turtsiĭa, 1912—1913 gg.* (Sofia, 1928—1930), published by the Bulgarian Ministry of War. A later work published by the same ministry is *Voĭnata mezhdu Bŭlgariĭa i drugite dŭrzhavi prez 1913 g.* (Sofia, 1941).

E. C. Helmreich's well-documented book, *The Diplomacy of the Balkan Wars, 1912—1913* (London, 1938), is still the basic study on the subject. The history of Bulgaria's involvement in the Balkan wars can be supplemented by A. Nazlumov's *Materiali za istoriĭata na voĭnata 1912—1913 g.* (Sofia, 1931) and such other works as I. Fisher's *Balkanskata voĭna 1912 – 1913* (Sofia, 1940) and I. Geshov's *The Balkan League* (London, 1915). A crucial documentation is the Carnegie Endowment – sponsored *Report of the International Commission to Inquire into the Causes and Conduct of the Balkan Wars* (Washington, D.C., 1914).

The Soviet historian V. A. Zhebokritskiĭ has contributed two important studies of Bulgaria in the Balkan War, *Bolgariíà nakanune balkanskikh voĭn 1912 – 1913 gg.* (Kiev, 1960) and *Bolgariíà vo vremíà balkanskikh voĭn 1912 – 1913 gg.* (Kiev, 1961). Other works on the history and diplomacy of the Balkan wars include Nikola Ivanov's two-volume study, *Balkanskata voĭna 1912 – 1913 gg.* (Sofia, 1924 – 1925), A. Ganchev's *Balkanskata voĭna 1912 – 1913 gg.* (Sofia, 1939), and A. Papanchev's *Edno prestupno tsaruvane: Ferdinand I, tsar na bŭlgarite* (Sofia, 1950).

Bulgarian diplomatic documents relating to World War I were published by Aleksandŭr Stamboliĭski's government in two volumes. The Hoover Institution has a number of works published by various ministries, including *Bŭlgarskata armiíà v svetovnata voĭna, 1915 – 1918* (Sofia, 1936 – 1943), published by the Ministry of War; *La Verité sur les accusations contre la Bulgarie*, 2 v. (Sofia, 1919), containing documents and facsimiles, published by the Ministry of Foreign Affairs; and *Doklad na Parlamentarnata izpitatelna komisiíà (Voĭnata, diplomaticheskata podgotovka i diplomaticheski prigovori)*, published in 1918 by the National Assembly's Parliamentary Inquiry Commission. Another interesting collection, compiled by Pancho Dorev, is the book *Vŭnshna politika i prichini na nashite katastrofi: Spomeni, fakti i dokumenti* (Sofia, 1924).

To these collections of documents can be added diplomatic memoirs, such as Vasil Radoslavov's *Bŭlgariíà i svetovnata kriza* (Sofia, 1923), written by Bulgaria's prime minister in World War I; K. T. Stambolski's *Avtobiografiíà, dnevnitsi i spomeni*, 3v. (Sofia, 1927 – 1932); and *Diplomaticheskata podgotovka na nashite voĭni* (Sofia, 1932), written by Bulgarian statesman Mikhail Madzharov. English-language sources include A. V. Nekliudov's *Diplomatic Reminiscences Before and During the World War, 1911 – 1917* (New York, 1920) and Anna Stancioff's *Recollections of a Bulgarian Diplomatist's Wife* (London, 1931).

The number of monographic studies on Bulgaria in World War I is rather low. Probably the most useful is *Bŭlgariíà pred Velikata voĭna* (Plovdiv, 1932), written by Aleksandŭr Girginov, a Bulgarian general, politician, and chairman of the Ministry of War's Commission on Military History. Another work by the same author is *Narodnata katastrofa* (Sofia, 1926), also concerned with World War I and the Balkan Wars. Two studies, both indictments of Bulgaria's role in World War I, were published soon after the war. Jacques Ancel's *L'Unité de la politique bulgare, 1870 – 1919* (Paris, 1919) and Victor Kune's *Bulgaria Self-Revealed* (London, 1919).

## THE PARIS PEACE CONFERENCE

The Hoover Institution has a large collection of materials relating to Bulgaria at the Paris Peace Conference, including Bulgarian documents presented at the conference. Among them are Bulgaria. Ministerstvo na Vŭnshnite Dela i na Izpovedaniiata. *The Accusations Against Bulgaria: Official Documents Presented to the Peace Conference by the Bulgarian Delegation* (Sofia, 1919) and *Statements and Annexes Which Deal with the Territorial Questions Affecting Bulgaria* (Sofia, 1919). A general overview of the period, from the Bulgarian point of view, is given in Iordan Ivanov's *Les Bulgares devant le Congrès de la paix* (Bern, 1919). Other materials include delegation documents distributed to the public at the conference and materials relating to Bulgaria issued by the Serbian, Romanian, and Greek delegations.

## THE INTERWAR PERIOD, 1918–1939

The Hoover Institution has the official law gazette, *Dŭrzhaven vestnik*, for this entire period, as well as the records of the National Assembly, *Stenografski dnevnitsi*. This type of major governmental source is supported by a fair collection of documentary publications of various ministries and departments. There are many books on the first premier after World War I, Aleksandŭr Stamboliĭski, and his Agrarian Union, among them Nikola Petkov's *Aleksandŭr Stamboliĭski. Lichnost i idei* (Sofia, 1930), Marko Turlakov's *Istoriia, printisipi i taktika na Bulg. Zeml. Naroden Sŭiŭz* (Sofia, 1929), and a collection of Stamboliĭski's speeches, *Stamboliĭski kato orator* (Pleven, 1929). Other materials on the same subject include Paul Gentizon's *Le Drame bulgare* (Paris, 1924); two works published by the Agrarian Union, Stoian Omarchevski's *Bŭlgarskite upravnitsi prez svetovnata voĭna. Fakti i dokumenti* and Nedielko Atanasov's *Po trudniia pŭt* (Sofia, 1931); and two important books by Kosta Todorov, a leftist Agrarian leader, *Balkan Firebrand* (Chicago, 1943) and *Politička istorija savremene Bugarske* (Belgrade, 1938). There are also more recent studies, such as Petko Kunin's *Agrarnoselskiiat vŭpros v Bŭlgariia* (Sofia, 1971), D. Tisher's *Za sŭiŭz mezhdu rabotnitsite i selianite, 1917–1923* (Sofia, 1964), G. S. Slavov's *Selskoto dvizhenie v Bŭlgariia i sŭzdavaneto na BZNS* (Sofia, 1976), and John D. Bell's *Peasants in Power: Alexander Stamboliski and the Bulgarian Agrarian Union* (Princeton, N.J., 1977).

The problem of Bulgaria's irredenta in Macedonia and Thrace is well covered by contemporary materials as well as by retrospective works. The Hoover Institution contains a substantial collection of material relating to the Internal Macedonian Revolutionary Organization (IMRO) both before and during the interwar period. Among the documents published by IMRO can be found a memorandum presented to the Paris Peace Conference, *Mémoire de l'Organisation intérieure révolutionnaire macédonienne aux présidents des délégations des grandes puissances à la Conférence de la paix* (Paris, 1919) and a similar memorandum presented to the Fifth Assembly of the League of Nations, *La Question macédonienne et la situation en Macédonie* (Geneva, 1924). Other IMRO publications are *Zagovorŭt protiv Todor Aleksandrov* (Paris, 1924) and a copy of the rare *Les Traîtres à la cause macédonienne* (Paris, 1929), a protest against fascist elements in the organization. In addition, there are several works issued by the Macedonian Political Organization in the United States of America and Canada, a Mikhailovist group, and two newspapers, *Makedonska tribuna* (Indianapolis) and *La Fédération balcanique* (Vienna). Another important source of IMRO history are the memoirs of Ivan Mikhailov, of which four volumes have been published thus far in Italy, between 1958 and 1973.

Other topics strongly documented within the Hoover Institution collection are the Balkan conferences and the Balkan Pact, the September 1923 uprising, the Zveno organization, and Communist party activities. Overall coverage of interwar events is strengthened by a moderate but well-chosen collection of political writings and memoirs. In addition to the catalogued books on Bulgaria mentioned above, the Hoover Institution has a collection of Bulgarian miscellany, consisting of about 900 books and pamphlets from Bulgaria, mainly from the interwar period. These materials deal with a wide range of subjects, including history, politics, and society in Bulgaria during the interwar and earlier periods. This large fund will eventually be integrated into the rest of the catalogued collection.

## WORLD WAR II

The Bulgarian involvement in World War II is not particularly strongly represented in the collection by Bulgarian publications dating from that period. The only complete contemporary record of that time at the Hoover Institution is the National Assembly's *Stenografski dnevnitsi*. However, the Institution has a solid collection of memoirs published later by participants in the partisan movement, as well as some collections of documentary materials and a number of monographic studies.

Bulgaria's official history of operations against Germany is given in *Otechestvenata voĭna na Bŭlgariia, 1941–1945*, 3v. (Sofia, 1961–1966), issued by the Ministry of Defense. Another documentary publication, edited by Petŭr Georgiev, is *Bulgariens Volk im Widerstand, 1941–1944: Eine Dokumentation . . .* (Berlin, 1962). To this should be added the collection of the Bŭlgarska Akademiiâ na Naukite, *Ustanoviâvane i ukrepvane na narodno demokratichna vlast, sept. 1944—mai 1945: Sbornik dokumenti* (Sofia, 1969), edited by V. Bozhinov. Bozhinov has also written a valuable study of the war years, based on materials of the Bulgarian Foreign Ministry, *Politicheskata kriza v Bŭlgariiû prez 1943—1944* (Sofia, 1957). Two English-language works are available on wartime Bulgaria. Marin Pundeff's dissertation, "Bulgaria's Place in Axis Policy" (University of Southern California, 1958) and Marshall L. Miller's *Bulgaria During the Second World War* (Stanford, 1975).

The Hoover Institution's collection of partisan memoirs is fairly broad and consists of over fifty titles dealing with various aspects of underground movements in Bulgaria. Among the most informative are T. Balkanski's *Nashite partizanski pŭtishta: Spomeni* (Sofia, 1967), S. Dzhakhov-Turchina's *Iz debrite na "Eledzhik": Partizanski spomeni* (Sofia, 1966), T. Ivanov's *Dŭlg kŭm vremeto: Partizanski zapiski* (Sofia, 1963), and D. Ovadiiâ's *Partizanski dnevnik* (Sofia, 1963). Some memoirs are available in Russian translations, among them M. Grŭbcheva's *Vo imiâ naroda: Vospominaniiâ* (Moscow, 1965), A. Semerdzhiev's *Rodopskie partizany: Vospominaniiâ* (Moscow, 1965), and K. Vidinski's *Povodniki: Vospominaniiâ* (Moscow, 1965).

There are a large number of studies by other communist scholars concerning the events of World War II. The works of two Soviet historians deserve particular mention: L. B. Valev's two monographs, *Bolgarskiĭ narod v bor'be protiv fashizma nakanune i v nachal'nyĭ period vtoroĭ mirovoĭ voĭny* (Moscow, 1961) and *Iz istorii Otechestvennogo fronta Bolgarii: iiûl' 1942g.—sentiâbr' 1944g.* (Moscow, 1950); and M. Pozolotin's *Bor'ba bolgarskogo naroda za svobodu i nezavisimost' v period Vtoroĭ mirovoĭ voĭny* (Moscow, 1954). Also worth consulting are:

> Sterev, P. *Obshti borbi na bŭlgarskiiâ i grŭtskiiâ narod sreshtu khitlero-fashistkata okupatsiiâ* (Sofia, 1966).
>
> Filchev, L. *Bŭlgaro-sŭvetskata boĭna druzhba prez Otechestvenata voĭna, 1944—1945g.* (Sofia, 1961).
>
> Georgiev, G. *NOVA-boĭnata deĭnost na narodoosvoboditelnata vŭstani-cheska armiiâ, 1943—1944* (Sofia, 1974).
>
> Gosztony, P. *Das Eindringen der Roten Armee in Rumänien und Bulgarien im Jahre 1944* (Zurich, 1965).
>
> *Istoriiâ na antifashistkata borba v Bulgariiâ, 1939—1944*, 2v. (Sofia, 1976).

## THE POST—WORLD WAR II PERIOD

The postwar period is the most strongly represented period in the collection. The whole period is covered by an extensive collection of leading governmental and administrative sources and by documentary collections of the Communist party, the official ruling party since the last quarter of 1946. As such, many of its publications supplement and support postwar historical studies of the country. Material relating to this period is examined in greater detail in the following sections.

## LAW AND GOVERNMENT

Legal, governmental, and administrative sources are of great importance for research in almost any field of Bulgarian history. The Hoover Institution has a good collection of official Bulgarian law gazettes, parliamentary records, and collections of laws. On the other hand, publications of judicial and quasi-judicial decisions are not as well represented.

The Hoover Institution holds a large portion of the official Bulgarian law gazette, *Dŭrzhaven vestnik*. It contains all laws, edicts, cabinet resolutions, and ordinances, as well as judicial, commercial, and private announcements, legal notices, and governmental communications. *Dŭrzhaven vestnik* was published in 72 volumes from 1879 through 1950, when it was replaced as official organ by *Izvestiia na Prezidiuma na Narodnoto sŭbranie*. In 1962 the title *Dŭrzhaven vestnik* was resumed.

As noted above, the Hoover Institution also holds the records of the National Assembly, *Stenografski dnevnitsi*, for the period 1908 to 1946 and more recently from 1968 to the present. In addition to a number of separately published constitutions, the holdings contain several collections and studies of constitutional law, among them B. Spasov's *Dŭrzhavno pravo na Narodna Republika Bŭlgariia* (Sofia, 1968). For examination of earlier constitutional and institutional history, see:

> Girginov, A. *Dŭrzhavnoto ustroĭstvo na Bŭlgariia* (Sofia, 1921).
> Balamezov, S. *La Constitution de Tirnovo* (Sofia, 1925).
> Angelov, D. *Istoriia na bŭlgarskata dŭrzhava i pravo* (Sofia, 1959).
> Bulgaria. Ministerstvo na Pravosŭdieto. *Shestdeset godini Bŭlgarsko pravosŭdie, 1878—1941* (Sofia, 1941).

Holdings in the fields of civil and criminal law and procedure are also good. In criminal law, the major collection *Nakazatelen kodeks* (Sofia, 1956), compiled by D. Dimitrov, is particularly useful. For the study of state administration, P. Staĭnov's publications, among them *Administrativnite aktove v pravnata sistema na Narodna Republika Bŭlgariia* (Sofia, 1952) and *Administrativnoe pravo N.R. Bolgarii* (Moscow, 1960), are invaluable.

Current writing in the field of law is contained in the legal journal *Sotsialistichesko pravo*, published monthly by the Ministry of Justice, the Chief Prosecutor's Office, and the Supreme Court.

## ECONOMY AND STATISTICS

The Hoover Institution collection is well supplied with statistical material dating back to the liberation of the country in 1878. There are a large number of publications from the Central Statistical Office, covering the period 1886–1939, as well as publications of the Ministry of Finance, the Ministry of Commerce and Agriculture, and other ministries. Official statistics for the period 1914–1939 are given in *Mesechni statisticheski izvestiià na Glavnata direksiià na statistikata na Bŭlgarskoto Tsarstvo* and in the official statistical yearbook, *Statisticheski godishnik na Tsarstvo Bŭlgariià* (Sofia, 1909–1942).

Bulgaria's prewar economic development is discussed in Atanas ÎAranov's *La Bulgarie économique* (Lausanne, 1919). Another useful work on the same subject is Kiril G. Popov's *La Bulgarie économique, 1879–1911* (Sofia, 1920). An additional source is *Economic Notes from German and Austrian Newspapers* (London, 1914–1920), which covers the period 1914 to 1919 and was published by the British Ministry of Labour in 54 volumes. It includes Bulgaria and Turkey in its extensive coverage of economic conditions in enemy-occupied countries.

A Marxist history of Bulgaria's economic development is given in *Istoriià ekonomicheskogo razvitiià Bolgarii* (Moscow, 1961), a translation from the Bulgarian edition by Zhak Natan, a well-known academician. Works by V. Angelov on financial and economic conditions, V. Bakharov on Bulgarian industry, and a number of studies of Bulgarian agriculture are also found in the collection.

The amount of work done on postwar economic developments within the Soviet system is considerable. Studies of this type include George R. Feiwel's *Growth and Reforms in Centrally Planned Economies: The Lessons of the Bulgarian Experiences* (New York, 1977); Khristo Dorchev's *Die sozialistische Umgestaltung Bulgariens* (Berlin, 1960); *Ekonomicheskoe razvitie Narodnoĭ Respubliki Bolgarii* (Moscow, 1963), written by Kiril Lazarov, one of the postwar ministers of finance; Khristo Marinov's *Niàkoi ikonomgeografski problemi v razvitieto na bŭlgarskoto narodno stopanstvo vŭv vrŭzka s mezhdunarodnoto sotsialistichesko razdelenie na truda* (Varna, 1961); and *Narodnaià Respublika Bolgariià: Ekonomika i vneshniaià torgovlià* (Moscow, 1962), by two Soviet economists, S. D. Sergeev and S. Dmitrievich. Yet another important source of economic information on Bulgaria found at the Hoover Institution is the six-volume *Ikonomika na Bŭlgariià* (Sofia, 1971–1977).

In the field of economic planning, the Hoover Institution holds several editions of different five-year plans, as well as various commission reports and party directives on the subject. National economic plans are enacted by law and are published in the official gazette, *Dŭrzhaven vestnik*.

Discussion of current economic questions appears in *Izvestiià na Visshiià*

*Institut za Narodno Stopanstvo "Dimitŭr Blagoev"* (Varna, 1969−) and in *Planovo stopanstvo* (Sofia, 1949, 1969−). The latter is issued by Dŭrzhaven Komitet za Planirane.

## THE COMMUNIST PARTY

The early history of Bulgarian communism is documented in the Hoover Institution by several recent publications by the Bulgarian Communist Party:

*Bŭlgarska komunisticheska partiĭa. Dokumenti na tsentralni rŭkovodni organi: Sbornik, 1891−1903*, 2v. (Sofia, 1972, 1974).

*Materiali po istoriĭa na Bŭlgarskata komunisticheska partiĭa, 1885−1944* (Sofia, 1960).

*Rabotata na BKP v armiĭata, 1891−1918: Dokumenti i materiali* (Sofia, 1966).

*Internatsionalizmŭt na BKP: Dokumenti i materiali, 1892−1944* (Sofia, 1974).

*Obshtinskata politika na BKP, 1891−1944* (Sofia, 1974).

*Bŭlgarska komunisticheska partiĭa: Dokumenti na tsentralnite rŭkovodni organi, 1891−1899* (Sofia, 1972).

*Septemvriĭskoto antifashistko vŭstanie 1923: Dokumenti i materiali* (Sofia, 1973).

To such collections of material can be added the various editions of the early party leaders' works, among them Dimitŭr Blagoev's *Sŭchineniĭa*, 20v. (Sofia, 1957−1964), and Georgi Dimitrov's *Sŭchineniĭa*, 14v. (Sofia, 1951−1955). A number of biographies and other secondary materials contain information on these leaders.

This early period is also represented by a group of monographic studies, both in Bulgarian and Western languages. Among the latter, two are especially useful: Rothschild, J. *The Communist Party of Bulgaria: Origins and Developments, 1883−1936* (New York, 1959); and Oren, N. *Bulgarian Communism: The Road to Power, 1934−1944* (New York, 1971).

Representation of Communist party periodicals from the period prior to World War II is scattered since many were published illegally and in small quantities. However, the most important materials have been reprinted in *Rabotnicheski vestnik: Izbrani statii i materiali*, 3v. (Sofia, 1953−1955), which consists mostly of material from the party's interwar underground publications, and in *Rabotnichesko delo: Izbrani statii i materiali, 1927−1944* (Sofia, 1954), which Hoover has on microfilm.

The communist view of postwar development in Bulgaria can be found at the Hoover Institution in numerous documentary studies and monographs. Most of the various versions of official histories of the party published since the war can be found in the collection. Postwar events are covered in *Materiali po istoriiă na Bŭlgarskata komunisticheska partiiă, 9 septemvri 1944—1960* (Sofia, 1961), published under the editorship of Pavel Kostov. Other histories include *Materiali po istoriiă na Bŭlgarskata komunisticheska partiiă, 1925—1962g.* (Sofia, 1962) and *Istoriiă na Bŭlgarskata komunisticheska partiiă* (Sofia, 1969). These works are supplemented by numerous monographs, for example, K. Kukov's *Razgrom na burzhoaznata opozitsiiă, 1944—1947g.* (Sofia, 1966) and P. Gundev's *Razvitie na sotsialisticheskata demokratsiiă v Bŭlgariiă* (Sofia, 1965).

Major party leaders, among them Vasil Kolarov, Vŭlko Chervenkov, and Todor Zhivkov, are represented by numerous editions of their works, biographies, and bibliographes. Hoover also has several works relating to the trial of Traĭcho Kostov in 1949.

Decisions and policy statements made by the Bulgarian Communist Party between between 1891 and 1955 have been reproduced in *Bŭlgarskata rabotnicheska partiiă (komunisti) v rezoliŭtsii i resheniiă na kongresite, konferentsiite i plenumite na TsK* (Sofia, 1947—1955), which the Hoover Institution has on microfilm. The collection also contains the minutes of all postwar party congresses (fifth through tenth), printed in six volumes of *Stenografski protokol* (Sofia, 1948—1971). These are for the most part on microfilm, as are the minutes of the third conference (1950), also entitled *Stenografski protokol*. In addition to the minutes, the collection contains individual reports given to the congresses by Georgi Dimitrov, Vŭlko Chervenkov, and Todor Zhivkov, as well as various directives, resolutions, and a large number of reports issued by plenums of the Central Committee of the Bulgarian Communist Party.

The Hoover Institution holdings of documentary materials dealing with the Bulgarian Communist Party in the postwar years have strong research potential. The extensive documentary holdings are supported by quite comprehensive holdings of published collected works, speeches, and writings of the leading postwar party members.

## PARTY AND PRESS PUBLICATIONS

The Hoover Institution possesses an excellent collection of publications issued by the official party press. Of postwar newspaper titles, *Rabotnichesko delo* (Sofia), the official daily organ of the Bulgarian Communist Party's Central Committee, is the best represented. The collection includes issues from 1946 to 1949 and from 1956 to the present. In addition to articles, *Rabotnichesko delo* prints decisions of the party and government and speeches by party and government leaders. Holdings of *Otechestven front* (Sofia), daily organ of the National

Council of the Fatherland Front, which gives wide coverage to the work of the Bulgarian People's Council and the activities of the Fatherland Front, run from 1962 to the present. Other Bulgarian newspapers received at the Hoover Institution include *Zemedelsko zname* (Sofia), daily organ of the Agrarian People's Union; *Trud* (Sofia), daily organ of the Central Council of the Trade Unions; *Narodna armiĭa* (Sofia), daily organ of the Ministry of National Defense; and five other titles.

A few of the 36 periodicals currently received should be mentioned. Two of the most important are *Novo vreme* (Sofia) and *Partien zhivot* (Sofia). The library has complete holdings of the first from 1947 and of the second from 1969. *Novo vreme* is a theoretical monthly issued by the Communist party's Central Committee and prints party documents in addition to articles on theoretical problems and economic and ideological issues. *Partien zhivot* is the monthly organ of the Communist party's Central Committee and deals with party life and work.

Among the periodicals are three titles of a documentary nature: Bulgaria. Laws, Statutes, etc. *Normativni aktove*; Bulgaria. Laws, Statutes, etc. *Dŭrzhaven vestnik;* and Bulgaria. Narodno Sŭbranie. *Stenografski dnevnitsi*.

A selective list of other periodicals currently received by the Hoover Institution on Bulgaria or from Bulgaria includes:

*Armeĭska mladezh*
*Armeĭski komunist*
*Bulgaria Today*
*Bŭlgaro-sŭvetska druzhba*
Bŭlgarska Komunisticheska Partiĭa. Tsentralen Komitet. *Osvedomitelen biŭletin*
*Bŭlgarski profsŭĭuzi*
*Bŭlgarski voin*
*Izvestiĭa na Voenno-Istoricheskoto Nauchno Druzhestvo*
*Kooperativno zemedelie*
*Mezhdunarodna politika*
*Narodna prosveta*
*Narodnostopanski arkhiv*
*Politicheska prosveta*
*Problemi na truda*
Radio Free Europe. *Bulgarian Press Survey*
Radio Free Europe. *East Europe: Bulgaria. Background Reports and Situation Reports*
*Sofia News*
*Statistika*
*Voennoistoricheski sbornik*

## ARCHIVAL COLLECTIONS

Bulgaria is the partial subject of a number of collections in the Hoover Institution Archives, including the Allied and Associated Powers Treaties Collection, 1914–1920 (13 folders), the Joseph S. Roucek Collection, 1920–1949 (37 manuscript boxes), and the World War II Balkans Collection (1 manuscript box). Two small collections also deal with Bulgaria exclusively: the selected writings of Georgi M. Dimitrov, émigré agrarian politician, 1923–1972 (1 manuscript box); and an unpublished study, ''An Operational Geography of Bulgaria from a Geopolitical Viewpoint,'' by former Bulgarian general staff officer Doncho D. Gerganoff.

# CZECHOSLOVAKIA

The Czechoslovak Collection at the Hoover Institution consists of over 24,500 volumes (books and pamphlets), about 150 newspaper titles, and over 300 periodical titles. The collection officially begins with Czechoslovak independence in 1918, but includes important background materials concerning the development of the Czech and Slovak national movements, especially for the period of the First World War. In addition, important sources for Czechoslovak history are found in other collections, particularly those of Austria and Hungary.

This survey covers the Czechoslovak Collection in four chronological sections: pre-independence (to 1918); the First Czechoslovak Republic (1918−1939); World War II and the German occupation (1939−1945); and postwar and socialist Czechoslovakia (1945 to present). Within each chronological section, the collection is surveyed with regard to three types of resources: government documents and documentary collections; memoirs, collected writings, and speeches; and special subject collections. Newspapers and periodicals for all chronological periods are listed at the end of this survey.

## PRE-INDEPENDENCE PERIOD (TO 1918)

Materials pertaining to the Czech and Slovak lands before independence include scattered references from before 1867, dealing with the genesis of Czech and Slovak nationalism and pan-Slavism. Research materials for the post-Ausgleich era up to the beginning of World War I are more abundant, although they remain selective in both primary and secondary resources. The collection within this period is richest for the World War I years since this period was one of the main priorities for the Hoover Institution collection from its inception.

## Government Documents and Documentary Collections

*Austro-Hungarian Documents.* One of the primary resources at the Hoover Institution for research on this period is the collection of Hapsburg government documents, especially Austrian publications dealing with Bohemia, Moravia, and Silesia; and Hungarian publications on Slovak and Sub-Carpathian Ruthenian lands (to these may be added German government documents on Upper Silesia). The collection of Austro-Hungarian government documents is most comprehensive for the First World War and the period immediately preceding it. Holdings consist of legislative and judicial records, legal collections, statistical and economic studies, propaganda ephemera, and other works.

The Hoover Institution has a small but excellent collection of documents in manuscript form in its archives that relate to Czechoslovak affairs during the First World War. These include correspondence, reports, and speeches of Hungarian leaders such as Eszterházy, Madrassy-Beck, and Tisza; a collection of reports on the war and its aftermath by the Hungarian Ministry of Foreign Affairs; and manuscripts on the mobilization of Austro-Hungarian armed forces, along with a number of other diaries, transcripts, and political ephemera.

Austro-Hungarian published documents pertaining to Czech and Slovak lands include:

> Austria (1866–1918). Reichsrat. *Abgeordnetenhaus, Herrenhaus, und Delegation des Reichsrates: Protokollen* (Vienna, 1891–1918).
> Czechoslovakia. Sněm. *Stenografické zprávy Sněmu Království Českého* (Prague, 1908–1914).
> Hungary. Országgyűles Förendiház. *Napló: Stenographic records* (Budapest, 1901–1918).
> ———. ———. *Documents* (Budapest, 1910–1919).
> ———. Országgyűles Képviselöház. *Documents* (Budapest, 1901–1918).

For a detailed description of the Austro-Hungarian holdings of the Hoover Institution, see the article, "Austro-Hungarian Material 1867–1918 at the Hoover Institution, Stanford University," *Austrian History Newsletter,* no.2 (1961).

*Czech and Slovak Semiofficial Documents.* The Hoover Institution possesses an important collection of the published documents of the Czechoslovak National Council (Národní Rada), the supreme body that represented the aspirations of the Czechs and Slovaks before the Allied powers. Included in this collection are the National Council's official organ, *Československá samostatnost: L'Indépendance tchèque* (Paris, August 1915–August 1918), and another serial, *La Nation tchèque.* Large sets and files of memorandums, declarations, pamphlets, and propaganda material are also held by the Hoover Institution, including some rare documents in the archival collection of the George Herron Papers (December 1917–December 1919).

Also available is a 24-volume retrospective documentary collection of the council, entitled *Červánky svobody, sborník časových letáků* (Prague), that contains writings published in the years 1914–1918 by council members.

## Memoirs, Collected Writings, and Speeches

The Hoover Institution has a rich collection of the contemporary and commemorative works of the founders of Czechoslovakia and the leaders in its efforts for independence. It consists of writings by those Czechoslovak leaders who remained in their homeland in World War I (V. Klofáč, V. Červinka, J. Buřival, V. Choc, J. Netolický, J. Vojna, K. Kramář, K. Čulen, I. Dérer, V. Dyk, I. Gessay, G. Habrman, G. Opočenský. V. Šrobár, J. Preiss, J. Hajšman, B. Šmeral, A. Rašín, M. Hodža, P. Šámal, F. Juriga, F. Soukup, J. Jesenský, I. Stodola, J. Kvapil, J. Machar, and others); those who were active in exile (T. G. Masaryk, E. Beneš, B. Borský, A. Brusilov, J. Dürich, M. Janin, F. Kopecký, S. Kratochvíl, S. Osuský, B. Pavlů, and others); and those who served in the Czechoslovak Legions (R. Gajda, J. Skácel, J. Slanička, J. Švec, F. Vondráček, and others). In addition to this memoir material, the Hoover Institution possesses the writings of less well known leaders of the Czechoslovak national movement (J. Herben, J. Kaizl, etc.), as well as memoirs of Austrian and Hungarian leaders (I. Burian, O. Czernin, L. Bilinski, J. Redlich, K. Stürgkh, E. Plener, C. von Hotzendorf, G. Andrássy, L. Biro, M. Károlyi, I. Tisza, and others).

## Special Subject Collections

*The Czech Maffia.* Among the special subject holdings of the Hoover Library are materials concerning the secret committee of Czech political leaders within the Austro-Hungarian empire known as the Česká Maffie. This group organized resistance in the homeland and maintained contact with leaders abroad. The most significant sources for this organization are the memoirs of its leaders and those of the exile leaders, many of whom are mentioned in the preceding section. Also available is a small but selective set of published documentary papers on the "maffie," supplemented by a great number of studies published after World War I, of which the following are the most valuable:

> Paulová, Milada. *Dějiny maffie: Odboj Čechů a Jihoslovanů za světové války, 1914–1918*, 2v. (Prague, 1937–1939).
> ———. *Jihoslovanský odboj a česká maffie* (Prague, 1928).

————. *Tajný výbor maffie a spolupráce s Jihoslovany v letech, 1916–1918* (Prague, 1968).

Hajšman, Jan. *Česká maffie: Vzpomínky na odboj doma* (Prague, 1934).

————. *Maffie v rozmachu: Vzpomínky na odboj doma* (Prague, 1933).

Šišić F. *Dokumenti o postanku Kraljevine Srba, Hrvata i Slovenaca, 1914–1918* (Zagreb, 1920).

Soukenka, J. *Karel Kramář, 1914–1918* (Prague, 1931).

Stojanović, N. *Jugoslovenski odbor (Članci i dokumenti)* (Zagreb, 1927).

*Political Reprisals and Trials.*   The fate of Czech and Slovak national leaders who were arrested and interned as political prisoners by Hapsburg authorities during the war is documented at the Hoover Institution in a good collection of records of their trials that includes transcripts, documented proceedings, newspaper reports, and memoirs of those prosecuted (see the section Memoirs, Collected Writings, and Speeches above). Secondary works on the trials published after the war from both Czech and Austrian viewpoints are also available at the Hoover Institution.

*Czechoslovak Legions.*   Another strength of the Hoover Institution collection in a specific subject area for this period is its holdings on the Czechoslovak Legions, the military units of Czechs and Slovaks that were organized and fought for the Allies on the Western, Italian, and Russian fronts during the First World War.

Materials on the legions on the Western and Italian fronts are adequate, but coverage of the legion in Russia is excellent. Among the most important materials are the memoirs of the officers and participants in the Russian legion, along with those of the Czech political leaders involved with the legion; these works include:

Dürich, Josef. *V. českých službách: Vypsání mého pobytu za hranicemi, 1915–1918* (Klášter nad Jizerou, 1921).

Gajda, Rudolf. *Moje paměti* (Prague, 1920).

Skácel, Jindřich. *S generálem Syrovým v Sibiři* (Prague, 1923).

Slanička, Josef. *Ze slavných dob České družiny: Vzpomínky starodružiníka* (Prague, 1929).

Vondráček, František. *Husité dvácatého století: Deník ruského legionáře* (Prague, 1922).

Russian views of the Czechoslovak Legion are given in several books available at the Hoover Institution Library:

Dragomiretskiĭ, V. *Chekhoslovaki v Rossii, 1914–1920* (Moscow, 1928).

Karzhanskiĭ, N. *Chekho-slovaki v Rossii: Po neizdannym ofitsial'nym dokumentam* (Moscow, 1918).

Lazarevskiĭ, V. A. *Rossiia i chekhoslovatskoe vozrozhdenie: Ocherki chesko-russkikh otnosheniĭ, 1914—1918* (Paris, 1927).
Popov, F. *Chekhoslovatskiĭ miatezh i samarskaia uchredilka* (Moscow and Samara, 1933).

Besides these memoirs and Russian accounts, the Hoover Institution possesses a small number of serials published by segments of the Czechoslovak Legion in Russia, such as *Čechoslovak* (Petrograd, 1915—1917).

Finally, there are various important interwar and post—World War II publications on the Russian legion, including documentary collections and monographs. In addition, there are studies on the legions by such Marxist historians as A. K. Klevanskiĭ, J. Kvasnička, V. Olivová, O. Říha, and M. Vietor.

*Political Parties.* The Hoover Institution's holdings on the development of political life among the Czechs in the Hapsburg monarchy are abundant, but corresponding materials on the Slovaks are meager. Among the primary sources on Czech party politics at the Hoover Institution, one notable collection is the stenographic records for 1918—1920 of the Czech Social Democratic party (Československá Sociálně Demokratická Strana), entitled *Protokoly XII—XIII radného sjezdu československé sociálnídemokratické strany dělnické*. . . . The earlier activities of the Czech Social Democrats from 1874 to 1905 are covered in Austrian Social Democratic party records available at the Hoover Institution.

The Hoover Institution's holdings of important histories of political activities and parties among Czechs and Slovaks include the following:

Brugel, L. *Geschichte der österreichischen Sozialdemokratie*, 5v. (Vienna, 1922—1925).
Klíma, A. *Počátky českého dělnického hnutí*, 2v. (Prague, 1948).
Opočenský, J. *Konec monarchie rakousko-uherské* (Prague, 1928).
Slovenská Akadémia Vied. Historický Ustav. *Dokumenty k slovenskému narodnému hnutiu v rokoch 1848—1914*, 3v. (Bratislava, 1962—1972).

# THE FIRST CZECHOSLOVAK REPUBLIC, 1918—1939

## Government Documents

The Hoover Institution has almost complete files of the laws and decrees and government gazettes for this period, including Czechoslovak Republic. Laws, statutes, etc. *Sbírka zákonů a nařízení* (Prague, 1918—1945); and *Úřední list Československé Republiky* (Prague, 1918—1945).

Records of the activities of the National Assembly of the Czechoslovak republic are represented in the Hoover Institution holdings by a nearly complete holding of the interwar stenographic minutes: Czechoslovak Republic. Poslanecká Sněmovna. *Těsnopisecké zprávy o schůzích Poslanecké Sněmovny Národního Shromáždění Republiki Československé* (Prague, 1920–1938).

The bulletins published by the different ministries of the First Czechoslovak Republic are well represented at the Hoover Institution. Some of the more important ministerial publications include:

Czechoslovakia. Ministerstvo Národní Obrany. *Věcny věstník Ministerstva Národní Obrany* (1925–1935).

———. Ministerstvo Financí. *Věstník Ministerstva Financí Republiky Československé* (1925–1938).

———. Ministerstvo Spravedlnosti. *Věstník Ministerstva Spravedlnosti* (1919–1936; in Green Library).

———. Ministerstvo Zdravotnictví. *Věstník Ministerstva Zdravotnictví*, (1919–1938).

Holdings for economic and social statistical studies and reports for the interwar Czechoslovak republic are good, including important collections of reports and statistical overviews.

Documents for the First Czechoslovak Republic are abundant. These important collections of governmental and diplomatic documents and correspondence were published both before and after World War II by private, official, semiofficial, and foreign diplomatic institutions. The Hoover Institution holdings of interwar publications include:

Czechoslovak Republic. Ministerstvo Zahraničních Věcí. *Archív diplomatických dokumentů československých*, 2v. (Prague, 1927–1928).

———. Národní Shromáždění. *Důvodová zpráva k vládní předloze o ratifikaci mírových smluv* (Prague, 1920).

———. ———. *Z cizích parlamentů . . . ročník 1–38* (Prague, 1920–1938).

———. Treaties, etc., 1918–. *Osnovy československo-německých ujednání červnových z roku 1920* (Prague, 1920).

*Deset let Československé republiky*, 3v. (Prague, 1928).

Hoover Institution holdings of postwar publications of documentary collections include:

*Bojový odkaz roku 1919: Spomienky bojovníkov za Slovenskú Republiku rád a za Maďárskú Republiku rád* (Bratislava, 1960).

César, Jaroslav. *Hnutí venkovského lidu v českých zemích v letech 1918–1922: Prameny k ohlasu Velké říjnové socialistické revoluce a vzniku ČSR* (Prague, 1958).

Kejik, František. *O zahraniční politice ČSR: Fakta a dokumenty* (Prague, 1951).

Král, Václav. *Die Deutschen in der Tshechoslowakei, 1933–1947: Dokumentensammlung* (Prague, 1964).

*Německý imperialismus proti ČSR, 1918–1939* (Prague, 1962).

Říha, Oldřich. *Vliîanie Oktîabrskoĭ revoliûtsii na Chekhoslovakiîu* (Moscow, 1960).

Olivová, Věra. *Československo-sovětské vztahy v letech 1918–1922* (Prague, 1957).

*Souhrnná týdenní hlášení prezidia zemské správy politické v Praze o situaci v Čechách 1919–1920: Prameny* (Prague, 1959).

## Memoirs and Collections of Writings

The Hoover Institution possesses a rich collection of published memoirs and writings of the founders and leaders of the Czechoslovak republic of the interwar years, including those of Masaryk, Beneš, Kramář, Osuský, Dérer, Habrman, Herben, Peroutka, Veselý, Soukup, Hodža, Hurban, Bláho, Klofáč, Černý, and Nejedlý.

The Hoover Institution holdings of memoirs of communist leaders active in the period of the First Czechoslovak Republic include those of Gottwald, Novotný, Široký, Fučík, Šmeral, Šverma, Kopecký, Prechtl, Hybeš, and Zápotocký.

## Czechoslovak Miscellany

In addition to catalogued materials dealing with Czechoslovakia before World War II, the Hoover Institution has over 1,200 books and pamphlets, mainly from the interwar period, that are listed alphabetically by author and title in the miscellany catalog in the Reference and Reading Room. This list includes works dealing with political, social, and economic affairs in the period before 1938.

## Special Subject Collections

For a great number of specific subjects pertaining to the First Czechoslovak Republic, the Hoover Library and Archives have extensive published and unpublished sources. Holdings on three of these many subjects are of particular value and importance.

The Institution possesses a sizable collection dealing with the formation and activities of the major political parties of interwar Czechoslovakia. This collection includes newspapers, journals, programs, manifestos, platforms, minutes of meetings, collections of speeches, and other official and semiofficial publications of Czechoslovak political parties. Parties that are extensively represented include the Agrarian, the Socialist Democratic, the National Socialist, the Populist, the National Union, the Sudetendeutsche, and the Communist parties.

Another major asset is a rich collection of published and unpublished sources on the Paris Peace Conference, including the delegation documents and propaganda of the Czechoslovak representatives, along with those of all other interested delegations (Austria, Hungary, the Carpatho-Ruthenians, Poland, and the Great Powers). To these must be added the records and minutes of the meetings and councils of the peace conference. An abridged bibliography of the collection can be found in Nina Almond and Ralph M. Lutz's, *An Introduction to a Bibliography of the Paris Peace Conference (Collections of Sources, Archives Publications, and Source Books),* (Stanford: Stanford University Press, 1938).

Other sources on the peace conference are unpublished materials in the Hoover Institution Archives, including the collections of Štefan Osuský, Herbert Hoover, George Herron, James Logan, V. C. McCormick, L. H. Gray, W. G. Atwood, W. B. Cousey, L. Hutchinson, F. L. Polk, and W. B. Ryan.

A third subject area in which the Hoover Institution excels is the short-lived Slovak Soviet Republic. This small but significant collection includes incomplete runs of the communist newspapers *Červené noviny* (Budapest, 1919) and *Armáda proletáru* (Bratislava, 1919), as well as a number of pamphlets, bulletins, leaflets, and other propaganda of the Slovak and Hungarian revolutionaries. The materials in Hungarian of the Béla Kun government also have pertinent information on the Slovak republic. These primary printed sources are supplemented by memoirs of Slovak and Hungarian Communists who were participants in those soviet republics, including those of F. Munich, T. Szamuely, and others, as well as by histories published later.

## WORLD WAR II AND THE OCCUPATION

Following the dismemberment of Czechoslovakia in 1938–1939, four governments emerged. The Czech lands became the German "Protectorate of Bohemia and Moravia" and were directly incorporated into the Reich. Slovak lands, except for those annexed by Hungary along with Ruthenia, were formed into the "Slovak Autonomous State," an Axis satellite. In addition, two other different sorts of governments were organized: an official government-in-exile in London led by Edvard Beneš and a nonrecognized government made up of Czech and Slovak Communists in Moscow under the leadership of Klement Gottwald.

## The Protectorate of Bohemia and Moravia

Government documents for the German occupation include the legal gazette (decrees of the existing government), Czechoslovakia. Bohemia and Moravia (German Protectorate). *Sbírka zákonů a nařízení Protektorátu Čechy a Morava;* the official gazette (decrees of the German commander in the protectorate), *Amtsblatt des Protektorates Böhmen und Mähren (Úřední list Protektorátu Čechy a Morava)* (Prague, 1939–1945); and the general German legal gazette, Germany. Laws, Statutes, etc. *Reichsgesetzblatt* (Berlin, 1939–1945).

These contemporary documentary sources, along with runs of occupation newspapers and periodicals, are supplemented by postwar publications consisting of various primary and secondary sources.

One of the most widely covered aspects of the German occupation is the resistance against it. Works held at the Hoover Institution on this subject deal with such topics as the student resistance, the underground network, the assassination of Heydrich, the massacre at Lidice, and the Prague uprising. Among the most significant histories of the resistance are:

> Janáček, F. *Dva směry v začiatkoch narodného odboja, oktober 1938–jún 1940* (Bratislava, 1962).
>
> Pavlík, B., ed. *KSČ v boji za svobodu: Činnost a boj Komunistické Strany Československa v době od mnichovské kapitulace až k národním osvobození* (Prague, 1949).
>
> Topek, F. *Lidé stateční a tí druzí* (Hradec, 1966).

Regional histories of the occupation and resistance abound as well. Especially informative are:

> Frajdl, Jiří. *Květen 1945 ve východních a severovýchodních Čechách: Sborník dokumentů* (Havlíčkův Brod, 1965).
>
> Jiřik, Karl. *Osvobození Ostravy ve světle vzpomínek a kronik* (Prague, 1965).
>
> Kotík, Jaromir. *Velká Bíteš za okupace: Letopis 1938–1945* (Velká Bíteš, 1965).
>
> *Květen 1945 ve středních Čechách: Sborník dokumentů a vzpomínek, na revoluční dny 1945* (Prague, 1965).
>
> *Středočeské kapitoly z dějin okupace, 1939–1942* (Prague, 1965).

Other important sources at the Hoover Institution Library are the transcripts of trials of collaborators and war criminals and the memoirs of both German occupation authorities and Czech resistance leaders.

## The Slovak Autonomous State

The Hoover Institution does not possess contemporary published documents of the Slovak Autonomous State, except for an encyclopedic almanac, *Slovenská vlastiveda*, 4v. (Bratislava, 1943–1946). Unpublished sources are available, however, in the Hoover microfilm holdings of the German Foreign Ministry archives; for example, the files of conferences and correspondence of German and Slovak leaders.

By far the most important source on wartime affairs in Slovakia at the Hoover Institution are the handwritten journals of Stefan Tiso, the brother of the Slovak prime minister. This diary was written from August 1944 to May 1945 and covers the period of the Slovak uprising and the end of the autonomous state.

Another significant source for the end of the Slovak Autonomous State is the large archival collection of the Czechoslovak Eastern Armies, established by Czech and Slovak communist leaders in Moscow and supported by the Soviets.

The library holds a formidable collection of published documents and secondary sources on the Slovak Autonomous State that appeared after the war, particularly since 1962. Abundant materials on Slovak resistance, especially the uprising of 1944, are held at the Hoover Institution, including documentary publications, reprints, general and regional histories, and Communist party accounts.

## The London Exile Government

The official publications of this provisional government preserved at the Hoover Institution include its official gazette, *Úřední věstník Československý* (London 1940–1944); a nearly complete set of memoirs and works of its ministers; contemporary publications of documents, such as *Czechoslovak Sources and Documents* (New York, 1942–1945) and *Czechoslovakia Fights Back* (Washington, D.C., 1943); and contemporary monographs, for example, *Four Fighting Years* (London and New York, 1943).

In addition to these contemporary works on and by the London government, the Hoover Institution Library has postwar interpretations of its affairs. Of interest is the Marxist history by Bohuslav Laštovička, *V Londýně za války: Zápasy o novou ČSR 1939–1945* (Prague, 1961).

## The Czechoslovak Communist Leadership in Moscow

The Hoover Institution's holdings on the Moscow government are important in the realm of military affairs since they include the archives of the group's eastern front armies. The communist exile group in Moscow headed by Klement Gottwald was allowed to establish this military organization with Soviet help.

This force, along with Soviet armies, liberated Czechoslovakia and influenced the formation of the postwar government.

These holdings consist of the following types of sources:

1) a large amount of correspondence between the various brigade commanders and Czechoslovak representatives in Moscow, for example, Ludvík Svoboda and Gottwald, Čepička, Kopecký, and others. There is some correspondence between Svoboda and the general staff of the Red Army, including correspondence with Stalin and Khrushchev (then in the general staff of the Red Army as communication officer of the NKVD). Also included is German correspondence from the German prime minister for the protectorate, K. H. Frank, with SS units and with German army commanders;

2) numerous handwritten regimental diaries;

3) a large collection of telegrams and radiograms with military orders (including numerous ones from Khrushchev);

4) various reports by commanders, including many secret reports on the outcome of their campaigns;

5) an extensive collection of military maps and plans;

6) a strong collection of the army's various publications.

Among the last is *Naše vojsko* (Paris, December 1943—May 1945) and about ten additional titles, some of which do not cover the military. One of these is the Slovak Communist Party's central organ, *Pravda* (Bratislava, 1945), which appeared in Slovakia during the uprising. Another is *Čas* (Bratislava, 1945), the central organ of the Democratic party of Slovakia. This whole collection is far too large to allow mention of all the unique items within it.

Other holdings include an almost complete set of the published documents of the Moscow group and the memoirs of its leaders (K. Gottwald, Z. Fierlinger, V. Kopecký, R. Slánský, and others). The interaction between the Moscow communist leaders and the London exile government is also chronicled in a number of works at the Hoover Institution.

## POSTWAR AND SOCIALIST CZECHOSLOVAKIA, 1945 TO PRESENT

The Hoover Institution collection on the Czechoslovak republic for the years following World War II is quite comprehensive for the period 1956 to the present, with significant gaps for the immediate postwar period (1945—1955). Materials pertaining to the Czechoslovak Communist Party are the largest of the subject areas covered and complement areas where there are lacunae in government materials.

## Government Documents

The collection of published government documents for the Czechoslovak Socialist Republic is the mainstay of Hoover Institution holdings for this period. The holdings are strongest for the post-1956 period and more limited, although extremely useful, for the immediate postwar period. Below are abbreviated lists of the main documents possessed by the Hoover Institution, arranged according to type.

*Government Gazettes.* Czechoslovak Republic. Laws, Statutes, etc. *Sbírka zákonů a nařízení státu Československého* (Prague, 1945–1947); *Sbírka zákonů republiky Československé* (Prague, 1957– ); and *Úřední list Československé Republiky* (Prague, 1953–1961).

*National Assembly Documents.*
    *Přehled o činnosti Národního Shromáždění ČSSR* (Prague, 1964–1968).
    *Těsnopisecké zprávy o schůzích Národního Shromáždění ČSSR* (Prague, 1955–1960 [incomplete], 1960–1964).
    *Zpráva o schůzích Národního Shromáždění ČSSR* (Prague, 1964–1968).

For 1968, the Hoover Institution has individual official reports printed as pamphlets and in the press. These contemporary publications are supplemented by documentary and semidocumentary collections on the Assembly's work published in the West.

*Statistical Documents.* Czechoslovak Republic. Státní Úřad Statistický. *Statistická ročenka Československé Socialistické Republiky; Statistika; and Zprávy.*

## Communist Party Documents

The basic sources for post-1948 government affairs are the documents of the ruling Communist party. Of particular importance for studying the relation of party to government are the following: Komunistická Strana Československa Ústřední Výbor. *Usnesení a dokumenty ÚV KSČ* (Prague, 1958, 1960, 1962– ): as well as statutes of the party, published in separate volumes after their adoption at party congresses, such as Komunistická Strana Československa. Congress. *Stanovy Komunistické strany Československa: Schválené XII sjezdem KSČ dne 8 prosince 1962, doplněné a upravené XIII. sjezdem KSČ 4 června 1966* (Prague, 1966); and programs of the party published in the protocols of party congresses.

The minutes of the congresses since the ninth (1949) are available at the Hoover Institution.

## MEMOIRS, COLLECTED WRITINGS, AND SPEECHES

The library is richly endowed with memoir and commemorative literature of the leaders and statesmen of postwar Czechoslovakia, in particular of leading members of the Czechoslovak Communist Party. Personalities that are well represented in monographic editions include K. Gottwald, A. Novotný, J. Šverma, and R. Slánský. The memoirs and works of other party functionaries, such as V. Kopecký, J. Krejčí, J. Dolanský, P. Reiman, Z. Fierlinger, and V. Clementis, have been published in collective works, for example, A. Novotný's *Projevy a stati* (Prague, 1964), and in such journals as *Nová mysl* (Prague, 1952, 1954–).

Works of party leaders of the postwar generation have also been published. These new leaders include V. Bilák, O. Černík, V. Daubner, A. Dubček, J. Duriš, E. Erban, J. Fojtík, J. Hájek, M. Hruškovič, A. Indra, J. Janík, D. Kolder, J. Lenárt, J. Loerincz, B. Lomský, F. Penc, L. Pezlár, O. Šik, V. Slavík, K. Šmidke, L. Štrougal, and L. Svoboda.

## SPECIAL SUBJECT COLLECTIONS

### The Immediate Postwar Period, 1945–1948

The early period of postliberation Czechoslovakia and the programs of the National Front are documented at the Hoover Institution in the previously mentioned materials on the Moscow and London exile governments and in a number of published sources, such as:

Chalupa, V. *The National Front in Czechoslovakia* (Chicago, 1958).
*První vláda osvobozené Československé republiky* (Prague, 1945).
Šlechta, E. *Národní Fronta-pevná jednota lidu* (Prague, 1955).
*Ustavení Československé vlády Národní fronty Čechů a Slováků a její první projevy* (Prague, 1945).

On the local "national committees" that were formed in these first few years, the Hoover Institution possesses a number of works, including K. Bertelmann's *Vývoj národních výborů do ústavy 9. května, 1945–1948* (Prague, 1964) and Komunistická Strana Československa. Ústřední Výbor. *Národní výbory* (Prague, 1946).

The crises between communist and noncommunist elements in the government and society in Czechoslovakia are represented by a large collection of different studies, including:

*Československá revoluce v letech 1944—1948: Sborník příspěvků z konference historiků k 20. výročí osvobození ČSSR* (Prague, 1966).
*Československo na cestě k socialismu: Dokumenty o vzniku a vývoji lidové demokracie v Československu do února 1948* (Prague, 1965).
Dvořáková, Eva. *Československá společnost a komunisté v letech 1945—1948* (Prague, 1967).
Jech, Karel. *Prebudená dedina k dejinám revolúcie na našom vidieku v rokoch 1945—1948* (Bratislava, 1963).
Opat, Jaroslav. *O novou demokracii, příspěvek k dějinám národné demokratické revoluce v Československu v letech 1946—1948* (Prague, 1966).

The materials at the Hoover Institution on the 1948 communist coup consist of speeches by those involved, documentary and semidocumentary works, secondary studies, and other important books from both the communist and Western points of view.

## The Purges

The collection of the Hoover Institution on the political trials that were held from the 1950s until 1962 consists of such published accounts as:

Clementis, Vlado. *Listy z väzenia* (Bratislava, 1968).
*Die Revolution rehabilitiert ihre Kinder: Hinter den Kulissen des Slánský-Processes* (Vienna, 1968).
*War Conspirators Before the Court of the Czechoslovak People* (Prague, 1950).

The most important holding of the Hoover Institution concerning the purges is a complete copy of the manuscript of the "Kaplan Report," a candid and critical study of the purge trials of the 1950s by a special committee of the Communist party under Dubček in 1968. Abridged editions of the report have been published in English and German: Komunistická Strana Československa. Ústřední Výbor. Komise pro Vyřizování Stranických Rehabilitací. *Czechoslovak Political Trials* (Stanford, 1971); and Komunistická Strana Československa. Ústřední Výbor. Komise pro Vyřizování Stranických Rehabilitací. *Das unterdrückte Dossier* (Vienna, 1970). Neither is complete. The manuscript at the Hoover Institution is complete in both text and documentation.

## Socialist Economic Development

The Hoover Institution possesses impressive holdings on the economic development of the republic under socialism, both in its Stalinist and reform phases. Sources for this subject are found in Communist party publications, including party congress protocols *(Protokoly Sjezdu KSČ)*, yearbooks *(Usnesení a dokumenty ÚV KSČ)*, and party labor legislation *(KSČ o úloze odborů při výstavbě socialismu: Sborník usnesení a dokumenty* [Prague, 1962]). Documentary sources, in addition to the statistical publications listed above, are available in the Hoover Institution in such official and semiofficial collections as:

Gaspar, Michal. *Plánovacie akty a ich funkcia v riadení národného hospodárstva ČSSR* (Bratislava, 1963).

Girášek, Jordan. *Finančné hospodárenie národných výborov* (Bratislava, 1968).

*Khozîaĭstvennyĭ kodeks Chekhoslovatskoĭ Respubliki: Zakon ot 4 iîunîa 1964 goda* (Moscow, 1966).

Nikodým, Dušan. *Kontrola v štátnej a hospodárskej správe ČSSR* (Bratislava, 1969).

Spišiak, Ján. *Hospodárske právo a vedecké plánovanie v čs. federácii* (Bratislava, 1968).

General studies of Czechoslovak economic development include:

Czechoslovak Republic. Státní Úřad Statistický. *25 (i.e. dvacet pět) let Československa: Statisticko-ekonomický přehled vývoje socialistického Československa v letech 1945–1970* (Prague, 1970).

*Stručný hospodářský vývoj Československa do roku 1955 (pod redakcí Rud. Olšovského)* (Prague, 1969).

Barvík, Jaromír, et al. *Vývoj Československé ekonomiky a hospodářská politika KSČ* (Prague, 1971).

Individual topics in economic planning and development are covered at the Hoover Institution in such works as:

Čermák, Václav. *Vývoj Československé ekonomické reformy* (Prague, 1970).

Čvančara, F. *Zemědělská výroba v číslech* (Prague, 1962).

Czechoslovak Republic. Federální Statistický Úřad. *Ekonomický vývoj 1968: ČSR, SSR. kraje, okresy* (Prague, 1969).

————. Státní Úřad Statistický. *25 (i.e. dvacet pět) let Československa: Statisticko-ekonomický přehled vývoje socialistického Československa v letech 1945–1970* (Prague, 1970).
Janhuba, Alois. *Základy ekonomiky ČSSR* (Brno, 1973).
*K štrukturálnym problémom rozvoja ekonomiky Slovenska* (Zost. Michal Senčak) (Bratislava, 1970).
Kazimour, Jan. *Technický a economický rozvoj ČSSR* (Prague, 1975).
*Nationalization en Tchécoslovaquie* (Prague, 1946).
Němec, B. *Druhá československá pětiletka, 1956–1960: Názorné pomůcky* (Prague, 1958).
Janovič, J., et al. *Oblastné problémy rozvoja poľnohospodářstva v ČSSR* (Prague, 1968).
*Pracovní síly v československém hospodářství* (Prague, 1970).
*První Československý pětilety plán* (Prague, 1949).
*Rozvoj Slovenska v socialistickom Československu* (Bratislava, 1965).
Šik, Ota. *K problematice socialistických zbožních vztahů* (Prague, 1965).

## The Soviet Invasion of 1968

With regard to the events of 1968, the Hoover Institution has collected many official and clandestine ephemeral-underground newspapers, brochures, leaflets, as well as special editions of the following newspapers:

*Lidová demokracie,* organ of the Czechoslovak People's Party
*Literární listy,* organ of the Union of Czechoslovak Writers
*Mladá fronta,* the youth daily
*Práce,* the daily of the Revolutionary Trade Union Movement
*Pravda,* organ of the West Bohemian Regional Committee of the Communist party
*Rudé právo,* organ of the Communist party's Central Committee
*Svobodné slovo,* organ of the Socialist Party of Czechoslovakia

In addition to the published sources, the Hoover Institution has also acquired some unpublished materials (letters, lists, etc.) and has put together a collection of clippings from the U.S. and European press regarding the events leading to and following the Warsaw Pact invasion.

## The Federalization of 1969

The reorganization of Czechoslovakia into a federation with separate state governments for Czech and Slovak lands (Česká Socialistická Republika and Slovenská Socialistická Republika) following the 1968 revolution is documented at the Hoover Institution, aside from government documents, in the following works:

Bidlo, Bořivoj, et al. *Organizace státní správy Československé socialistické republiky* (Prague, 1970).
*Československá federace* (Prague, 1969).
*Česko-Slovenská federace (Dokumentační redakce J. Munclinger)* (Prague, 1969–1970).
Trella, R., and Chovanec, J. *Nové štátoprávne usporiadanie ČSSR* (Bratislava, 1971).
Vaněček, Václav. *Česká národní rada, Sněm českého lidu* (Prague, 1970).

## Human Rights in Czechoslovakia

Since the 1968 Warsaw Pact invasion, several cases involving human rights and their violation in Czechoslovakia have occurred, the most important and recent being the publication of Charter 77 and its aftermath. Besides having photocopies of documents and correspondence concerning this affair (provided by Prof. H. Gordon Skilling), the Hoover Institution is collecting all published materials concerning the democratic opposition in Czechoslovakia. Among the works received are:

*Acta Persecutionis: A Document from Czechoslovakia. Presented to the XIV International Congress of Historians* (San Francisco, 1975).
Kavan, Jan. *Socialistyczna opozycja w Czechosłowacji: Dokumenty, 1973–1975* (London, 1976).
Mlynář, Zdeněk. *Politická situace Kolem Charty 77* (Toronto, 1977).
Pelikán, Jiří. *Socialist Opposition in East Europe: The Czechoslovak Example* (New York, 1977).
Preisner, Rio. *Kritika totalitarismu* (Rome, 1973).
*Zpráva dokumentacní komise K231* (Toronto, 1973).

At present the library is arranging with European sources to obtain copies of all clandestine publications emanating from Czechoslovakia and reaching the West. Opposition periodical publications are also collected (see the section Serial Collection below).

## CZECHOSLOVAK COMMUNIST PARTY

The Hoover Institution possesses an outstanding collection of sources relating to the growth and activities of the Communist party in Czechoslovakia since 1945 and good resources for the previous periods. These include the original and reprinted protocols of all Communist party congresses from 1923 to the present (all original editions from 1949 on), as well as records of the plenums of the party's Central Committee from 1958 to 1960 and from 1962 to the present *(Usnesení a dokumenty ÚV KSČ)*.

Other important sources are the numerous memoirs and writings of leading members of the party (see the section Memoirs, Collected Writings, and Speeches). The periodical and newspaper collection at the Hoover Institution (see below) is another major source for information on Communist party affairs, in particular the party press and information organs.

The Hoover Institution has a large number of secondary historical works on the Communist party in Czechoslovakia, including the following general histories: *Prehl'ad dejín KSČ na Slovensku* (Bratislava, 1971); *Příruční slovník k dějinám KSČ*, 2v. (Prague, 1964); and Reimann, P. *Dějiny Komunistické strany Československa* (Prague, 1931).

Regional and local histories of the party include:

*Bojovali-zvítězili: Vzpomínky komunistů Jihočeského kraje* (České Budějovice, 1961).

Hrbek, R. *Revolučné hnutie robotníkov západného Slovenska, 1918—1938* (Bratislava, 1970).

Jiřík, Karel. *Z dějin dělnického hnutí na Kladensku: Sborník práci k 40. výročí vzniku KSČ* (Prague, 1962).

Laštovka, Vojtěch. *KSČ na Klatovsku* (Plzeň, 1963).

Mlynárik, Ján. *Od októbra 1917 ku vzniku KSČ: Revolučné hnutie na strednom a severozápadnom Slovensku v rokoch 1917—1921* (Banská Bystrica, 1967).

Pecka, Emanuel. *Historický mezník: K počátkům činnosti Komunistické strany Československa v jižních Čechách* (České Budějovice, 1960).

Peša, Václav. *Z dějin Komunistické strany Československa na Brněnsku: Od vzniku KSČ 1921 do osvobození v květnu 1945* (Brno, 1962).

Pleva, Jan. *Príspevok k dejinám bolševizácie KSČ na Slovensku a Zakarpatsku* (Bratislava, 1962).

Plevza, V. *KSČ a revolučné hnutie na Slovensku, 1929—1938* (Bratislava, 1965).

Sommer, Karel. *Z boju dělnické třidy a KSČ na Prostejovsku v letech 1921—1928* (Brno, 1965).

Splíchal, Václav. *Za bolševizácí KSČ v Jihlavském kraji* (Brno, 1964).

*Studie z dejín KSČ a robotnickeho hnutia na Slovensku, 1917—1923* (Bratislava, 1968).

## CZECHOSLOVAK SERIAL COLLECTION

One of the strongest points of the Czechoslovak Collection is its impressive collection of serial publications, which consists of over 300 periodical titles and some 150 files of newspapers. These serials cover the entire period from the 1860s to the present. Particularly well documented are World War I, the 1930s, World War II, and the late 1960s and 1970s.

Many titles of both periodicals and newspapers are represented by scattered issues only. Frequently these partial runs and scattered issues are among the rarest items.

The following is a list of some of the more impressive and longer retrospective runs of newspapers. The dates shown do not necessarily mean that every issue is held, but most runs are relatively complete.

*Bojovník* (Bratislava, 1969–1974)
*Čechoslovan* (Kiev, 1916–1917).
*Čechoslovák* (London, 1939–1945)
*České slovo* (Munich, 1955–1967)
*Československá samostatnost* (Paris, 1915–1918)
*Hlas revoluce* (Prague, 1956–1975)
*Lidová demokracie* (Prague, 1945–1952, 1968–1974)
*Lidové noviny* (Prague, 1940–1951 [scattered issues])
*Literární listy* (Prague, 1968–1969)
*Mladá fronta* (Prague, 1946, 1948 [scattered issues], 1968–1970, 1972–1974)
*Národní politika* (Prague, 1914–1919, 1940–1945)
*Národní listy* (Prague, 1914–1921, 1924, 1938, 1940–1941)
*Nedělní české slovo* (Prague, 1941–1944)
*Nové Československo* (London, 1941–1945, 1947)
*Nové Československo* (Paris, 1945–1946)
*Nové slovo* (Bratislava, 1968–1976)
*Noviny zahraničního obchodu* (Prague, 1963–1966, 1968–1971)
*Polední list* (Prague, 1942–1945)
*Práca* (Bratislava, 1962–1974)
*Rolnické noviny* (Bratislava, 1968–1970, 1972–1973)
*Sloboda* (Bratislava, 1968–1973)
*Smena* (Bratislava, 1968–1970, 1972–1974)
*Svobodné slovo* (Prague, 1945–1951 [scattered issues], 1962–1969, 1971–1973)
*Večerní české slovo* (Prague, 1939–1945)

*Večerní Praha* (Prague, 1962–1964, 1968–1969, 1971–1973)
*Večerník* (Bratislava, 1968–1969, 1972–1973)

In addition to these Czech and Slovak titles, certain German- and Hungarian-language newspapers in the Hoover Collection are valuable for research on Czechoslovak history.

*Arbeiterzeitung* (Brno)
*Magyarország* (Budapest)
*Népszava* (Budapest)
*Neues Pester Journal* (Budapest)
*Pester Lloyd* (Budapest)
*Pesti hírlap* (Budapest)
*Pesti napló* (Budapest)
*Prager Abendzeitung* (Prague)
*Prager Abendblatt* (Prague)
*Prager Presse* (Prague)
*Prager Tagblatt* (Prague)
*Sozialdemokrat* (Prague)

Currently the Hoover regularly receives five newspapers from Czechoslovakia:

*Hospodářské noviny* (Prague, 1964– )
*L'ud* (Bratislava, 1962– )
*Práce* (Prague, 1945–1948, 1962– )
*Pravda* (Bratislava, 1962– )
*Rudé právo* (Prague, 1945– )

As previously mentioned, the Hoover Institution has among its holdings more than 300 titles of Czech and Slovak periodicals. Many of the titles are, in fact, short runs or runs with substantial gaps. Some of the more complete and more important titles in the collection are:

*Bratislava* (Prague, 1927–1937)
*Česká osvěta* (Prague, 1936–1940)
*Česká revue* (Prague, 1898, 1914–1922)
*Český časopis historický* (Prague, 1921–1938, 1946–1949)
*Dnešek* (Prague, 1946–1948)
*Moderní stát* (Prague, 1928–1940)
*Naše doba* (Prague, 1894–1941, 1946–1949)
*Naše revoluce* (Prague, 1923–1932)
*Naše vojsko* (Prague, 1936–1938)

*Obzor národo-hospodářský* (Prague, 1899–1941)
*Prudý* (Bratislava, 1922–1925)
*Politická revue* (Prague, 1937–1938)
*Slovanský přehled* (Prague, 1899–1914, 1925–1935, 1938–1939)
*Sociální problémy* (Prague, 1931–1938)
*Sociologická revue* (Brno, 1930–1939, 1946–1948)
*Stát a právo* (Prague, 1956–1957, 1959–1960, 1963–67)
*Svobodný zednář* (Prague, 1925–1938)
*Vojenské rozhledy* (Prague, 1922–1924, 1928, 1931, 1933)
*Vojenský svět* (Prague, 1933–1934)

In addition, a total of 37 periodical titles are currently received, 31 from Czechoslovakia, and 6 published outside of Czechoslovakia by opposition groups. Some samples are:

PUBLISHED IN CZECHOSLOVAKIA:

*Czechoslovak Digest*
*Czechoslovak Economic Digest*
*Dikobraz*
*Ekonomický časopis*
*Historia a vojenství*
*Mezinárodní vztahy*
*Nová mysl*
*Plánované hospodářství*
*Politická ekonomie*
*Právník*
*Právny obzor*
*Práce a mzda*
*Problemy mira i sotsializma* (in Russian)
*Slovanský přehled*
*Sociálná politika*
*Život strany*

PUBLISHED OUTSIDE CZECHOSLOVAKIA:

*Listy: Časopis československé socialistické opozice* (Rome)
Radio Free Europe. Research department. *Czechoslovak Press Survey* (New York)
Radio Free Europe. Research Department. *East Europe: Czechoslovakia. Background Reports and Situation Report* (New York)
*Slovakia* (Middletown, Pa.)
*Spektrum* (London)
*Svědectví* (Paris)

## ARCHIVAL SOURCES ON CZECHOSLOVAK
## HISTORY, 1918 TO PRESENT

In addition to voluminous published sources, the Hoover Institution possesses several important archival collections on Czechoslovak history since 1918. The Ladislav K. Feierabend Collection consists of correspondence, speeches and writings, memoirs, photographs, and printed matter relating to agricultural administration, Czechoslovakia in World War II, Czechoslovak foreign relations with Germany and the Soviet Union, and generally dealing with Feierabend's career as a Czechoslovak government official. The papers cover the period 1922−1975 (20 manuscript boxes; personal papers closed until 1998).

The Joseph Lettrich Collection consists of correspondence, appointment books, speeches and writings, reports, memorandums, clippings, newsletters, printed matter, photographs, and other material, 1940−1969, relating to Lettrich's activities as organizer of the Slovak national resistance movement, 1944−1945; president of the National Slovak Council and the Slovak Democratic party, 1945−1948; member of the Czechoslovak parliament, 1945−1948; founder of the Council of Free Czechoslovakia (Washington, D.C.); and member of various émigré organizations, 1948−1969 (33 manuscript boxes).

The Štefan Osuský Collection consists of correspondence, memorandums, reports, clippings, printed matter, memorabilia, photographs, etc., pertaining to Osuský's career as Czechoslovak ambassador to Great Britain (1918−1920) and to France (1920−1940); to foreign and domestic affairs of Czechoslovakia; and to international relations, primarily in Western and Central Europe between the two world wars (42 manuscript boxes, 1 album, and 2 card files).

The Juraj Slavík Collection consists of correspondence, speeches and writings, reports, dispatches, memorandums, telegrams, clippings, and other materials, 1934−1966, relating to Slavik's service as minister and envoy to Poland (1936−1939), minister of interior (1940−1945), minister of foreign affairs (1945−1946), and ambassador to the United States (1946−1948), and dealing with political developments in Czechoslovakia, Czech emigration and émigrés, and anticommunist movements in the United States (32 manuscript boxes).

Besides these four major archival units, there are 32 smaller collections of manuscripts also touching upon Czechoslovak affairs. Among the smaller collections are CBS Broadcast Scripts (Czechoslovak Crisis, 1938); E.Chaloupný Papers; Československý Armádní Sbor v SSSR; William Duncan Papers; European Socialist Parties Collection; Lieutenant Kapnist Papers; Zdeněk Kryštůfek Papers; Joseph S. Rouček Papers; Miroslav Schubert Papers; Jan Slovik Papers; the Štefan Tiso Diary; and Eduardas Turauskas Papers.

The Greek Collection of the Hoover Institution, although relatively small (about 3,000 volumes), is useful for researching certain subjects and certain periods. Although for the pre-1936 and 1949−1967 periods sources are limited to a few primary ones, mostly in Western languages, the period from 1936 to 1949 is well covered by both Greek- and Western-language materials. Topics best covered in this period include Greece's role in World War II, the Axis occupation, the national resistance, guerrilla warfare, and the Greek Civil War. For the period of the military regime of 1967−1974, as well as for contemporary political affairs, the Hoover Institution collection of materials, although still limited, is growing.

This survey summarizes Hoover Institution holdings for each period and topic in Greek affairs since 1900. Basic primary sources (government documents, newspapers, etc.) are covered first, followed by a sampling of the Hoover Institution's holdings in secondary sources, emphasizing Greek works. Finally, serial holdings and archival materials are outlined.

## THE GRECO-TURKISH WAR, 1897

The Greco-Turkish War of 1897 is documented at the Hoover Institution not only by a number of scattered Western sources, but also by two voluminous Greek studies: Mazarakēs-Aenian, A. *Historikē Meletē 1821−1897 kai ho polemos tou 1897,* 2v. (Athens, 1950); and Spēliopoulos, A. *Historia tou Hellēno-Tourkikou polemou epi tei basē pollōn diplomatikōn kai historikōn engraphōn,* 2v. (Athens, 1897).

## 1909-1914

For the period of the military revolution of 1909, the rise of Eleutherios Venizelos, and the Balkan wars, a number of works, both Western and Greek, are available at the Hoover Institution, including:

Dragoumēs, Ion. *Ho Hellēnismos mou kai hoi hellēnes: Hellēnikos politismos* (Athens, 1927).

Driault, E. and Lheriter, Michel. *Histoire diplomatique de la Grèce de 1821 à nos jours,* 5v. (Paris, 1925−1926).

Enepekidēs, P. *Hē doxa kai ho dichasmos apo ta mystika archeia tēs Viennēs, 1908−1916* (Athens, 1962).

Malainos, M. *Hē epanastasis tou 1909* (Athens, 1965).

Markezinēs, S. B. *Politikē historia tēs neōteras Hellados,* 4v. (Athens, 1960−1968).

Vlachos, Nikolaos. *Historia tōn kratōn tēs Chersonēsou tou Haimou, 1908−1914* (Athens, 1954).

Vournas, Tassos. *Goudi: To kinēma tou 1909* (Athens, 1957).

Zorogiannidēs, Kōnstantinos. *Hēmerologion poreiōn kai polemikōn epichēireseōn, 1912−1913* (Thessalonikē, 1975).

During the first decade of this century, a multifaceted struggle was carried on among Balkan states for the control of Macedonia and its population. The Greek side of this conflict is presented in a number of memoirs and histories, including:

Augerinos, Melpomenēs. *Makedonia: Apomnēmoneumata kai diplomatika paraskēnia . . . apo 1908−1912* (Athens, 1914).

Chatzēkyriakos, G. *Skepseis kai entypōseis ek periodeias ana tēn Makedonian, 1905−1906* (Athens, 1962).

Dakin, Douglas. *The Greek Struggle in Macedonia* (Thessalonikē, 1965).

Georgiou, C. G. *Ho Yermas kai ta gegonota tou Makedonikou agōna* (Thessalonikē, 1966).

Karavangelēs, Germanos. *Ho Makedonikos agōn* (Thessalonikē, 1959).

Souliōtēs-Nikolaidēs, A. *Ho Makedonikos agōn: Hē "Organōsis Thessalonikēs," 1906−1908* (Thessalonikē, 1959).

## WORLD WAR I, 1914−1918

For the history of Greece during World War I, the Hoover Institution has some limited primary sources, including two years of the government gazette of the pro-Allied provisional government of Eleutherios Venizelos: *Ephēmeris tēs Prosōrinēs Kybernēseōs tou Basileiou tēs Hellados* (Chania, September 1916; Thessalonikē, 1916–1917). Newspaper coverage for Greece during World War I consists of scattered wartime holdings of the Athens newspapers *Akropolis, Chronos, Empros,* and *Hestia–Nea Hellas* and *L'Indépendant* of Thessalonikē, as well as substantial runs of *Patris* (Athens, 1915, 1916, 1918), *Le Messager d'Athènes* (1915–1916), and *Journal des Hellènes* (1916–1918).

On the problems of Greek political division over neutrality, Allied intervention, and Greece's role in the First World War, the following secondary works, among others, may be found at the Hoover Institution:

Adamov, Evgeniía A. *Evropeĭskie derzhavy i Gretsiía v epokhu mirovoĭ voĭny* (Moscow, 1922).

Bujac, Jean L. *Les Campaigns de l'armée hellénique, 1918–1922* (Paris, 1930).

Cosmin, S. P. *Dossiers secrets de la Triple Entente: Grèce, 1914–1922* (Paris, 1969).

Enepekidēs, P. *Hē doxa kai ho dichasmos: Apo ta mystika archeia tēs Viennēs, 1908–1916* (Athens, 1962).

*L'Entente et la Grèce pendent la grande guerre . . . ,* 2v. (Paris, 1926).

Frangulis, A. F. *La Grèce et la crise mondiale,* 2v. (Paris, 1926).

Greece. Genikon Epiteleion Stratou. *Ho Hellēnikos Stratos kata ton Prōton Pankosmion Polemon, 1914–1918,* 2v. (Athens, 1958–1961).

———. Hypourgeion tōn Exōterikōn. *The Greek White Book: Diplomatic Documents, 1913–1917* (New York, 1918); and *Supplementary Diplomatic Documents, 1913–1917* (New York, 1919).

———. ———. *Documents diplomatiques, octobre 1915–juin 1916* (Athens, 1921).

Leon, George B. *Greece and the Great Powers, 1914–1917* (Thessalonikē, 1974).

Theodoulou, C. A. *Greece and the Entente* (Thessalonikē, 1971).

Venterēs, Georgios. *Hē Hellas tou 1910–1920,* 2v. (Athens, 1970).

## POST-WORLD WAR I GREECE AND THE GRECO-TURKISH WAR, 1919–1922

Abundant information on the diplomatic activity of Greece at the Paris Peace Conference can be found in the Greek delegation's documents as well as in several of the books mentioned above.

A little-known episode in post–World War I Greek history is the participation of Greek armed forces in the Russian Civil War in the southern Ukraine in 1919. Books on this topic at the Hoover Institution in Greek are:

Doukas, Sophronios. *Apo tēn Sovietikēn Rōsian: Entypōseis, kriseis, perigraphai* (Athens, 1922).
Greece. Genikon Epiteleion Stratou. *To Hellēnikōn Ekstrateutikon Sōma eis mesēmbrinēn Rōsian, 1919* (Athens, 1955).
Oikonomakos, Petros. *Periorismenē drasis: Hē 534 moira stē Rōsia choris aeroplana* (Athens, 1970).
Paulidēs, Eleutherios. *Ho hellēnismos tēs Rōsias kai ta 33 chronia tou en Athēnais Sōmateiou tōn ek Rōsias hellēnōn* (Athens, 1953).

The climactic events of the immediate postwar period for Greece were its mandate in Asia Minor and its disastrous defeat in the Greco-Turkish War of 1919–1922. The history of this catastrophe is covered in a number of Western and Greek works, including:

Bujac, Jean L. *Les Campagnes de l'armée hellénique, 1918–1922*, 2v. (Paris, 1930).
Greece. Genikon Epiteleion Stratou. *Hē ekstrateia eis tēn Mikran Asian, 1919–1922*, 10v. (Athens, 1957–1967).
Mostras, Vasileios D. *Hē Mikrasiatikē epicheiresis* (Athens, 1969).
Mpoulalas, Kleanthos. *Hē Mikrasiatikē ekstrateia, 1919–1922* (Athens, 1959).
Nikolopoulos, Chrēstos B. *Me tous "myrious tou 1921"* (Athens, 1922).
Pantazēs, K. G. *Symbolē eis ten historian tēs Mikrasiatikēs ekstrateias, 1919–1922* (Athens, 1966).
Prōtonotarios, Stylianos. *Hē prodotheisa Hellas: Ta aitia tēs katastrophēs tēs Mikras Asias kai tēs Anatolikēs Thrakēs* (Athens, 1922).
Psyrouches, Nikos. *Hē Mikrasiatikē katastrophē* (Athens, 1975).
Smith, Michael L. *Ionian Vision: Greece in Asia Minor, 1919–1922* (New York, 1973).
Toynbee, Arnold. *The Western Question in Greece and Turkey* (Boston, 1922).

Archival materials on the subject of the Asia Minor defeat and its aftermath in interwar Greece can be found in the Frank R. Buchalew Papers, Ruth A. Parmelee Papers, Arnold J. Toynbee Letters, and the Mary Tsipouras Memoir (see the section Selected Archival Materials below).

## GREECE AS A REPUBLIC, 1922−1936

For the 1922−1936 period, primary sources consist, in addition to those mentioned above, of several publications of the Ministry of the National Economy and a limited number of documents from other ministries. Newspaper holdings for the same period include scattered runs of *Eleutheron Bēma* (Athens), *Salpinx* (Athens), and *Makedonia* (Thessalonikē), as well as sizable holdings of the French-language newspapers *Journal des Hellènes* (Paris, 1922−1930), *Le Messager d'Athènes* (Athens, 1922−1925), and *Le Progrès* (Thessalonikē, 1931, 1933, 1934). Holdings of histories, memoirs, and political writings for the period at the Hoover Institution include:

Daphnēs, Geōrgios. *Hē Hellas metaxy dyo polemōn, 1923−1940*, 2v. (Athens, 1955).

Eddy, Charles B. *Greece and the Greek Refugees* (London, 1931).

*Hē ethnosōtērios epanastasis tēs 14 Septembriou 1922* (Athens, 1923).

Mears, E. G. *Greece Today: The Aftermath of the Refugee Impact* (Stanford, 1929).

Merkourēs, Stamatēs. *Geōrgios Kondylēs, 1879−1936* (Athens, 1954).

Pentzopoulos, Dimitri. *The Balkan Exchange of Minorities and Its Impact upon Greece* (Paris, 1962).

Saraphēs, Stephanos. *Historikes anamnēseis* (Athens, 1952).

Svolopoulos, Kōnstantinos. *Hē Hellēnikē exōterikē politikē meta tēn synthēkēn tēs Lōzannēs* (Thessalonikē, 1977).

Venizelos, Eleutherios. *Gnōmai* (Athens, 1945).

Vlachos, Spyros. *Stratiōtika apomnēmoneumeta* (Athens, 1970).

The period of the Metaxas dictatorship (1936−1941) is well covered by government documents, including complete holdings of the government gazette of the Metaxas regime: *Ephemeris tēs kybernēseōs tou Basileiou tēs Hellados* (Athens, 1936−1941). In addition to this major source, the Hoover Institution has a number of publications of the Undersecretariat of Press and Tourism (Hyphypourgeion Tourismou), including such histories of the regime as: *To ergon tēs tetraetias 1936−1940 me gegonota kai arithmous* (Athens, 1940); *To kratos tēs tetartēs augustou kata to 1937* (Athens, 1938); *4 (i.e., tetartē) augustou, 1936−1938* (Athens, 1938); and *Tessara chronia diakyberneseōs I. Metaxa*, 3v. (Athens, 1940).

Newspaper sources for this period at the Hoover Institution are *Le Messager d'Athènes* (Athens, 1937−1940) and *Eleutheron Bēma* (Athens, 1940−1941).

Political writings, memoirs, and secondary works for the Metaxas period, besides some of those mentioned above, include:

Chrēstidēs, C. *Kindynoi ki' elpides tou Hellēnismou* (Athens, 1936).
Kaphatarēs, Geōrgios. *Logos pros tou Hellēnikou laou* (Grenoble, 1938).
Linardatos, Spyros. *Hē exōterikē politikē tēs tetartēs augoustou* (Athens, 1975).
————. *Hē 4ē (tetartē) augoustou* (Athens, 1975).
Malainas, Miltiadēs. *4ē (tetartē) augoustou: Pōs kai diatē epeblēthē hē diktatoria tou I. Metaxa* (Athens, 1947).
Metaxas, Iōannēs. *Logoi kai skepsēs*, 2v. (Athens, 1969).
————. *To prosopiko tou hēmerologio*, 4v. (Athens, 1951–1960).


## WORLD WAR II AND THE RESISTANCE MOVEMENT

The most traumatic period of twentieth-century Greek history was the period from the Metaxas dictatorship through the 1940s, which saw Greece at war with the Axis, under occupation, and torn by civil war. Some works held at the Hoover Institution attempt to present a picture of large parts of this period, including:

Koutsakos, Dēmētrios. *Hē hellēnikē pragmatikōtes tēs teleutaias de-kaetias, 1935–1945* (Nicosia, 1945).
Makkas, Leōntios. *Ethnikai agōniai kai prosdokiai, 1937–1945* (Athens, 1946).
Nikoloudēs, T. *Hē hellēnikē krisis* (Cairo, 1945).
Richter, Heinz. *Greichenland zwischen Revolution und Konterrevolution, 1936–1946* (Frankfurt am Main, 1973).
Woodhouse, Christopher M. *The Struggle for Greece, 1941–1949* (London, 1975).

Diplomatic sources and studies of Greece's entry into World War II include:

Ciano, G. *The Ciano Diaries, 1939–1943* (New York, 1946).
Grazzi, E. *Il principio della fine* (Rome, 1945).
Greece. Hypourgeion tōn Exōterikōn. *Greek White Book* (Washington, D.C., 1943).
————. ————. *Hē italikē epithesis kata tēs Hellados* (Athens, 1940).
Linardatos, Spyros. *Hē exōterikē politikē tēs 4ēs augoustou kai ho polemos tou, 1940–1941*, 2v. (Athens, 1976).
Malakassēs, John T. *The Foreign Policy of the Metaxas Regime vis-à-vis London at the Eve of the Greco-Italian War* (Ioannina, 1977).

Mondini, Luigi. *Prologo del conflitto Italo-Greco* (Rome, 1945).
Sellēnas, S. *Hē Hellas eis ton polemon* (Athens, 1946).

On the military aspects of the six-month conflict between Greece and the Axis, the Hoover Institution has important holdings of official histories and other secondary works. These include such favorable accounts of Greece's prewar military preparations as: *Ho Ethnikos Stratos tēs sēmeron* (Athens, 1940); Greece. Genikon Epiteleion Stratou. *Hē pros polemon proparaskeuē tou hellēnikou stratou, 1923–1940* (Athens, 1969); and Oikonomakos, Petros. *Hē Hellēnikē Aeropōreia* (Athens, 1975).

On the military campaigns in Greece in 1940–1941, the Hoover Institution has a fair collection of Western works, including Mario Cervi's *Storia della guerra di Grecia* (Milan, 1966), C. G. Cruickshank's *Greece, 1940–1941* (London, 1976), Alex Buchner's *Der deutsche Griechenland-Feldzug* Heidelberg, 1947), Costa de Loverdo's *La Grèce au combat* (Paris, 1966), and others. The library also has a select collection of Greek works on the war in 1940–1941, including:

Greece. Genikon Epiteleion Stratou. *Ho Hellēnikos stratos kata ton Deuteron Pankosmion Polemon,* 4v. (Athens, 1959–1966).
Gregoriadēs, Neokosmos. *Ho Pankosmios Polemos, 1939–1945* (Athens, 1945).
Katheniōtēs, Demetrios. *Hai kyriōterai stratēgikai phaseis tou polemou tou, 1940–1941* (Athens, 1946).
Kokkinos, Dionysios A. *Hoi dyo polemoi, 1940–1941* (Athens, 1945).
Papamichalopoulos, Z. N. *Ho polemos Hellados kai Axōnos, 1940–1941* (Athens, 1945).
Papagos, Alexandros. *The Battle of Greece, 1940–1941* (Athens, 1949).
———. *Ho polemos tēs Hellados, 1940–1941* (New York, 1946).
Sakellariou, Alexandros. *Hē theseis tēs Hellados eis ton Deuteron Pankosmion Polemon,* 2v. (Athens, 1945).
Svolopoulos, D. K. *Ho polemos tōn Hellēnōn tou 1940–1941,* 2v. (Athens, 1945).

Holdings of general works, memoirs, and opinions on the war of 1940–1941 at the Hoover Institution include such works as:

Kotzias, Kōstas. *Hellas, ho polemos kai hē doxa tēs* (New York, 1945).
Kyrou, Achilleus. *Sklavomenoi Niketai* (Athens, 1945).
Marcantonatos, L. G. *A Athènes pendant la guerre: Journal d'un témoin, octobre 1940–avril 1941* (Thessalonikē, 1976).
Vlachos, G. A. *Arthra tou Polemou* (Athens, 1945).

On the occupation period, 1941−1944, the Hoover Institution has a significant collection of primary and secondary sources. Chief among the former is a complete run of the government gazette of the occupation regime, *Hellēnikē politeia: Ephēmeris tēs Kybernēseōs* (Athens, 1941−1944), and the corresponding government gazette of the Greek government-in-exile, *Ephēmeris tēs Kybernēseōs tou Basileiou tēs Hellados* (London and Cairo, 1941−1944). In addition to these sources, a number of individual primary sources are useful for studying the occupation of Greece. One is the clandestine legal pronouncements of the Political Committee of National Liberation (PEEA), the provisional government of the left-wing National Liberation Front (EAM), *Diataxeis gia tēn autodioikēsē kai tē laikē dikaiosynē*, as well as other legislation published in the two postwar issues of *Archeion ethnikēs antistasēs*. An excellent study of the legal procedure of the EAM is offered in Demetrios Zepos's *Laïkē dikaiosynē eis tas eleutheras periochas tēs hypo katochēn Hellados* (Athens, 1945).

Reports of the occupation regime in the city of Athens are found in *Dēmos Athēnon: Hen etos draseōs tou Dēmou Athēnōn, 1941−1942* (Athens, 1942) and *Dyo akomē etoi draseōs tou Dēmou Athēnōn, 1942−1944* (Athens, 1944).

Newspaper holdings at the Hoover Institution for the occupation period consist of *Eleutheron Bēma* (Athens, 1941−1944), *Ēnomenos Typos* (Athens, 1944), *Le Messager d'Athènes* (Athens, 1941), and the exile newspaper *Hellas: National Greek Weekly* (London, 1942−1945).

The main outgrowth of the Axis occupation of Greece was the formation and growth of resistance organizations. The most influential of these organizations was the leftist EAM, a coalition of socialist and agrarian parties headed by the Communist Party of Greece. It not only galvanized large segments of the urban population in Greece, but also fielded a guerrilla army that numbered about 50,000 men at the time of liberation. The EAM's views on wartime and postwar political affairs can be found in its postwar publications. Those found in the Hoover Institution include:

*Anatolikes synoikies Athēnas, 1941−1945* (Athens, 1945).
Glēnos, Dēmētrēs. *Ti einai kai ti thelei to Ethniko Apeleurōtiko Metopo* (Athens, 1944).
*Hē katastasē stēn Hellada kai ta aitia tēs* (Athens, 1946).
*Leukē Biblos: Maēs 1944−Martēs 1945* (Trikkala, 1945).
*Leukē Biblos: Parabaseis tēs Varkizas* (Athens, 1945).
*Leukē Biblos: "Dēmokratikos" Neophasismos* (Athens, 1945).
*Maurē Biblos: To eklogiko praxikopima* (Athens, 1946).
*Odēgies sto dēmokratiko politē gia tous eklogikous katalogous* (Athens, 1945).
Partsalidēs, Mētsos. *Diplē apokatastasē tēs ethnikēs antistasēs* (Athens, 1978).

*Physē kai proorismos tou E.L.A.S.* (Athens, 1946).
*Hoi pragmatikes aities tou Hellēnikou dramatos* (Athens, 1947).
Roussos, Petros. *Perissotero phos ston ethniko apeleutherotiko agona tou Hellēnikou laou* (New York, 1945).
Thesprōtos, Dēmos. *Autokritikē-Giate chathēke ne laikē exousia tou EAM, 1940−1945* (Athens, 1976).

Other historical and memorial works on the EAM and its subsidiaries include: Petros Antaios's *Historia tēs EPON* (Athens, 1977), Thanasēs Chatzēs's *Hē nikēphora epanastase pou chathēke, 1941−1945* (Athens, 1977), and Kleon Papaloizos's *Ethnikē Allēlengye* (Athens, 1977).

Other views of the resistance can be found in a number of secondary works, many of which deal in part with organizations in the city of Athens:

Dēmotakēs, N. *Mystikos Polemos, 1941−1944* (Athens, 1948).
*Ektelesthentes tēs katochēs* (Athens, 1976).
Gatopoulos, D. *Historia tēs katochēs,* 4v. (Athens, 1945−1947).
Ioannidēs, G. *Hellēnes kai xenoi kataskopoi stēn Hellada* (Athens, 1952)
Kōtsēs, Spyros. *Midas 614* (Athens, 1976).
Mpastias, K. *Arachnē no.44: Hē hellēnobretanikē kataskopeia sta chronia tēs katochēs, 1941−1944* (Athens, 1946).
Mpenetatos, Dionysios. *To Chroniko tēs katochēs* (Athens, 1963).
Psathas, D. *Antistasē, 1941−1945* (Athens, 1946).
Voltairakes, A. *Ego eis tēn hypēresian tēs Gestapo* (Cairo, 1943).

The Hoover Institution has a unique collection of underground newspapers and journals published during the occupation. These issues are valuable as primary sources for the study of resistance groups and the problems that concerned them. All parts of the political spectrum, from royalists to communists, are represented in the 42 titles in the serial collection. A work that can serve as a guide to these clandestine materials is N. A. Anagnōstopoulos' *Paranomos typos katochēs, 1941−1944* (Athens, 1960), which, although incomplete, can be used as a research aid for these serials.

The Hoover Institution has significant holdings of materials (books, pamphlets, and periodicals) on guerrilla warfare in Greece during the occupation. Western memoirs and histories include:

Eudes, Dominique. *The Kapetanios* (New York, 1972).
Hamson, Denys. *We Fell Among the Greeks* (London, 1946).
Jecchinis, Chris. *Beyond Olympus* (London, 1960).
Myers, E. G. *Greek Entanglement* (London, 1955).
Woodhouse, Christopher. *Apple of Discord* (London, 1948).

Holdings of Greek memoirs and histories on armed resistance in the country-side are abundant in the Hoover Institution collection. General studies on the military side of the resistance and the growth of the Greek partisans include:

Enepekidēs, P. *Hē Hellēnikē Antistasis, 1941–1944* (Athens, 1964), based on German archival materials.

Grēgoriadēs, Phoivos. *To Antartiko-ELAS-EDES-EKKA (5/42)*, 5v. (Athens, 1964).

Kouvaras, Kostas. *O.S.S. me tēn kentrikēn tou EAM* (Athens, 1976).

Pyromaglou, Komnēnos. *Hē ethnikē antistasis* (Athens, 1947).

—————. *Ho Doureios Hippos* (Athens, 1958).

Besides these and other histories, there are many works on specific guerrilla organizations and units, especially those of the ELAS (National Popular Liberation Army), the military arm of the EAM. Books on the ELAS include such collective works and albums as *St'armata, st'armata: Chroniko tēs ethnikēs antisasēs, 1940–1945*, 4v. (Athens, 1967); *Hē epopoiia tēs ethnikēs antistasēs tou Hellēnikou laou* (Athens, 1946); and studies and memoirs of the ELAS resistance organization and units in various areas of Greece, including

FOR CENTRAL GREECE:

*Hoi Antartes tēs XIII Merarchias tēs Roumelēs* (Lamia, 1944).

Dēmētriou-Nikēphoros, M. *Antartēs sta Vouna tēs Roumelēs*, 3v. (Athens, 1965).

—————. *Hē katochē sta vouna tēs Roumelēs: Meta to Gorgopotamo* (Athens, 1965).

Geladopoulos, Ph. *13ē Merarchia tou ELAS-Ta ephodia kai ho kouvalētēs* (Athens, 1975).

FOR THESSALY:

Angeloudēs, Antōnēs. *Vrontaei ho Olympos* (Athens, 1945).

Phlountzēs, Antōnēs. *Stratopeda Larisas-Trikalōn, 1941–1944* (Athens, 1977).

Arseniou, Lazaros. *Hē Thessalia stēn antistasē* (Athens, 1966).

Sevastakēs, Alex. *Kapetan Boukouvalas To antartiko hippiko tēs Thessalias* (Athens, 1978).

FOR MACEDONIA AND THRACE:

*To Apospasma Vermiou* (Athens, 1946).

Kasapēs, Vangelēs. *Ston Korpho tēs Gkymprenas: Chroniko tēs ethnikēs antistasēs ston Evro*, 2v. (Athens, 1977).

Kōnstantaras, K. *Agōnēs kai diōgmoi* (Athens, 1964).

Metsopoulos, Thanasēs. *To 30° Syntagma tou ELAS* (Geneva, 1971).
Phloisvos, Telēs, *Ho ELAS kai hoi ethnoprodotes stēn Anatolikē, Makedonia kai Thrakē* (Kavalla, 1945).
Valioulēs, Stergios. *Politēs B' Katēgorias* (Athens, 1975).

FOR PELOPONNESOS:

Papasteriopoulos, E. *Ho Mōrias Sta Opla*, 4v. (Athens, 1975).
Vazaios. Emmanuēl. *Ta agnōsta paraskēnia tēs ethnikēs antistasēs eis tēn Peloponnesōn* (Corinth, 1961).

Among the most important materials on the ELAS is the history of Stephanos Saraphēs, its general military commander, *Ho ELAS* (Athens, 1946), which was later published in an abridged English edition under the title *Greek Resistance Army* (London, 1951). Other important sources, including ELAS documents, were published in the periodicals of the Greek resistance mentioned above and in the Yugoslav collection, Arhiv na Makedonija. *Egejska Makedonija vo NOB, tom I, 1944—1945* (Skopje, 1971).

Accounts of guerrilla forces fielded by other Greek resistance organizations are also available at the Hoover Institution Library.

FOR THE EDES-EOEA (GREEK DEMOCRATIC NATIONAL ARMY—NATIONAL BANDS OF GREEK GUERRILLAS):

Choutas, Stylianos. *Hē ethnikē antistasis tōn Hellēnōn* (Athens, 1961).
Myridakēs, Michaēl. *Agōnes tēs Phylēs: Hē ethnikē antistasis EDES-EOEA, 1941—1944* (Athens, 1948).
Papamanōlēs, T. G. *Katakaïmenē Ēpeiros* (Athens, 1945).
Pyromaglou, K. *Hē ethnikē antistasis* (Athens, 1947).

FOR THE EKKA-5/42 S.E. (NATIONAL AND SOCIAL LIBERATION—5/42ND EVZONE REGIMENT):

Dedousēs, I. *Thymios Dedousēs, lochagos-bouleutēs, ho ethnomartys agōnistēs, maios 1941—aprilios 1947* (Athens, 1949).
Kaïmaras, G. *Historia tēs ethnikēs antistaseōs tou 5/42 Syntagmatos Euzonōn Psarrou, 1941—1944* (Athens, 1953).
Pyromaglou, K. *Ho Geōrgios Kartalēs kai hē epochē tou* (Athens, 1966).
Vlachos, Spyros. *Apomnemoneumata*, 2v. (Athens, 1972).

FOR THE EOK (NATIONAL ORGANIZATION OF CRETE):

Petrakēs, E. L. *Hē Ethnikē Organōsis Krētēs (EOK): Tmēma Herakleiou Kata tēn Germanikēn katochēn* (Herakleion, 1953).
Theodorakēs, A. *Hē ethnikē antistasis Krētēs, 1941—1945*, 3v. (Herakleion, 1971).

FOR THE YBE-PAO (DEFENDERS OF NORTHERN GREECE—PATRIOTIC LIBERATION ORGANIZATION):

Chrysochoou, A. I. *Hē katochē en Makedonia*, 6v. (Thessalonikē, 1949–1951).

AND FOR THE E.S. (ETHNIKOS STRATOS):

Antōnopoulos, Kosmos. *Ethnikē antistasis, 1941–1945*, 3v. (Athens, 1964).

Although many of these studies of the ELAS and other partisan groups are tinged with biases and polemics, they nonetheless give a picture not only of their own organizations but also of opposing forces.

The problem of military collaboration with the occupation forces is covered in a number of works, including those on armed resistance mentioned above. Although most studies are resoundingly critical of the collaboration that occurred during the occupation, a number of apologetic works on the subject of collaboration by participants in the Tagmata Asphaleias (Security Battalions) and other formations have appeared. Among these are:

Antōnopoulos, K. *Hē ethnikē antistasis, 1941–1945*, 3v. (Athens, 1964).
Chrysochoou, A. *Hē katochē en Makedonia*, 6v. (Thessalonikē, 1949–1951).
Stavrogiannopoulos, V. *Hē zōē tēs katochēs kai ta Tagmata Asphaleias* (Athens, 1972).
———. *Pikres Anamnēseis* (Athens, 1974).
Tsakalotos, T. *Hē machē tōn oligōn* (Athens, 1971).

In addition to its monograph and pamphlet holdings, the Hoover Institution has runs of four periodicals devoted entirely or partially to the study of the national resistance: *Archeion ethnikēs antistasēs* (Athens, 1946), *Ethnikē antistasē* (Athens, 1975), *Historikon Archeion tēs ethnikēs antistaseōs* (Athens, 1958–1962), and *Historikē Epitheorēsē* (Athens, 1962–1967).

The political division of Greece between forces of the left and right occurred not only in occupied Greece, but also among the forces of the Greek government-in-exile, as is evidenced by the mutinies of Greek forces fighting with the Allies in the Middle East. Works at the Hoover Institution that throw light on these events include:

Athanasiadēs, G. *Hē prōtē praxē tēs Hellēnikēs tragōdias: Mesē Anatolē, 1941–1944* (Athens, 1975).
Loverdo, Costa de. *La Bataillon sacré* (Paris, 1965).

Manetas, Ioannēs K. *Hieros Lochos, 1942—1945* (Athens, 1977).
Tsouderos, Emmanouēl. *Hellēnikes anomalies stē Mesē Anatolē* (Athens, 1945).

The memoirs and biographies of political and military leaders are valuable sources for the wartime and postwar period of Greece. Besides those mentioned above, the Hoover Institution holdings include the following biographical sources:

Chatzēpanagiōtes, G. *Hē politikē diathēkē tou Arē Velouchiōtē* (Athens, 1975).
Kanellopoulos, Panagiotēs. *1935—1945 Enas apologismos* (Athens, 1945).
Kartalēs, Georgios. *Pepragmena* (Athens, 1945).
Kodros, M. *Ho Basileus eis tōn agōna: 15 historikai hēmeromēniai* (Athens, 1945).
Lagdas, Panos. *Arēs Velouchiōtēs* (Athens, 1976).
Papandreou, Geōrgios. *Hē apeleutherōsis tēs Hellados* (Athens, 1947).
———. *Keimena*, 2v. (Athens, 1962—63).
Rallēs, G. *Ho Iōannēs Rallēs homilei ek tou taphou* (Athens, 1947).
Tsirimōkos, Ēlias. *Alexandros Svolos: Hē dikē mas aletheia* (Athens, 1962).
Tsouderos, Emmanouēl. *Gnōmes kai logoi* (Athens, 1946).
———. *Logoi: Aprilios 1941—martios 1942* (New York, 1942).
Venezēs, Ēlias. *Archiepiskopos Damaskēnos* (Athens, 1952).
———. *Emmanouēl Tsouderos* (Athens, 1966).

Archival materials at the Hoover Institution on World War II can be found in the G. D. Athanassopoulos Memorandum, the Greek Resistance Posters Collection, the Joseph S. Roucek Collection, the Leften Stavrianos Collection, the Costa Couvaras Papers, and the World War II—Balkans Collection (see below).

## THE DECEMBER 1944 UPRISING

Besides EAM and other documents, the Hoover Institution has the following secondary works, among others, concerning the December 1944 uprising and British intervention:

Damonidēs. *Ho tritos gyros* (Athens, 1945).
Iatridēs, John O. *Revolt in Athens: The Greek Communist "Second Round", 1944—45* (Princeton, N.J., 1972).
Karagiōrgēs, Kōstas. *Gyro apo to dekembrē* (Athens, 1945).

Papandreou, Geōrgios. *Hē apeleutherōsis tēs Hellados* (Athens, 1945).
Petsopoulos, Giannes. *Ta pragmatika aitia tēs diagraphēs mou apo to K.K.E.: Kritikē mias politikēs kairoskopias kai prodosias* (Athens, 1946).
*Hē symphonia tēs Varkizas* (Athens, 1945).
Zevgos, Giannēs. *Hē laïkē antistasē tou dekemvrē kai to neohellēniko zētēma* (Athens, 1945).

## THE GREEK COMMUNIST PARTY

Since the Communist Party of Greece (KKE) played such a significant role in the events of wartime and postwar Greece, a section on the Hoover Institution's holdings on the KKE is appropriate. Primary and secondary sources on the early socialist movements in Greece include Giannēs Kordatos's *Historia tou Hellēnikou Ergatikou Kinematos* (Athens, 1931), George B. Leon's *The Greek Socialist Movement and the First World War: The Road to Unity* (Boulder, Colo., 1976), and G. Sklēros's *Erga* (Athens, 1976).

Official documentary collections of the Communist Party of Greece are available for the years 1918 to 1945 at the Hoover Institution under the titles:

Kommounistikōn Komma Helladas. Kentrikē Epitropē. *To KKE apo to 1918 eōs to 1931*, 2v. (Athens, 1947).
———. ———. *Pente chronia agōnēs 1931–1936* (Athens, 1946).
———. ———. *Deka chronia agōnēs 1935–1945* (Athens, 1946).
———. ———. *Episēma keimena tou KKE,* 4v. (Athens, 1975).

The documents of congresses and organizational meetings of the Greek Communist Party from 1918 to 1945 can be found in the above collections, while later congresses and meetings are found in the following works:

Kommounistikōn Komma Helladas. Kentrikē Epitropē. *To 7o (ebdomo) synedrio tou KKE,* 4v. (Athens, 1945).
*VIII s''ezd Kommunisticheskoĭ partii Gretsii, avgust 1961 g.* (Moscow, 1962).
*To 9o (enato) synedrio tou KKE* (Athens, 1977).
*Hē panhelladikē organotikē syskepsē* (Athens, 1946).

Histories of the KKE available at the Hoover Institution include:

Dēmētriou, Panos. *Hē diaspasē tou KKE,* 2v. (Athens, 1975).
Katsoulēs, Giōrgos D. *Historia tou Kommounistikou Kommatos Helladas, 1918–1933,* 4v. (Athens, 1976– ).

Kousoulas, Dēmētrios G. *Revolution and Defeat: The Story of the Greek Communist Party* (London, 1965).
Solaro, Antonio. *Historia tou Kommounistikou Kommatos Helladas* (Athens, 1975).
Vonitsos-Gousias, Giōrgēs. *Hoi aities gia tis ēttes, tē diaspasē tou KKE kai tēs hellēnikēs aristeras,* 2v. (Athens, 1977).
Zachariadēs, Nikos. *Theseis gia tēn historia tou KKE* (Athens, 1945).

Holdings of periodical publications of the Greek Communist Party are mainly limited to the 1940s and the 1970s. For the occupation and postwar years, the Hoover Institution holds scattered underground issues of *Rizospastēs,* a reissue of the wartime run of *Kommounistikē Epitheorēsē,* and postwar runs of *Kommounistikē Epitheorēsē* (1945–1947), *Morphosē* (1945–1947), and *Ho Rizos* (1945–1947).

## THE GREEK CIVIL WAR, 1946–1949

Primary materials on the Greek Civil War (1946–1949) include Ethniko Apeleutherotiko Metopo. *Daily Press Review* (Athens, 1946); and Ethniko Apeleutherotiko Metopo. *Press Bulletin* (Athens, 1947) as well as the following:

Greece. Hyphypourgeion Typou kai Plērophorion. *Deltion* (Athens, 1945–1953).
Prosōrinē Dēmokratikē Kybernēsis Hellados. *Livre bleu sur l'occupation americano-anglaise, sur le régime monarcho-fasciste, sur la lutte du peuple grèc* (Athens, 1948).
———. *Second Blue Book on the Anglo-American Intervention, on the Monarcho-fascist Regime, on the People's Struggle for Liberty* (Athens, 1949).
*Third Blue Book on the Anglo-American Intervention, on the Monarcho-fascist Regime, on the People's Struggle for Liberty* (n.p., 1950).

Newspapers of the period held by the Hoover Institution consist of *Eleutheria* (Athens, 1944–1945), *Hellēnikon Haima* (Athens, 1945–1948), *Hestia* (Athens, 1946–1949), *Le Messager d'Athènes* (Athens, 1945–1949), and *Ho Rizos* (Athens, 1945–1949).

Secondary works at the Hoover Institution on the Greek Civil War include:

Averoff-Tossizza, Evangelos. *Le Feu et la hache: Grèce 1946–1949* (Paris, 1973).

Greece. Genikon Epiteleion Stratou, *Ho Hellēnikos Stratos kata ton Antisymmoriakon agōna (1946–1949)*, 2v. (Athens, 1970–1971).
Grēgoriadēs, Phoivos. *Historia tou Emphyliou Polemou 1945–1949: To deutero antartiko*, 4v. (Athens, 1965).
Kiriakidis, G. D. *Grazhdanskaîa voîna v Gretsiī, 1946–1949* (Moscow, 1972).
O'Ballance, Edgar. *The Greek Civil War, 1944–1949* (London, 1966).
Pejov, Naum. *Makedoncite i Graǵanska vojna vo Grcija* (Skopje, 1968).

Archival sources on the Greek Civil War can be found in the Robert T. Frederick Papers, Joseph S. Roucek Collection, Leften Stavrianos Collection, and the Reports of the U.S. Embassy in Greece.


## 1949–1967

The Hoover Institution collection for this period of Greek affairs consists mostly of Western-language materials. Few government documents are held for this period, with the exception of some statistical and economic reports. Newspaper holdings consist of *Hestia* (Athens, 1949–1951) and *Le Messager d'Athènes* (Athens, 1949–1958).

Secondary sources for this period include:

Karagiōrgas, Geōrgios. *Apo ton IDEA stēn chounta* (Athens, 1975).
Meynaud, Jean. *Les Forces politiques en Grèce* (Lausanne, 1965).
Sosialistikos Synaspismos. *Ta eklogika systēmata* (Athens, 1961).
Paralikas, Dēmētrios. *To alēthino prosopo tou I.D.E.A. kai tou A.S.P.I.D.A., 1944–1974* (Athens, 1978).
Theodoropoulos, S. K. *Ap to "Dogma Trouman" sto "Dogma Chounta"* (Athens, 1976).

Archival materials of this period can be found in the Robert T. Frederick Papers and the Leften Stavrianos Collection.


## THE GREEK JUNTA, 1967–1974

Materials on this period are more abundant than for the previous period. Among the primary sources are a number of government documents, including reports of the ministries of Finance and Justice, as well as the statistical yearbook of Greece since 1969. Newspapers for this period consist of *Eleutheros Kosmos* (Athens, 1971–) and *Ta Nea* (Athens, 1971–).

In addition to these sources, the Hoover Institution has runs of such exile publications as *Eleutheria* (Waltham, Mass., 1970−1975), *Eleutherē Patrida* (London, 1971−1974), and *Grecia* (Rome, 1971−1974). Scattered issues of clandestine opposition serials are available in the pamphlet collection as well. Secondary works in Greek acquired thus far by the Hoover Institution include:

Darakē-Mallē, Maria. *Hoi Esatzedēs* (Athens, 1976).
Diakogiannēs, Kyriakos. *Giatē pēra meros stē synomosia tēs chountas kai tēs C.I.A. kata tou Andrea Papandreou kai tēs Hellēnikes Dēmokratias* (Montreal, 1979).
Kakaounakēs, Nikos. *2650 Meronychta synomōsias,* 2v. (Athens, 1976).
Meynaud, Jean. *To Stratiōtiko praxikopēma tou apriliou tou 1967* (Montreal, 1970).
Papazoglou, Mēna. *Phoitetiko kinēma kai diktatoria* (Athens, 1975).
Pezmazoglou, Geōrgios I. *Mia dekaetia, 1967−1976* (Athens, 1976).
Zigdēs, Ioannēs G. *Protimēsa tēn phylakē* (Athens, 1977).

## POST-JUNTA PERIOD, 1974 TO PRESENT

Although at the time of writing the number of works on this period was still limited, some acquisitions should be cited, including:

Eliou, Elias. *Politika keimena* (Athens, 1977).
Karas, Stavros. *Ideologia kai politikē sto KKE esōterikou* (Athens, 1977).
Mpakogiannēs, Paulos. *Anatomia tēs Hellēnikēs politikēs* (Athens, 1977).
Papandreou, Andreas. *Apo to P.A.K. sto PA.SO.K.* (Athens, 1976).
―――. *Hē Hellada stous hellēnes* (Athens, 1976).

## SERIAL HOLDINGS

Besides the underground newspapers mentioned previously, the Hoover Institution has 36 periodical and 32 newspaper titles. Among the most useful of the earlier serials for research are:

*Antaios* (Athens, 1945−1946, 1948−1951)
*Les Balkans* (Athens, 1932−1933, 1937−1939)
*Diethnes Scheseis* (Athens, 1962−1965)
*L'Hellénisme contemporaine* (Athens, 1949−1952)
*Nea Oikonomia* (Athens, 1946−1947)
*Politikē Epitheorēsē* (Athens, 1945−1946)

Greek newspapers and periodicals currently received at the Hoover Institution consist of:

| Newspapers | Periodicals |
|---|---|
| *Kathēmerinē* (Athens) | *Anti* (Athens) |
| *Rizospastis* (Athens) | *Greece. Eastern Mediterranean: Economic & Social Information* (Athens) |
| *Ta Nea* (Athens) | *Greece. Economic News* (Athens) *Hellenews* (Athens) *Politika themata* (Athens) |

## SELECTED ARCHIVAL MATERIALS ON GREECE AND CYPRUS

*Costa G. Couvaras Papers:* Reports and transcriptions of radio messages relating to the activities of the Greek resistance organization EAM-ELAS during World War II, collected by the head of the Office of Strategic Services Pericles mission to Greece, 1944–1945. Includes reports by German, Greek collaborationist, and EAM-ELAS officials and a statement by C. G. Couvaras relating to the origins of the Greek Civil War (1/2 manuscript box).

*Henry Crouzot Manuscript:* Manuscript copy of *History of the Cyprus Conflict, 1946–1959*, commissioned by the Carnegie Foundation (1 manuscript box).

*Robert T. Frederick Papers:* Correspondence, diaries, writings, memorandums and photographs, 1928–1967, of Maj. Gen. R. T. Frederick, U.S.A., including materials on the U.S. Military Mission to Greece in 1951 (8 manuscript boxes).

*Greek Political Opposition Collection:* Correspondence, reports, printed matter and photographs, 1967–1970, relating to the Greek junta and to Greek and international opposition to the military regime (2 manuscript boxes).

*George Grivas Collection:* Writings, public statements and proclamations, pamphlets, leaflets, and correspondence relating to the activities of the Greek underground Ethnikē Organōsis Kypriakou Agōnos (EOKA), 1955–1959, including the original manuscript of *EOKA'S Struggle* by George Grivas (2 manuscript boxes).

*Ruth A. Parmelee Papers:* Diaries, notes, correspondence, reports, clippings, and printed matter pertaining to refugee war relief and medical service in Greece, Israel, and Turkey, 1922–1945 (5 manuscript boxes).

*Leften S. Stavrianos Collection:* Papers of the noted historian, 1942–1963, including press releases and digests, reports, memorandums, clippings, pamphlets, and other materials relating to political and military developments in Greece and Cyprus, with emphasis on the Greek Civil War period, 1944–1949 (4 manuscript boxes).

*Mary W. Tsipouras Memoir:* Memoir of the wife of a Greek army colonel, 1923, relating to her husband's role in the military revolution of 1922 and the overthrow of King Constantine I (1 folder).

*Arnold J. Toynbee Letters:* Letters of the British historian and his wife to friends and relatives in England, 1921–1923, relating to their observations of conditions in Greece and Turkey during the Greco-Turkish War (1 folder).

*U.S. Embassy in Greece:* Reports, 1947–1948, prepared by the American embassy in Athens, describing the organization and activities of the embassy, the U.S. Information Service in Athens, and conditions in Greece (1 folder).

*World War II Balkan Collection:* Studies, reports, handbooks, maps, photos, diagrams, and printed matter, 1941–1944, relating to political, economic, social, and military conditions in the Balkans, including Greece (1 manuscript box).

# ( HUNGARY )

The Hungarian Collection consists of about 13,000 monographs, 200 periodical titles (22 titles currently received), 42 newspaper titles (4 titles currently received), and a unique archival collection. Exchange programs recently established with the library of the Institute of Party History and the Széchényi National Library in Budapest will strengthen the acquisition program in the future.

In collection building, first priority is given to the period from 1914 to the present; primary and secondary sources, (official) documents, memoirs, biographies and autobiographies, and studies relating to wars and revolutions; political, economic, and social problems, and antigovernment and left-wing labor movements; as well as the congresses, conferences, sessions, and activities of the Central Committee of the Hungarian Workers' Party and of the Social Democratic party. Second priority is given to the period from 1867 to 1913.

The collection also contains a considerable amount of material, chiefly secondary sources, on questions and problems of nationalities in Hungary, Hungarian minorities in annexed territories (especially in Transylvania), the Trianon Peace treaty and its settlement, anti-Semitism in Hungary, the history of the Hungarian labor movement, Imre Nagy, and Cardinal Mindszenty.

The material concerning Hungary at the Hoover Institution may be grouped in the following periods and categories:

Pre−World War I
World War I, and the short-lived revolutionary Hungarian Soviet Republic of 1918
Paris Peace Conference of 1920
The interwar period, 1918−1939
World War II, 1939−1945
Post−World II period, 1945−1960
1960 to the present
Émigré publications, newspapers and periodicals, government documents, and reference tools

Officially, the Hungarian Collection at the Hoover Institution starts with 1918, the year Hungary declared independence from Austria and proclaimed itself a republic. Holdings on the pre−1918 history of Hungary are, however, substantial. Some of this early material, approximately 130 titles, is cataloged under the Austro-Hungarian monarchy. Many works deal with the minorities within the empire. As a rule, these are cataloged under the particular nations that gained independence after 1918 (for example, Czechoslovakia).

## GENERAL CHARACTERISTICS

Primary and secondary coverage of World War I, the short-lived revolutionary Hungarian Soviet Republic of 1919 (March 21−August 2), the Paris Peace Conference of 1920, the 1956 uprising, and the period since 1960 (particularly the role of the Communist party) is very good to excellent. Below are rough topical and chronological ratings for the stronger areas of the collection.

TOPICAL RATING:

*Government publications:* good for 1914 to mid-1920s and 1960 to the present; official gazettes cover 1914 to the present.
*Newspapers:* excellent, 1914−1930 and 1956-present; fair to good, 1930−1939; haphazard, 1940−1950.
*Periodicals:* weak before 1956; fairly comprehensive thereafter.
*Hungarian-language monographs:* generally follow these same trends, with the weakest representation for the 1930s and 1950s.

CHRONOLOGICAL RATING:

*1914−1920:* good to excellent for most sources and subjects.
*1921−1930:* monographic sources, especially political biography, in Western languages rather than Hungarian; newspapers especially good for 1921−1932; good for statistics and government gazettes.
*1938−1945:* fair for newspapers, poor for government and scholarly publications issued during the period; Hungarian-language materials covering the period but published after 1960 are, however, considerable.
*1945−1948:* once the weakest part of the collection, this period has been strengthened recently.
*1956−1961:* in comparison with the outstanding coverage of the Hungarian Revolution, the five years following it leave much to be desired; newspapers and periodicals are excellent, however.
*1961−1971:* good to excellent, especially for the years after 1965; coverage in the latter half of Communist party publications is virtually complete.

The following description discusses the stronger areas of the collection. Those serials and government publications that span more than one period are placed in periods of origin. Unless otherwise noted, all serials are published in Budapest.

## WORLD WAR I AND AFTERMATH

Laws, decrees, and other official legal pronouncements may be found in *Magyar Törvénytár* up to 1948, except for a period in 1919, when the revolutionary Béla Kun regime (see below) had its own gazette. After 1948, the equivalent publication is *Magyar Közlöny*, which is available at the Stanford University Green Library. Specifically applicable to the war period are *Magyarországi Rendeletek Tára;* a collection of decrees published by the Ministry of the Interior for 1915–1919; *Háborúval kapcsolatos törvények és rendeletek gyüjteménye: Hivatalos kiadás*, 9v. (1915–1918); and *Háborús gazdasági törvények és rendeletek*, 6v. (1915–1918).

Hungarian parliamentary activity is reasonably well represented for the 1900–1945 period by a combination of stenographic records *(Napló)*, documents *(Irományok)*, and proceedings *(Jegyzőkönyvek)*. Holdings of departmental and ministerial bulletins and gazettes are less noteworthy. However, holdings of books and pamphlets published by several executive agencies, especially the ministries of Foreign Affairs, Interior, Agriculture, and Justice, are substantial. In this category, the most valuable, indeed unique, record relates to World War I. It is a six-volume collection of documents from the office of the prime minister, Count István Tisza, for 1914–1918. The material is a typewritten copy of the originals, which were destroyed during the Second World War. It is cataloged as part of the Tisza Collection under the title "Abschriften aus den Staatsarchiven des Kön. Ungarischen Minister-Presidenten, 1914–1918."

For official, published statistics, the Hoover Institution and the Green Library share coverage of the basic annual, *Statisztikai évkönyv*, known and published in English since 1957 as the *Statistical Yearbook of Hungary*. The World War I years are covered only in the French edition, *Annuaire statistique hongroise: Nouveau cours*, of which the Institution holds the years 1913–1941. An important supplementary collection of monographs on such special topics as foreign trade, agriculture, and demography is *Magyar statisztikai közlemények*, held jointly by Stanford and the Hoover Institution for 1902–1942.

### Memoirs

A rich source of material on World War I is the extensive holdings of memoirs and similar writings of leading political figures of the period. Examples are the works of Count István Tisza, the minister-president through the war years:

*Lettres de guerre, 1914–1915* (Paris, 1931) and *Összes munkái* (Budapest, 1923). Equally useful are the memoirs and writings of Count Mihály Károlyi, the leader of the Party of Independence, successor to Count Tisza in 1918 as prime minister, and in January 1919, the first president of the Hungarian republic. The institution holds both the English and German translations of his memoirs, which cover the years 1914–1918: *Fighting the World: The Struggle for Peace* (London, 1924) and *Gegen eine ganze Welt* (Munich, 1924). *Memoires of Michael Károlyi* (New York, 1957), translated from Hungarian, is also in the collection. Works of the two leading Hungarian political figures of the era are supplemented by addresses, sermons, and speeches of such others as Count A. Apponyi, L. Bíró, G. Bernády, and V. Molnár.

## Documentaries

The collection has an extremely good group of monographic and documentary studies, such as a five-volume compendium of maps on the war with registers and lists of decorated heroes. There are also various studies in Hungarian, such as those of Károly Lengyel and of the communist scholar József Galántai. Among publications in Western languages are those by Gyula Andrássy, Harry H. Bandholtz, Cecil Street, and Bertrand Auerback.

Also important are Austrian government statements on Austro-Hungarian relations during the First World War; for example, the seventeen-volume *Österreich-Ungarns letzter Krieg, 1914–1918* (Vienna, 1931–1938), published by the Österreichisches Bundesministerium für Heereswesen und vom Kriegsarchiv. Statistical materials on the war published by the Austrian government include *Berufsstatistik der Kriegstoten der Öst.-Ung. Monarchie* (Vienna, 1919), published by the Statistischer Dienst des Deutsch-österreichischen Staatsamtes für Heereswesen, and *Magyarország véradója, melyet a Habsburgoknak fizetett, 1914–1918-ig: Winkler Vilmos osztrák hadügyminiszteri titkárnak a wieni volt cs. és kir. Külügyminisztérium hiteles aktáiból megállapított adatai alapján* (Budapest, 1919). The two-volume *Külügyminisztérium, Károly viszatérési kiserletei* (Budapest, 1921) details the deposed Austrian Emperor Karl I's relations with Hungary.

In manuscript material, the Hoover Institution possesses a collection of miscellaneous documents transmitted to it in 1932 by the Royal Hungarian Ministry of Foreign Affairs. The set covers various events in Hungary from about 1915 to 1920, including the resignation of Count Mihály Károlyi's government; protocols of the council of Peidl's ministry; military reports on conditions in the army; revolutionary propaganda in the army from 1916 through 1918; return of war prisoners; various official plans and measures taken against the bolshevik movement, 1916–1918; documents relating to minorities, especially the Southern Slavs; and documents relating to land division, 1918–1920.

## Newspapers and Periodicals

The institution's longest run of a newspaper published in Hungary is *Pester Lloyd*. This German-language daily is available for 1914—1921 and for 1931—1944. The set consists of morning and afternoon editions, usually carrying the same numbering. *Pesti hírlap* (1913—1938) is also available on microfilm for October 1939 to December 1940 and March, April, and July 1941. Published daily except Monday, some of its issues contain articles in English. Other papers include:

> *Az est* (1914—1928; apparently the only holdings in the United States)
> *Budapesti közlöny* (1916—1927)
> *Magyarország* (1914—1935)
> *Pesti napló* (1914—1926)
> *Fővárosi közlöny* (1913—1928)

Shorter runs concentrating more closely on the years before, during, and after World War I include *Népszava* (1906—1921). This newspaper was founded on February 1, 1906, and continued publication until March 20, 1944. Again, this seems to be the only extended set in the United States since the Library of Congress has holdings only for 1941 through March 1944. The newspaper resumed publication on February 18, 1945, under the same title and has now become the central organ of Hungary's trade unions. The Hoover Institution has the post-1944 run of this title.

The weakness of the collection in pre-1956 periodicals lies not so much in paucity of titles (more than 300 for 1914—1927) as in discontinuities within sets. Typical coverage within a range of years is but 10 to 30 percent. Many of the titles date from the 1916—1920 period when Hoover Library acquisitions were just beginning and when the emphasis necessarily was placed more on breadth than on completeness or depth. The following listing of periodicals relating roughly to the World War I era is limited to those titles that are at least 40 percent complete within the cited time spans:

> *Az érdekes újság* (1914—1917)
> *Déli hírlap* (1917—1919)
> *Egyetemi lapok* (1912—1918)
> *Huszadik század* (1907—1917; 1914; 1919)
> *Magyar Tudományos Akadémiai almanach* (1911—1913; in the Green Library)
> *Nemzetközi élet* (1914—1918)
> *Tolnai világlapja* (1911—1918)
> *Történeti szemle* (1915—1930; complete for 1915—1918, incomplete after 1919)

## THE INTERWAR PERIOD, 1918–1939

Although documentation on the interwar period does not match the excellent coverage for the World War I period, the holdings are useful for research. Laws and statutes are well covered in *Magyar Törvénytár*, and stenographic records and documents of the parliament are available for the years 1927–1947; holdings on the National Assembly, which replaced the parliament from 1920 to 1926 are represented for the period of its duration.

Newspaper coverage of these years is contained in such papers as *Pester Lloyd* (1920–1921, 1931–1939), *Pesti hírlap* (1919–1938), *Magyarország* (1920–1939), *Pesti napló* (1920–1926), *Az est* (1920–1936), *Nemzeti újság* (1919–1936), *Magyar front* (1932–1939), *Népszava* (1939), and *Sonntagsblatt* (1934–1938; in 1936 renamed *Neues Sonntagsblatt*). Periodical holdings for the interwar period are rather weak. The catalog lists over 300 titles for the period 1914–1927; most, however, consist of partial sets (about 10 to 30 percent complete), and many are represented by only one or two issues.

### Hungarian Soviet Republic, 1919

The internal disunity of the Károlyi government contributed to its downfall and the subsequent establishment in March 1918 of the Hungarian Soviet Republic led by Béla Kun. Although the soviet republic fell after 133 days, it was a prolific source of propaganda. A recent bibliography, *A Magyar Tanácsköztársaság plakátjal* (Budapest, 1969), states that the total number of individual leaflet and pamphlet titles published between March 21 and August 2 was 680. Of these, the Institution has approximately 450.

Holdings of newspapers and periodicals that more or less appeared and disappeared with the soviet republic include complete files of the republic's official gazette, *Tanácsköztársaság*; the government's two official newspapers, *Népszava* (organ of the Social-Democratic party); and *Vörös Újság* (organ of the Hungarian Communist Party); and eleven other newspapers and numerous periodical titles from the period. This material is supplemented by 32 issues of the official publication of the Socialist-Communist party during the republic, *Kommunista Könyvtár*. The People's Commissariat of Education published the 59-volume *A Közoktatásügyi Népbiztosság Kiadása* and the 20-volume *Veröffentlichungen*. The collection also contains circulars and other documents issued by the People's Commissariat of Justice.

The Hoover Institution possesses the original telegrams reporting on the new regime sent by a Mr. Rosta, correspondent for the newspaper *Leipziger Volkszeitung*, to his paper during this period. The retyped text of the original telegrams comes to 347 pages.

The collection of Hungarian communist propaganda fliers consists of seven volumes: the first three are leaflets in the Hungarian language, the fourth has leaflets published in English and French, the fifth in German, the sixth in Romanian, and the seventh contains leaflets in Hungarian published by the Romanian occupation forces after the fall of the republic.

The Institution holds manuscript material on communist activities in Hungary prepared by the Association of German Anticommunist Leagues. "Ungarn unter Bolschewismus" consists of two volumes and covers the period from 1917 to 1928, including the Hungarian Soviet Republic. The second manuscript, "Bolschewismus-Ungarn-Europa," consists of six parts; part two contains Lenin's statements about the Hungarian Soviet Republic, part three covers the Comintern's relations with Hungary, 1919—1935, and part four summarizes the history of the Hungarian Soviet Republic. The material consists of quotations from non-German-language sources translated incompletely into German.

Of important documentary value are personal narratives of the participants in the events in Hungary that led to the Revolution of 1918 and the establishment of the Hungarian Soviet Republic. Unique among these are two unpublished accounts: S. A. Andrushkevich's "Poslĭedniiâ Rossiiâ" (handwritten: Sonica, Yugoslavia) and Vladimir P. Antichkov's "Vospominaniiâ" (typescript: San Francisco, 1936).

The Hungarian Collection holds some 40 volumes of the work of Béla Kun, published both during the revolutionary period and after, as well as his wife's memoirs, which appeared in Hungary in 1966. Other Hungarian communist personalities of this period whose writings are held include G. Alpári, V. Böhm, E. Bogár, I. Bogár, B. Fogarasi, G. Hevesi, J. Kelen, J. László, J. Pogány, J. Révai, T. Szamuely, B. Szántó, and B. Vágó.

Of the many monographs on the revolutionary period in the Hoover Library, two publications are especially important: Rudolf Tőkés's *Béla Kun and the Hungarian Soviet Republic* (New York, 1967) and Tibor Hajdu's *A magyarországi tanácsköztársaság* (Budapest, 1969).

## Paris Peace Conference

Although it is impossible to list the several hundred ephemeral pamphlets held as Hungarian delegation propaganda, the first four items listed below are illustrative of official notes and memorandums while the fifth typifies the nationalistic special pleading that went on in Paris:

> Hungary. Fegyverszüneti Bizottság (1918–1919). "Exchange of Notes, November 13, 1918–March 21, 1919, between the Hungarian Armistice Commission and Representatives of the Allied and Associated Powers in Budapest: Concerning the Execution of the Padus and Belgrade Armistices" (typescript: Budapest, 1919).
> ————. Peace Conference Delegations, 1920. *The Hungarian Peace*

*Negotiations: An Account of the Work of the Hungarian Peace Delegation at Neuilly s/S., from January to March 1920* . . . , 3v. (Budapest, 1920—1922).

————. ————. "Mémoire du gouvernment hongrois à la Commission des réparations relatif à l'exécution de l'article 181 de Traité de Trianon" (microfilm copy negative: Paris, 1922).

————.————. *Notes Presented to the Peace Conference*, 7v. (Budapest, 1920—1921).

Maygar Revizios Liga, Budapest. *Publications of the Hungarian Frontier Readjustment League*, 8v. (Budapest, 1927).

## WORLD WAR II

World War II is rather poorly covered by contemporary official and scholarly publications, but better covered by newspapers and periodicals. Those periodicals with the most complete runs are *Láthatár: Kisebbségi kultúrszemle* (1937—1944), *Külügyi szemle: Külpolitika* (1939—1944), and *Magyar szemle* (1940—1943, monthly). From among newspapers, the best holdings are *Pester Lloyd* (1939—1944), *Pesti hírlap* (1939—1941), *Magyar front* (1939—1941), *Deutscher Volksbote* (1939—1942), *Népszava* (1939—1942), and *Magyarország* (1939—1944).

These World War II holdings are supplemented by a voluminous collection of postwar memoirs, documents, and scholarly monographs sponsored predominantly by the Hungarian Communist Party. Noteworthy are the memoirs of Admiral Horthy, regent of Hungary, and the writings of Miklós Kállay, *Nagy idok sodrában* (Budapest, 1943) and *Hungarian Premier: A Personal Account of a Nation's Struggle in the Second World War* (New York, 1954). These are supplemented by collections of documents published by the Hungarian Academy of Sciences under the title *Magyarország és a második világháború: Titkos diplomáciai okmányok a háború előzményeihez és történetéhez* (Budapest, 1961). In 1975 the Hoover Archives acquired the handwritten original copy of Horthy's 495-page autobiography. Also of importance is the monograph entitled *Confidential Papers of Miklós Horthy*, published for the first time by the communist regime in 1965. These documents were reproduced primarily to detract from Horthy's popularity and to document his alleged cooperation with the Nazis. Other memoirs on this period were done by Stephen Kertész, secretary general of the Hungarian delegation to the Paris Peace Conference, and Vilmos Nagy, defense minister in 1942 and 1943. The recently published *Magyarország honvédelme a II. világháború előtt és alatt, 1920—1945*, 3v. (Munich, 1972—1973) by Lájos Dálnoki Veress, commander of the Second Army of Hungary in 1944, describes the role of the Hungarian armed forces and the economic and political background of the period.

The number of books from the communist view has increased in the past few years. The two basic works are István Pintér's *Magyar anti-fasizmus és ellenállás* (Budapest, 1975), which basically summarizes the anti-Nazi activities of the Communist party, and Dezső Nemes's *Magyarország felszabadulása*, 2d rev. ed. (Budapest, 1960). Both authors occupy high political posts in Hungary. Also of importance is the recently published work by György Ránki, *Emlékiratok és valóság Magyarország második világháborús szerepéről: Horthysta politika a második világháborúban* (Budapest, 1964), as well as the Russian study of Hungary during the Second World War by Andreï I. Pushkash, *Vengriiä v gody vtoroĭ mirovoĭ voĭny* (Moscow, 1966). The Hoover Archives holds unpublished writings of Col. F. Koszorus, dealing with Hungarian, German, Soviet, and international military strategy during World Wars I and II.

## POST–WORLD WAR II PERIOD, 1945–1960

On December 23, 1944, a provisional national government was formed in Debrecen under Soviet auspices. Following the election on November 4, 1945, a coalition government called the Hungarian National Independence Front was established with members from five parties: the Smallholders', the Communists, the Social-Democrats, the Citizen Democrats, and the National Peasants'. The leader of the coalition government was Zoltán Tildy, head of the anticommunist Smallholders' Party. On February 1, 1946, a republic was proclaimed with Zoltán Tildy as president and Ferenc Nagy, also of the Smallholders' Party, as premier. Between 1947 and 1948, the Hungarian Communist Party seized power and absorbed the Social-Democrats into the renamed Hungarian Workers' Party. It has since been the ruling party.

The postwar collection offers good research possibilities on all historical political, governmental, and related subjects. The period 1960–1970 is represented most comprehensively; 1945–1959 has the weakest representation, although it is still adequate for research.

The basic source for acts passed by the government is *Magyar Törvénytár,* which is complete for 1945–1948. For the post-1948 period, there was a new gazette, *Magyar Közlöny,* which can be found at Stanford's Law Library. These basic sources are supplemented by a number of cumulative collections such as the four-volume set, covering 1945–1958, *Hatályos jogszabályok gyüjteménye, 1945–1960.* Besides these, the Institution also possesses copies of individual laws as they were published, many of them in English translation. National Assembly decisions and edicts and decisions of the Presidium and other bodies for the years 1945 to 1948 are also contained in a rare four-volume collection,

*Hatályos jogszabályok gyüjteménye, 1945—1948: Készült a Magyar Forradalmi Munkás Paraszt Kormány 2011/1959 (LLL.18) sz.* határozata alapján (Budapest, 1960), edited by Ferenc Nezvál, Géza Szénási, and Tivadar Gál. After 1948, the directives of the Communist party (after 1956, called the Hungarian Workers' Party) are the factual source for laws. For the period 1956 to 1962, the party's publication, *Magyar Szocialista Munkáspárt határozatai és dokumentumai* (Budapest, 1962) acts as such. Further decrees appear in such official party monthlies as *Pártélet* (1956—1970), *Társadalmi szemle* (1957—1970), and the daily *Népszabadság* (1942—1970), which are all in the collection for the years indicated.

## The 1945—1948 Period

The collection of newspapers is excellent and includes *Magyar nemzet* (1946—1949), the official organ of the Patriotic People's Front, geared to the noncommunist masses; the National Peasant's Party's *Szabad szó* (1946—1949); the Smallholders' Party's, *Kis újság* (1946—1949); and the Hungarian Workers' Party's *Szabad nép* (1947—1950).

Of special research value for the interwar and early postwar years are the Rusztem Vámbéry papers. During the interwar period, Vámbéry was a lawyer and well-known left-wing politician. He was a member of the Revolutionary Governing Council of the Hungarian Soviet Republic in 1919; from 1924 to 1939 he edited the liberal social science journal *Századunk;* and from 1914 to 1938 he was vice-chairman of the Liberal-Radical Kossuth party. As a lawyer he was well-known as defense attorney in many political trials of communist and other left-wing politicians. His most famous client was Mátyás Rákosi. After the Second World War, Vámbéry was appointed by the Dinnyes government as ambassador to the United States. In 1948 he resigned his position, making New York his home.

His archives deposited at the Hoover Institution include a number of his diaries, original manuscripts of some of his publications, unpublished manuscripts and drafts, and many manuscripts of articles and books by his associates and friends, as well as a sizable collection of letters to and from friends. In addition, the Hoover Archives has the dispatches of S. M. Finger, written in 1953 while he was a foreign service officer in the American legation in Budapest, relating to various aspects of the Hungarian economy between 1950 and 1952. Two important monographs, among several others in the holdings, analyze and sum up the general political and social developments in Hungary after World War II: Balogh, Sándor. *Parlamenti és pártharcok Magyarországon, 1945—1947* (Budapest, 1975); and Szabó, Bálint. *A szocializmus utján: A felszabadulást követő negyedszázad kronológiája* (Budapest, 1970).

## The Revolution of 1956

The Hoover Library holds works by a number of well-known Communists, including Rákosi, Gerő, Révai, Rajk, Imre Nagy, Hegedus, and Lukács. The lives and activities of these persons are also documented with memoirs and biographies.

The Hoover Institution's collection of primary sources on the Hungarian Revolution of 1956 and its subsequent suppression by the Soviet army is probably unique outside of Hungary. One very rare holding includes some 30 items of proclamations and programs of the various parties that sprang up during the revolution. Researchers compiling information for bibliographies have pointed out the scarcity of these materials in the Western world. Among them are seven leaflets published by youth organizations in support of Imre Nagy; the "First Declaration" of the revolutionary government, October 28, 1956; a list giving all the representatives of the new government by name as well as position held; orders of the Soviet military forces after intervention, for example, surrender of arms, work orders, and time of curfew. Also included in this collection are the majority of Hungarian newspapers published during the period between October 29 and November 3:

> *Igazság*, the revolutionary Hungarian army and youth paper
> *Kis újság*, paper of the independent Smallholders' Party
> *Magyar függetlenség*, the Hungarian National Revolutionary Committee's paper
> *Magyar honvéd*, the Hungarian army's paper
> *Magyar ifjuság*, paper of the Young Workers' Revolutionary Council
> *Magyar nemzet*, an independent political daily
> *Magyar világ*, an independent daily
> *Népszabadság*, the Hungarian Socialist Workers' (communist) Party's paper
> *Népszava*, the Hungarian Trade Union Central Council's paper
> *Hétfői hírlap*, an independent Hungarian newspaper
> *Szabad ifjuság*, the revolutionary Hungarian youth paper
> *Szabad nép*, central paper of the Hungarian Workers' Party
> *Szabad szó*, central paper of the National Peasants' Party
> *Új Magyarország*, the National Peasants' Party daily
> *Valóság*, an independent Hungarian daily

These primary holdings are cataloged under the name of Theodore Kurayak, who collected most of these materials and sold them to the Institution in 1963, in the special collections holdings.

A recent purchase, the Nagy Collection, consists of more than 400 items, many of them brief, typed memoirs of people active in the revolution. It includes mimeographed resolutions of various Hungarian groups; records of a worldwide association established by Hungarian "freedom fighers"; United Nations reports and pamphlets; and issues of Western-language newspapers, which reported the anti-Soviet revolt. Also in this collection, as well as in the Kurayak Collection, are antirevolutionary pamphlets published by communist front organizations.

The outpouring of eyewitness accounts, alleged documentation, and analysis of the three-week Hungarian uprising has been so great as to defy treatment in this brief space. We can mention only a few items issued after the fact by the regime of János Kádár. On microfilm are excerpts from the government record of the trials of Imre Nagy, Pál Maléter, and others for "antistate activities and high treason." *Tájékoztató az amnesztia rendeletről* (Budapest, 1963) gives information about the amnesty granted by the communist regime. There is a small but unique compilation (cataloged as a pamphlet) entitled "Excerpts from American and European Dailies, June–July, 1956, dealing with Rákosi's Resignation and the Poznań Revolt" (typewritten in Hungarian with English translations: n.p., 1956). At the head of the title is "Free Hungary: A Periodical of the National Opposition Movement."

## 1960 TO THE PRESENT

The relative scarcity of official publications during the uncertain years immediately following the 1956 uprising is partly compensated by many newspapers and journals. These same media help to fill an earlier gap, from March 1955 through 1956, during which the speeches and declarations of the principal Hungarian Communists, Mátyás Rákosi, Ernő Gerő, and János Kádár, appear to have been published in no other form. The facts of censorship mean that fleeting issues of periodicals may become the only records of dissent. At the same time, such serial publications are used to convey current orthodoxies. Thus, the Hoover Institution has devoted considerable effort since 1962 to the purchase of newspapers and journals dating from 1956. Another area of intensive acquisition is Communist party documentation.

The following lists give newspapers and journals in two groups, the first consisting of files containing issues since 1956, the second of titles dating from 1962.

FROM 1956:

*Acta historica*
*AMTA Társadalmi-történeti tudományok osztályának közleményei*
*Hadtörténelmi közlemények*

*Hungarian Review* (in English)
*Közgazdasági szemle*
*Nemzetközi szemle*
*Népszabadság*
*New Hungary* (in English)
*Párttörténeti közlemények*
*Társadalmi szemle*
*Történelmi szemle*

FROM 1962:

*Állam és igazgatás*
*Béke és szocializmus*
*Gazdaság*
*Hungarian Law Review* (in English)
*Hungarian Trade Union News* (in English)
*Magyar hírlap*
*Magyar nemzet*
*Munka*
*Népszava*
*New Hungarian Quarterly* (in English)
*Pártélet*

## THE HUNGARIAN COMMUNIST PARTY AND HUNGARIAN WORKERS' MOVEMENT

The Hungarian Communist Party (A Kommunisták Magyarországi Pártja) was officially founded by Béla Kun on November 21, 1918. However, the historical background that led to the establishment of the Communist party goes back into the late nineteenth century to the birth of what came to be known as the "Hungarian workers' movement." The Hoover Institution's holdings of material on this socialist movement consist mostly of works published after 1960. The collection includes such documentary publications as *A Magyar munkásmozgalom történetének válogatott dokumentumai,* 6v. (Budapest, 1951–1962), which was published by the Institute of Party History of the Central Committee of the Hungarian Socialist Workers' Party. It is considered the most comprehensive source of documentary material on the pre-1918 workers' movement (volume one covers the period 1848–1890; volume two, 1890–1900; volume three, 1900–1904; volume four, 1908–1917; volume five, November 7, 1917–March 21, 1919; volume six, March 21, 1919–August 1, 1919).

Other works on the socialist and workers' movements in Hungary prior to 1918 are:

Erényi, Tibor, and Kovács, Endre, eds. *Az I Internacionálé és Magyarország* (Budapest, 1964).

Magyar Szocialista Munkáspárt. *A magyar forradalmi munkásmozgalom története*, 3v. (Budapest, 1966–1970).

Mailáth, József. *Szociálpolitikai tanulmányai és beszédei* (Budapest, 1903).

Pogány, József. *A Munkáspárt bűnei* (Budapest, 1917).

Váss, Henry, ed. *Munkásmozgalomtörténeti lexikon* (Budapest, 1972).

Vince, Edit S. *Küzdelem az Önálló Proletárpárt Megteremtéséért Magyarországon, 1848–1890* (Budapest, 1963).

Another work of a more general nature dealing with this early period is Minister of Education G. Fukász's history of bourgeois radicalism in Hungary, *A Magyarországi Polgári Radikálizmus Történetéhez, 1900–1918* (Budapest, 1960). A. Hevesi's *Vengerskoe krestiânstvo i ego bor'ba* (Moscow, 1927) deals with the Hungarian peasantry and its historical struggle and is devoted to the pre- and post-1918 periods. In recent years the number of English-language publications and translations of Hungarian documentary works on this subject has been rising. The Hoover Institution Library has a fairly large amount of monographic material (both treaties and document collections) on labor laws and legislation relating to Hungary. In 1974 the Institute of Party History began publishing a series of memoir literature pertaining to the history of the Hungarian working class movement by contemporary participants, under the series title *Tanúságtevők: Vissza emlékezések a magyarországi munkásmozgalom történetéből* (Budapest, 1968–). This series also includes biographical dictionaries for national and local labor leaders and other activists. The documentation of regional labor activism, both in agriculture and industry, is considerable. Bibliographies of general works and of periodicals and newspapers on this subject are also available.

The clandestine interwar activities of Hungarian Communists are documented in the Hoover Institution by such publications as: Imre, Magda. *Dokumentumok a Magyar forradalmi munkásmozgalom történetéből, 1919–1929* (Budapest, 1964); Borsányi, György. *Dokumentumok a Magyar forradalmi munkásmozgalom történetéből, 1929–1935* (Budapest, 1964); and Pintér, István. *Dokumentumok a Magyar forradalmi munkásmozgalom történetéből, 1935–1945* (Budapest, 1964).

The activities of the interwar Hungarian communist "emigrants" in Moscow and other countries and their underground activities are documented at the

Institution by such works as: Mályus, Elemér. *The Fugitive Bolsheviks* (London, 1931); Guttmann, Heinrich. *Die magyarische Pest in Moskau* (Leipzig, 1921); Szabó, Ágnes. *A KMP Első Kongresszusa* (Budapest, 1963); and Horváth, Zoltán. *A KMP Második Kongresszusa* (Budapest, 1964). The "fugitive Bolsheviks" evaluated the "lessons" of the ill-fated proletarian dictatorship in Hungary, and many of them published works, especially in Vienna. Many of these are preserved at the Hoover Institution in their original interwar editions.

The Institution has large holdings of documentary materials dealing with the Hungarian Communist Party in the postwar period. Among these are the published stenographic records of all party congresses, except for the second (1951). These are supplemented by the holdings of party decrees in one form or other, published speeches, works of all leading party members, and nearly complete sets of official party press publications. These are further supplemented by all post-1956 party documentary publications relating to various political developments. Similar holdings of publications for the 1945–1955 period are less complete.

A collection of documents on the foreign policy of the Hungarian Communist Party and on the interbloc relations for 1956 to 1963 is being acquired in manuscript and printed form (especially in English-language translations) by János Radványi. In 1967, Radványi, a former, high-ranking Hungarian communist diplomat, requested political asylum in the United States, came to study and write at Stanford, and published *Hungary and the Super-Powers: The 1956 Revolution and Realpolitik* (Stanford, 1972). The documents used by Radványi for his book on Hungarian foreign relations were then turned over to the Hoover Institution.

Other useful documents published by the Hungarian Communist Party or by one of its suborganizations include:

*A Kommunista Világmozgalom Fejlődése* (Budapest, 1967).

*A Magyar és a nemzetközi munkásmozgalom, 1945–1966: A Marxizmus-Leninizmus esti egyetem tankönyve. Kézirat gyanánt* (Budapest, 1967–1968).

*A Magyar Szocialista Munkáspárt határozatai és dokumentumai, 1956–1962* (Budapest, 1964).

*Hogyan dolgozzunk a pártalapszervezet bizottságában* (Budapest, 1968).

*Törvények és rendeletek hivatalos gyüjteménye, 1964: Közzeteszi az igazságügyminisztérium közreműködésével a Magyar Forradalmi Munkás-Paraszt Kormány Titkársága* (Budapest, 1965).

*Válogatott dokumentumok Csongrád megye munkásmozgalmának történetéből* (Szeged, 1970).

## CLANDESTINE PUBLICATIONS

At present the Hoover Institution is making every effort to acquire all clandestine and dissident publications emanating from Hungary. This undertaking is still in its infancy but several items have been acquired, such as *"0,1%"*, a digest of dissident writings; *Magyar füzetek*, a printed anthology of such texts with explanatory notes; and *Irodalmi újság*, a Hungarian literary monthly from Paris, which is the most representative organ of Hungarian dissident thought.

# POLAND

The Polish Collection was started early in 1919, when Prof. E. D. Adams, who had been appointed by Herbert Hoover to collect material for a library on World War I, contacted the Polish delegation to the Paris Peace Conference. He obtained the collection's first books and pamphlets on Poland and was assured that the government in Warsaw would be glad to contribute more material to the library. Acting on this promise, Prof. Ralph H. Lutz, also a member of the Adams team, visited Warsaw in September 1919 and received the full cooperation of the Polish government. He also contacted a prominent publisher and bookdealer, Dr. Stanislaw Arct, who helped select and locate important library and archival materials and, until World War II, served as the honorary curator of the Polish Collection and contributed greatly to its quality and growth.

Since 1919, the acquisition of materials on Poland has continued systematically. During a trip to Warsaw in 1939, Professor Lutz left $500 with Arct to secure acquisitions in Poland should war break out and direct contact be cut off. This foresight on the part of the director of the Hoover Library paid off after the termination of hostilities when Arct delivered a considerable amount of wartime material, mostly unique, clandestine publications and items issued by the German occupiers. After 1945, collecting activities in Poland were renewed and, despite some difficulties in the 1950s, developed satisfactorily. No other library in the United States can match the Hoover Institution's 50-year systematic collecting of material on Poland.

The period of coverage of materials on Poland starts with the aftermath of the abortive uprising of 1863–1864. In the three partition areas, political movements and parties were founded in the 1870s, as were cultural, social, and economic organizations whose activities paved the way for the development of Polish national life that climaxed in the rebirth of an independent Polish state in November 1918. The 40 years that preceded World War I were the formative period of modern Poland. General works on Polish history covering the pre- and post-1864 period are included in the collection.

The collection documents political, social, and economic changes, first on Polish soil occupied by the three partition powers (Austria, Germany, and Russia) and later during the twenty years of independence, the period of World War II, and finally the Polish People's Republic. Demography, military matters (particularly the revolutionary movements and paramilitary organizations before and during World War I and during World War II), minority questions, the large Polish emigration to foreign countries, and other specific matters are covered. About 80 percent of the material on Poland is in Polish. The remainder is in English, French, German, Russian, and other languages.

Within the collection's limited time period and subject scope, it is the strongest research collection on Poland in the United States. Its holdings of about 35,000 volumes and pamphlets, over 1,500 periodical titles, and 270 newspaper titles are supported by rich primary archival sources and collections of leaflets, posters, and other unique material. No other American library has such supporting strength since other libraries did not start their collecting activities on Polish history, politics, economics, and social affairs until 25 years or more after the Hoover Institution collection was founded. The collection is partially supported by the income from a modest endowment, the Witold Sworakowski Collection on Poland Fund. A printed listing of Hoover holdings of books, pamphlets, periodicals, and newspapers on Poland can be found in the pertinent volumes of the *Catalog of the Western Languages Collection of the Hoover Institution*, 63v., plus supplements (Boston: G. K. Hall, 1969–), which will provide the scholar, student, and librarian with detailed information on the collection.

## REFERENCE WORKS

All standard Polish-language reference works on Poland, as well as the few in other languages, are in the collection. The encyclopedias start with the oldest Orgelbrand edition, Samuel Orgelbrand, *S. Orgelbranda encyklopedja powszechna*, 18v. (Warsaw, 1898–1912) and include *Illustrowana encyklopedia Trzaski, Everta i Michalskiego*, 5v. (Warsaw, 1927–1928). The collection also has the latest edition of *Wielka encyklopedia powszechna PWN*, 13v. (Warsaw, 1962–1970). Specialized encyclopedias include the rare gazetteer *Słownik geograficzny Królestwa Polskiego i innych krajów słowiańskich*, 16v. (Warsaw, 1880–1904), which covers ethnographic Poland and all neighboring areas with a Polish population and remains the classic geographical reference work on a large area of East Central and Eastern Europe. Recent general and regional geographic reference books on Poland, all contained in the collection, are less extensive and less detailed. Atlases of Poland and an extensive map collection are additional geographical reference tools.

Another specialized reference work, the *Encyklopedia nauk politycznych*, 4v. (Warsaw, 1936–1939), was never fully published, but the first three volumes are in the collection. Biographic reference tools are very well represented, including the still unfinished and continuing *Polski słownik biograficzny*, 24v. (Kraków, 1937–1979; thus far covering A–O) and *Czy wiesz kto to?* (Warsaw, 1938). A few recently published specialized biographical publications are also in the collection's holdings.

Bibliographic reference works are equally well represented in the collection. The biweekly *Przewodnik bibliograficzny* (Warsaw, 1946–) published by the National Library provides the most detailed information on all publications issued in Poland over the past 30 years. Another biweekly, *Nowe książki* (Warsaw, 1947–) provides more detailed information on a selection of items and has a rather commercial character. A bibliography of Polish bibliographies by Wiktor Hahn, *Bibliografia bibliografii polskich do 1950 roku*, 3rd ed. (Wrocław, 1966) is also available. A bibliography of Polish history, *Bibliografia historii polskiej*, 19v. (1944–1972), edited by Jan Baumgart, is an important research tool for historians. The following special bibliographies have been prepared on the basis of Hoover Library holdings and are available to the student and scholar in duplicated form to facilitate the location of rare library or archival material:

> Sworakowski, Witold S. *Bibliography of Books, Pamphlets and Articles in Periodicals Dealing with Federation Plans for Central and Eastern Europe Developed During the Second World War* (Stanford, 1954).
> ———. *List of Archive Material Dealing with Federation Plans for Central and Eastern Europe Developed During the Second World War* (Stanford, 1954).
> ———. *List of the Polish Underground Collection in the Hoover Library* (Stanford, 1948).

Finally, dictionaries of the Polish language as well as Polish to English, French, German and Russian dictionaries are adequately represented. To the scholar and student these reference works will provide adequate support for advanced research on Polish affairs.

## POLAND UNDER RUSSIAN DOMINATION

Although the research collection on Poland covers the period since the abortive 1863–1864 uprising, it includes a certain amount of material covering earlier periods. Acquired mostly by gift or as part of larger collections, it provides outstanding background material for research on later years. Most of these materials consist of government documents, some modest archival units, and monographs on Poland before 1864.

The rare *Dziennik praw*, 4v. (Warsaw, 1810—1813) of the Duchy of Warsaw (1807—1812) created by Napoleon should be mentioned first. For the period of the Congress Kingdom, established at the Vienna Congress in 1815, the collection includes the complete set of *Dziennik praw-Dnevnik zakonov*, 70v. bound in 75v. (Warsaw, 1816—1870), which until 1835 appeared in Polish and French and later in Polish and/or Russian. Records of the State Council, which functioned at various times after 1815 under various names, and proceedings and legislation of these bodies are well covered in Russian government documents (see below).

The Platonov archival collection contains part of the papers of V. P. Platonov, minister for Polish affairs at the court of Russia, and originals of valuable memorandums of Aleksander Wielopolski, the actual chief of the government of the Kingdom of Poland in Warsaw. A considerable number of monographs on the period 1815—1863, including a documentary work on Wielopolski, *Aleksander Wielopolski, 1803—1877*, 4v. (Kraków, 1878), are in the collection.

The basic documentary sources on Russian rule over areas of the former Polish commonwealth are contained in the rich collection of Russian government documents, described in more detail in the survey of the Russian Collection. Those mentioned here are the most important Russian government documents that deal with the Polish area. The official law collection, Russia. Laws, statutes, etc. *Sobranie uzakonenii i rasporiazhenii pravitel'stva, 1914—1917*, 16v. (St. Petersburg, 1914—1917), covers the period of the First World War and contains the laws that Russian authorities issued for the Polish area. This primary set is supplemented by the official law gazette, Russia. Laws, statutes, etc. *Polnoe sobranie zakonov Rossiiskoi Imperii, sobranie I-III: 1649—1913*, 225v. (St. Petersburg, 1830—1913), which served as the basis for the implementation of laws and decrees for the entire empire and contains all legislation for the Kindgom of Poland after its full incorporation into the Russian empire. The vast compendium, Russia. Laws, statutes, etc. *Svod zakonov Rossiiskoi Imperii*, 33v. (St. Petersburg, 1857—1915), completes these legal sources.

After the revolution in Russia in 1905, which also extended to the Polish area, an elected legislative body, the state Duma, was created. Polish deputies, organized in the Polish Club, took an active part and at times played an important role. The stenographic records of the Duma, Russia. Gosudarstvennaia Duma, 1st-4th, 1906—1917. *Stenograficheskie otchety* (St. Petersburg, April 26, 1906—February 25, 1917), contain documentary evidence about these Polish political activities in Russia up to the collapse of the tsarist empire. The Russian Collection contains complete holdings of these records.

At the time of the 1905 revolution in Russia, two Polish socialist parties, the Polska Partia Socjalistyczna and the Socjal-demokracja Królestwa Polskiego i Litwy, instigated revolts and disorders in Congress Poland. These two parties and their political and revolutionary activities are well covered in monographs and collections of documents published before 1914 and after 1945. Rich archival material on these two parties can be found in the archives of the Russian Imperial Secret Police (Okhrana) in the Russian Collection.

With the outbreak of World War I, the Polish question in Russia gained new importance. In the fall of 1914, Grand Duke Nikolaï Nikolaevich issued the famous proclamation to the Poles promising an undefined "self-government" to Poland under Russian rule, to which were to be added Polish areas from Austria and Germany. Negotiations between the Polish Club in the Duma and the government led to the appointment by the tsar of a special Committee on Polish Affairs, which (until the fall of the tsarist regime) failed to produce any concrete solution of the Polish question. More details on material concerning this problem are mentioned below in the section World War I and the Paris Peace Conference.

In addition to the extensive monographic and documentary material on Russian-occupied Poland before 1914, the collection contains good coverage of memoirs, statistical data, and monographs, both in Polish and other languages, that are useful for detailed research on this period.


## POLAND UNDER AUSTRIAN DOMINATION

The Austrian documentation, which is very strong in the Hoover collection, provides primary sources for the study of the role and activity of the Poles in the Vienna parliament and government. Included are:

Austria (1866–1918). Reichsrat. Abgeordnetenhaus. *Stenographische Protokolle* (Vienna, 1866–1918).
———. ———. Delegation. *Stenographische Sitzungsprotokolle: Session 1–49*, 33v. (Vienna, 1868–1914).
———. ———. Herrenhaus. *Stenographische Protokolle* (Vienna, 1869–1918).

Gustav Kolmer's basic work, *Parlament und Verfassung in Österreich*, 8v. (Vienna, 1902–1914), is an abridged version of the first of the above titles and, while covering only the years 1848–1904, is an invaluable time-saver for researchers.

The official *Reichsgesetzblatt für die im Reichsrate vertretenen Königreiche und Länder, 1870–1918*, 6v. (Vienna, 1913–1918) is available in the library. Furthermore, the Austrian Collection contains many publications of particular ministries and central offices that partially deal with Galician affairs. Among them are *Hof und Staats Handbuch der Österreichisch-Ungarischen Monarchie, 1874–1918: Jhg. 30–43*, 14v. (Vienna, 1904–1917); and *Wiener Zeitung* (Vienna), a daily gazette published since 1703, containing not only official information but also current news and public announcements. The holdings of the Hoover Institution are incomplete, but include the years 1889–1953.

Finally, mention should be made of an almost complete set of the daily *Neue Freie Presse* (Vienna), which is available for the years 1864–1938.

The Polish Collection in the Hoover Institution has good coverage after 1861 of political, cultural, social, and economic developments in Galicia, an autonomous crown land under Austrian domination. The *Repertorium czynności galicyjskiego Sejmu Krajowego* comprises an abridged version of the proceedings of the Diet for the years 1861–1904, with the later years still missing. The political history of Galicia is analyzed in two works: Feldman, Wilhelm. *Stronnictwa i programy polityczne Galicji, 1846–1906*, 2v. (Kraków, 1907); and Buszko, Józef. *Sejmowa reforma w Galicji, 1905–1914* (Warsaw, 1956). Holdings of the publications of the autonomous administration are spotty. The political and cultural advances of the Galician Poles are, however, well covered by memoirs of contemporaries and in several periodicals published in Lwów and Kraków. The growing antagonism between the Poles and the Ruthenians in eastern Galicia is also covered in these publications.

Due to the political, cultural, and social freedom that the Poles enjoyed in Austria in the last decade before the outbreak of the war in 1914, Galicia became the "Piedmont" of the Poles in the Russian and German partition areas. Political exiles from Russia and Prussia were welcomed in Galicia. Polish youth, in violent opposition to russification and germanization, found haven at the Polish universities in Lwów and Kraków and at the Engineering College of Lwów. Several political and paramilitary organizations came into being, in secrecy at first, but later, after the Bosnian crisis in Austro-Russian relations (1910), operated in the open, with the tacit support of Austrian authorities. The most active of them was the Riflemen's Association (Związek Strzelecki) under Józef Piłsudski's leadership, which in August 1914 was renamed the Polish Legion and fought on the side of Austria against the Russians. The Supreme National Committee (Naczelny Komitet Narodowy, NKN), created with the full cooperation of the Polish Club in the Vienna parliament, became its political representative.

The Polish Collection covers both the developments of this decade and the period until October 1918, when the Polish representatives in the Reichsrat declared themselves in favor of restoration of an independent Poland, including Galicia, and walked out of the Austrian parliament.

## POLAND UNDER GERMAN DOMINATION

The Poles in the German partition area were exposed to a systematic germanization policy, aimed at achieving success for Germany's agelong "Drang nach Osten." Following the conclusion of the Holy Alliance by Austria, Prussia, and

Russia during the Vienna Congress in 1815, Prussia enacted this policy with growing strength. The Polish and German Collections at the Hoover Institution contain ample documentation of this period, covering both the German and Polish sides of this struggle.

The Institution's complete set of German parliamentary records reveals the struggle in the political arena of Germany: Reichstag. *Verhandlungen* (Berlin, 1871—1918), including the appendices and indexes, and the *Reichsgesetzblatt*. Holdings of the records of the Prussian parliament are spotty. Statistics, including the language results of censuses, agrarian statistics exposing the results of land expropriation, school statistics, and others, are well covered for the period 1899—1918.

Publications of the Deutscher Ostmarkenverein, the civic arm of the official anti-Polish policy, rare material in this country, are well represented in the collection. The official report of this organization, called the "Hakata" in Polish (from the initials of its founders), contained in *Die deutsche Ostmark* (Lissa, 1913); basic works supporting germanization, for example, Ludwig Bernhard's *Das polnische Gemeinwesen im preussischen Staat* (Leipzig, 1907) and Franz Wagner's *Polenspiegel* (Berlin, 1908); and other books and pamphlets intended to popularize the struggle against the "Prussian Poles" are valuable sources for research on this vast subject. German intentions during World War I to annex more Polish territories from Russia, supported by the Ostmarkenverein and German industrial circles, have fair coverage.

Polish resistance to this German policy is equally well represented. Holdings consist of items published in German Poland itself as well as in the Austrian partition area, where censorship was much milder. Roman Dmowski's *Niemcy, Rosya i kwestya polska* (Lwów, 1908) provided the ideological basis for the Polish resistance in Prussia. The rare volume by Wojciech Dzieduszycki, *Dokąd nam iść wypada* (Lwów, 1910), added fuel to Dmowski's anti-German conclusions. Memoirs of Polish participants in the parliamentary struggle, documentary studies, and popular publications about the Polish resistance in German-dominated Poland, the great anti-German demonstration in Kraków in 1910 commemorating the 500th anniversary of the Polish victory over the Teutonic Knights at Grunwald, and other contemporary subjects are well covered in the collection.

A wealth of materials on the Poles in Germany published in independent Poland, in the German Weimar Republic, and during the Hitler years, as well as publications that appeared after World War II about this still controversial struggle during the 1870—1918 period, have excellent coverage in the collection. (The Institution's holdings on German treatment of Poland, occupied by German armed forces during World Wars I and II, are discussed in other parts of this survey.)

# WORLD WAR I AND THE
# PARIS PEACE CONFERENCE

On August 16, 1914, in Austrian Poland (Galicia and Cieszyn Silesia) the NKN became the spokesman for the Poles and sponsor of the Polish Legions, an outgrowth of two paramilitary organizations created with tacit Austrian support in earlier years. Piłsudski became the commander of the legions, which on August 6 crossed into Russian Poland at the side of the Austrian army. Trusting that the Central Powers would defeat Russia, the NKN proposed a future "Austro-Polish solution" in which the liberated kingdom and Galicia would form part of a tripartite Hapsburg monarchy. The German partition area was not yet included in Polish unification plans.

The Polish Collection contains exceptionally complete documentation on the NKN, the legions, the attitudes of all Polish parties represented in the Vienna Reichsrat, and the Galician Diet. Worth noting here are: Naczelny Komitet Narodowy. *Dokumenty Naczelnego Komitetu Narodowego* (Kraków, 1917), compiled by the former chairman of the NKN, W. L. Jawarski; a unique carbon copy of *Brulion protokołów Delegacji NKN w Warszawie* (in the archives); Naczelny Komitet Narodowy. *Sprawozdanie Biura Prac Ekonomiczynch (NKN) za okres od 1 kwietnia 1915 do 31 marca 1917* (Kraków, 1917); Naczelny Komitet Narodowy. Sekcja Wschodnia. *Sprawozdanie Sekcji Wschodniej Naczelnego Komitetu Narodowego* (Kraków, 1917); a complete set of the very rare weekly published for the legions, *Wiadomości polskie* (Cieszyn and Piotrków, 1914−1919); a list of casualties of the legions, *Lista strat Legjonu Polskiego*, nos. 1−7, (Piotrków, 1915−1916); and a large number of pamphlets printed under the sponsorship of the NKN, among which should be mentioned the propaganda material directed to the population of the area of Russian Poland liberated by the legions. Among the newspapers published by the NKN in liberated Russian Poland are *Dziennik narodowy* (Piotrków, 1915−1916) and *Wici lubelskie* (Lublin, 1916−1920). More than a dozen dailies and weeklies published in Galicia and Cieszyn Silesia during the war and supporting the NKN are also in the holdings.

In Russian Poland the Poles, encouraged by the manifesto of Grand Duke Nikolaï Nikolaevich promising "self-government" after a victorious war and unification with the areas under Austrian and German domination, created the Polish National Committee (Komitet Narodowy Polski; KNP) in Warsaw on November 25, 1914. This committee was composed of all Polish deputies in the St. Petersburg Duma and representatives of the few civic organizations in Congress Poland and in other Polish centers of European Russia. Acting under the leadership of Roman Dmowski, the committee failed to obtain decisive influence over the Polish Legion (Legjon Puławski), a Russian-sponsored military force composed of Polish volunteers that never reached any considerable size or importance. After the occupation of Warsaw and most of the Congress Kingdom by the Germans and Austrians in August and September 1915 and due to the refusal of the Russian government to act on several proposals of the KNP to implement the Grand Duke's manifesto, Dmowski left for Western Europe in November 1915 to appeal to France and England for support. The committee continued its efforts without results until the fall of the tsarist regime in March 1917. A special Commission for Polish Affairs, appointed by the tsar, also failed to overcome the opposition of Russian rightist elements. These developments are well documented in two collections of documents issued later by the Soviet Central Archive: Russia (1917-RSFSR). Tsentral'noe Arkhivnoe Upravlenie. *Russko-polskie otnosheniiā v period mirovoĭ voĭny* (Moscow, 1926); and Russia (1917. Provisional government). Chrezvychaĭnaiā Sledstvennaiā Komissiiā. *Padenie tsarskogo rezhima*, 7v. (Leningrad and Moscow, 1924–1927). On the Polish side, Kazimierz Stanisław Kumaniecki's *La Question polonaise pendant la guerre mondiale* (Paris, 1920) contains the most important documents on this question. The memoirs of Roman Dmowski and Marian Seyda also deal with these affairs.

Unfortunately, the Polish press and periodicals published in Russian Poland and Russia during the war are represented in the collection only by sporadic issues. However, the Institution's excellent holdings of Russian newspapers, particularly those of a liberal tendency, contain much information on Polish affairs in Russia during World War I.

In German Poland just before the end of the war, the Polish members of the Reichstag and of the Silesian Landtag organized a joint representation in which the most important economic and cultural associations were also included. The interventions of Polish members in both houses concerning Polish affairs are available in the parliamentary stenographic records, contained in the German Collection. A few memoirs published later, particularly Marian Seyda's *Polska na przełomie dziejów*, 3v. (Poznań, 1927–1939), present personal accounts and documentation about events in this part of Poland during the war.

### Austro-German Occupation

In August 1915 Warsaw was occupied by the Germans, and a few weeks later practically all of former Russian Poland was taken by the Germans and Austrians. Both powers established governments in the occupied areas, with the Germans seated in Warsaw and the Austrians in Lublin. To show their favorable attitude toward the Poles, the occupation authorities permitted the creation of political parties, the establishment of Polish schools, including a Polish university in Warsaw, and the creation of trade unions. Although under military censorship, the Polish press mushroomed, and cultural life took on an openly national character. This reversal from Russian political and cultural suppression to moderately limited freedom produced an explosion of books, pamphlets, periodicals, newspapers, and leaflets in the Polish language that grew until the collapse of the Central Powers in November 1918. The majority of these publications pertinent to the collection's scope, and certainly the most important ones, is in its holdings.

The governments of both occupied areas issued numerous rules and regulations that are excellently covered in the collection. The most important of these include:

AUSTRIAN OCCUPATION:

Poland (Austrian occupation). Laws, statutes, etc. *Verordnungsblatt der K. und K. Militärverwaltung in Polen* (Lublin, February 19, 1915– October 19, 1918).

————. ————. *Sammlung der Verordnungen für die unter K. und K. Militärverwaltung stehenden Gebiete Polens* (Vienna, 1916).

————. ————. *Dziennik rozporządzeń C. i K. Zarządu Wojskowego w Polsce* (Lublin, 1917).

GERMAN OCCUPATION:

Poland (Territory under German occupation, 1916–1918). Laws, statutes, etc. *Bürgerliches Gesetzbuch des Königreichs Polen: Im Auftrag des Verwaltungschefs bei dem General-Gouvernement Warschau* (Berlin, 1915).

————. ————. General-Gouvernement, Warschau. *Verordnungsblatt für das General-Gouvernement Warschau (Dziennik rozporządzeń dla Jenerał-Gubernatorstwa Warszawskiego)* (Warsaw, 1915–1918).

Warsaw (Territory under German occupation, 1916–1918). *Handbuch für das General-Gouvernement Warschau: Auf Grund amtlicher Unterlagen, herausgegeben von E. Ginschel* (Warsaw and Poznań, 1917).

The collection further contains rules and regulations issued by the Austrian and German occupation authorities for particular countries and cities. A considerable number of broadsides and leaflets issued by occupation authorities is also available.

With a view to obtaining the full support of the Poles for the German and Austrian war effort against Russia and also to counteracting favorable intentions of the Western Allies concerning Poland's future, the emperors of Germany and Austria issued a manifesto on November 5, 1916, promising the creation of an independent Poland. On December 6, 1916, they named a Provisional State

Council with a council of ministers. A further step in this direction was the creation by the occupiers in September 1917 of a Council of Regents for the Kingdom of Poland.

In early November 1918, first the Austrian occupation forces and on November 11, the Germans, were disarmed, and the regents were in full control. On the same day Piłsudski returned from German imprisonment, and on November 14, 1918, the regents turned their power over to him as chief of state. Independent Poland was reborn.

The holdings of the collection on this period are excellent and are matched only by the holdings of the Polish National Library in Warsaw. They include the very rare, illegally printed weekly *Z dokumentów chwili* (Warsaw, 1916–1918; 110 issues) and the unique Wisłowski Collection of leaflets. Several collections of documents, the previously mentioned Kumaniecki and Filasiewicz volumes, publications of Piłsudski's underground Polish Military Organization (Polska Organizacja Wojskowa), Stefan Dąbrowski's *Walka o rekruta polskiego pod okupacją* (Warsaw, 1922), and finally memoirs, important monographs, and serials and newspapers are the raw material for advanced research on this period.

### Paris Peace Conference

On arriving in Western Europe, Dmowski at first tried to convince the French and British governments to apply pressure on Russia to grant Poland broad autonomy under Russian rule. At the same time he warned the Allies of the danger of a revolution in Russia. He made contact with Ignacy Paderewski in the United States, who was working to secure independence for Poland. Paderewski's influence with Colonel House, and through him with President Wilson, was successful. In Wilson's address to the Senate of January 22, 1917, before the fall of the Romanovs, Wilson declared himself in favor of a united and independent Poland. After the Russian revolution, when the Provisional Government of Russia acknowledged the need for reestablishing a free Poland, Dmowski created the Polish National Committee (Polski Komitet Narodowy, PKN) in Paris on August 15, 1917. After Wilson's Fourteen Points declaration, this body was recognized by the Western Allies as provisional representative of Poland. A branch of the PKN was active in the United States under Paderewski's leadership. These events are well documented in the collection.

After the defeat of the Central Powers and the armistice, Poland was invited to participate in the Paris Peace Conference, at which Paderewski and Dmowski were Poland's main representatives. Poland's requests to the conference are well documented in a large number of publications of the Polish delegation and various Polish societies and institutions. Its affairs at the conference are broadly documented in the official collection, Paris. Peace Conference, 1919. *Recueil des actes de la Conférence*, 8v. bound in 18 v. (Paris, 1922–1934); and in the rare report of the Polish Delegation to the Conference, Paris. Peace Conference, 1919. Poland. *Akty i dokumenty dotyczące sprawy granic Polski na Konferencji Pokojowej w Paryżu, 1918–1919*, 4v. bound in 1v. (Paris, 1920–1925). The Hoover Library also has a considerable number of documentary and monographic publications on the conference and all the published memoirs of its participants, which represent exceptionally strong support for the peace conference documentation mentioned above. This coverage of the Paris Peace Conference is outstanding among the materials in the Hoover Institution.

## INDEPENDENT POLAND, 1918–1939

Systematic acquistions have resulted in an outstanding research collection on the twenty years of Poland's independence. Holdings of parliamentary debates are complete for the Constituent Assembly, Poland (1918–1939). Sejm. *Sprawozdanie stenograficzne: Sejm Ustawodawczy* (Warsaw, 1919–1922); and for the Lower House, Poland (1918–1939). Sejm. *Sprawozdanie stenograficzne* (Warsaw, 1922–1939). The following documents cover the activities of the Senate: *Exposé sommaire des travaux de la Diéte et du Senat polonais, 1918–1927* (Warsaw, 1925–1929); and Poland. Senat. *Sprawozdanie stenograficzne z posiedzeń 131–157 Senatu Rzeczypospolitej* (Warsaw, 1926–1927). Holdings of both official serials containing laws enacted by parliament and decrees and declarations of the governments are complete for the years 1918–1939: Poland (1945–). Laws, statutes, etc. *Dziennik ustaw Rzeczypospolitej Polskiej* (Warsaw, 1918–1939); and *Monitor polski* (Warsaw, 1918–1939). Indexes to the *Dziennik ustaw* facilitate its use. A collection of laws and regulations, Poland (1918–1939). Laws, statutes, etc. *Ustawy i rozporządzenia z lat 1918–1934*, 8v. (Warsaw, 1935–1938), and similar official journals (*Dziennik urzędowy . . .*) of several ministries complete this field.

Rare government publications for the early period of plebiscites and temporary administration of some areas (Central Lithuania, Upper Silesia, Poznań area) are well represented.

### Statistics

The publications of the Central Statistical Office (Główny Urząd Statystyczny) for the period 1919–1939 are practically complete in the holdings and include specialized statistics on agriculture, industry, prices, and labor for certain periods, as well as the results of the censuses of 1921 and 1931. The interested student can find all the titles in the Hoover printed catalog.

## Silesia

Due to the special status of this province, which was created by the Geneva Convention of 1922, it enjoyed considerable autonomy and published its own government documents. It had a separate diet (Sejm Śląski) the stenographic records of which are in the holdings: Silesia. Sejm. *Sprawozdania stenograficzne z posiedzeń Sejmu Śląskiego* (Katowice, 1922–1939). The official gazette, *Gazeta urzędowa Województwa Śląskiego* (Katowice), is complete for the years 1922–1939. These official Silesian publications are much desired items for research on the Silesian question, which was a bone of contention between Poland and Germany during the interwar period.

## Political Parties

The main weakness of the new Polish state was the large number of political parties, both Polish parties and parties of the national minorities, of which the Ukrainians, Belorussians, Germans, and Jews were the most numerous. During the 1918–1939 period, these parties changed names many times and combined into blocs, making a complete listing confusing and useless. The scholar and student can find in the holdings of the collection coverage of party programs, political maneuvers, election propaganda, and similar material in proportion to the strength of the respective parties. Coverage is excellent for the Stronnictwo Narodowe, Polska Partia Socjalistyczna, and Polskie Stronnictwo Ludowe "Piast," but becomes weaker for the smaller, short-lived parties. The coverage for the comparatively small Communist Party of Poland (Komunistyczna Partia Polski), which never obtained more than 5 percent of the vote in elections to the Sejm, is excellent. It includes unique leaflets from the early period (including the 1918 leaflet announcing the formation of the party), pamphlets, and rare periodicals. The material published on this party after the formation of People's Poland in 1945 is abundant.

The Bezpartyjny Blok Współpracy z Rządem, which became the governing party after Piłsudski's coup d'état in 1926, is well covered, as is the center-leftist bloc, the Centrolew, which became troublesome for the government in the 1930s. The Front Morges, a loose group formed by Ignacy Paderewski, General Władysław Sikorski, Wincenty Witos, and several socialists, is represented by some scarce material and by the memoirs of its participants.

Special mention should be made of the broad coverage of the press of this period, newspapers and periodicals alike. Unfortunately, this coverage is uneven and often in short runs. The conservative *Kurjer Warszawski* (Warsaw, 1919–1921, 1924–1928), the socialist *Robotnik* (Warsaw, 1918–1921, 1923–1928, 1931–1938), the socialist *Naprzód* (Kraków, 1918–1921, 1924–1928), and the nonpartisan newspaper *Łodzianin* (Łódź, 1918–1920, 1924–1928) have the longest runs. Holdings of some 30 other newspapers are in short runs of one to three years. The very irregular communist press is comparatively well covered; it appeared illegally or under various covers, and the collection includes many ephemera of which only a few issues appeared.

A rich collection of writings by Polish political leaders of the period of independence adds considerable strength to the material mentioned above. These include over one hundred volumes of memoirs and other publications by prominent political authors, such as Norbert Bralicki, Józef Beck, Leon Biliński, Adam Ciołkosz, Lidia Ciołkosz, Ignacy Daszyński, Jan Dąbski, Roman Dmowski, Stanisław Grabski, Władysław Grabski, Józef Haller, Stanisław Haller, Tadeusz Hołówko, Stanisław Kot, Herman Lieberman, Juljusz Łukasiewicz, Mieczysław Niedziałkowski, Aleksandra Piłsudska, Józef Piłsudski, Stanisław Pozner, Marian Seyda, Władysław Sikorski, Stanisław Stroński, Władysław Studnicki, Jan Szembek, Wincenty Witos, and Zygmunt Zaręba.

## Polish-Soviet War, 1919—1920

Begun by the advance of Soviet troops into Poland after the retreating German army in February 1919, this war is still misinterpreted by some historians, and the rich documentation in the Hoover Library holdings, from both the Polish and the Soviet side, offers possibilities for further research. There is ample documentation on the origins of this war, particular campaigns, the peace feelers in the fall of 1919, psychological warfare by both sides, the Piłsudski-Petlura agreement concerning Ukrainian territories, and the armistice and the peace negotiations concluded with the peace treaty of Riga in March 1921. As it would take too much space to list the 200 or more items on the subject here, we refer the reader to the catalog for more detailed information. We emphasize here only that the coverage is outstanding.

## Polish-Czechoslovak Conflict over Cieszyn Silesia

Again, the coverage of this subject is outstanding and includes official documents of both sides, the political background of the Ostrava agreement of November 5, 1918, the Czechoslovak invasion, the short military operations, the interventions at the Paris Peace Conference, and the final settlement at Spa by decision of the major powers. The Spa settlement, however, did not end the Cieszyn question. Despite attempts to settle the treatment of the Polish minority in Czechoslovakia by bilateral negotiations and conventions, the Polish government tried to improve its position. This led to tensions between the states, which culminated in October 1938 in the return of that part of Cieszyn Silesia with a Polish majority to Poland. Although this transfer was initiated by President Beneš and was not included in the Munich agreement, it is still a controversial question between the two states, dimmed only by Moscow's influence in Prague and Warsaw. The collection contains full documentation on the 1939 territorial change and on the entire problem.

## The 1920 Plebiscites

The Versailles treaty imposed plebiscites to be held in Upper Silesia and East Prussia. The Upper Silesia plebiscite in particular produced much trouble, and there were three armed uprisings by local Poles attempting to secure the area for Poland. The collection has strong documentation on the uprisings, the plebiscite, and the final decision of the League of Nations dividing the area between Poland and Germany.

## Poland's Economy

Statistical publications, discussions in the Sejm and Senate, publications of economic associations and banks, and finally monographs dealing with economic problems of the country are rich research sources for the study of Poland's economy during the period of independence. Some of these publications are in English and French. For details, see the Hoover Institution catalog under Poland, economic conditions, and under other related subject headings.

## WORLD WAR II

After a five-week campaign, Poland was occupied by German and Soviet troops. A Polish government-in-exile was established in Paris and published the following title: Poland. Ministerstwo Spraw Zagranicznych. *Official Documents Concerning Polish-German and Polish-Soviet Relations, 1933–1939: The Polish White Book* (New York, 1940; also published in French). The British, French, and German governments published similar documents. These documents, as well as the memoirs of diplomats and statesmen about the outbreak of the war, are in the collection.

The Germans annexed parts of the Polish territory, including Danzig (Gdańsk), to the Reich. The Soviet Union, after a plebiscite, annexed eastern Poland. Most of the remaining area was administered by the Germans as General Gouvernement Polen. The Wilno area was given by the Germans and Soviets to Lithuania. Ample documentation about this new partition of Poland is available in the collection.

During the war the Germans published Poland (Territory under German occupation, 1939–1945). Laws, statutes, etc. *Verordnungsblatt des General-gouverneurs für die besetzten polnischen Gebiete* (Kraków, 1939–1943) and a large number of other legal regulations and announcements, which are well represented in the collection. A large collection of photographs of German posters announcing executions and other repressions against the Polish population can be found in the archives of the Hoover Institution.

The Soviet documentation concerning eastern Poland under Soviet rule is limited to decrees published in the official publication, Russia (1917-RSFSR). Laws, statutes, etc. *Sobranie postanovleniĭ i rasporiazheniĭ pravitel'stva SSSR* (Moscow, 1917—) and in Soviet monographs. The few existing Polish publications on this subject are also in the collection.

Documentation on Lithuanian rule of the Wilno area is poorly covered. Polish eyewitness reports and monographs on the subject are scarce.

Underground movements were organized in all the occupied areas of Poland, with the one in the General Gouvernement the strongest. Some armed resistance groups were later united into the Home Army, which subordinated itself to the exile government and later in 1944 led the futile Warsaw uprising. Small communist armed squads took the name People's Army.

The underground organizations issued widely disseminated publications of which the Hoover Institution Collection has a considerable number and the largest collection outside Poland. Photographic reproductions of *Biuletyn informacyjny* (Warsaw, 1940—1945), the official organ of the government-in-exile and of the Home Army, are almost complete for the years 1940—1945. Holdings of five of the most important illegal periodicals of the Polish Peasant party are almost complete for the years 1940—1945. The few communist underground publications are also well represented in the collection.

The Polish government-in-exile published a large amount of documents, periodicals, and monographs, which are complete in the collection. A unique set of stenographic reports of the Rada Narodowa, a wartime semi-parliamentary representation, is available in typewritten form in the archives of the Hoover Institution. The official *Dziennik ustaw Rzeczpospolitej* (Warsaw, 1918—1939) and *Monitor polski* (Warsaw, 1918—1939) were continued in Paris and Angers and later in London. Entire sets for the years 1939—1945 are in the holdings. Another important wartime file, the entire correspondence between the Fifth Division of the Polish general staff and the command of the Home Army, is in the archives in photographic reproduction of the originals, which remain in London. A microfilm of General Sikorski's personal archive is in the possession of the Institution. Finally, the archives of some departments of the government-in-exile and the private papers of several Polish political and military leaders in exile and also in occupied Poland complete this strong archival support for research on Polish affairs during World War II.

Another strongly documented area concerns the Polish military forces formed abroad by the government-in-exile. The first divisions mobilized in France, the units created in the Middle East, the army and air force in England, and the army organized in the Soviet Union under General Władysław Anders's command from men and women released from Soviet forced labor camps, jails, and forced settlement in Central Asia and Siberia are excellently covered by rich archival sources, memoirs of commanders and participants, military studies on most campaigns, and other monographs. Among the campaigns in which Polish armed forces participated, the most important were the Narvik expedition, the defense of the southern wing of the Maginot Line, the air battle of Britain, the defense of Tobruk and the African campaign, the Italian campaign and the taking of Monte Cassino, the Normandy landing and the advance through northern France, Belgium, and Holland, and the penetration into Germany, including the battles of Arnhem and Wilhelmshaven. All are excellently covered in the holdings.

The Polish forces created in Russia under the sponsorship of the Soviet government (Kosciuszko Division and other units) and their campaigns against the Germans, including the battle for Berlin, are excellently covered in postwar Polish publications.

The Communist Party of Poland, revived late in 1943 under the name Polska Partia Robotnicza (Polish Workers' Party), created a National Council of the Homeland (Krajowa Rada Narodowa), whose executive body became the Polish Committee of National Liberation (Polski Komitet Wyzwolenia Narodowego). In January 1945, this committee was recognized by the Soviet Union as the provisional government of Poland. The holdings in the collection include a considerable amount of contemporary documentation originating with the committee and the provisional government, as well as publications about their activities issued in postwar Poland.

Important documentation on Polish-Soviet relations during the war and on the over one million Poles deported from Soviet-occupied Poland to forced labor camps, prisons, and exile in Siberia and Central Asia is contained in the archives of the Polish embassy in Moscow and the Kuibyshev and Anders archives, both available in the collection. Over 40,000 original release certificates from forced labor camps, more than 11,000 personal accounts of former Polish inmates in these Soviet places of confinement, official correspondence between the Polish embassy in Moscow and Soviet authorities, and invaluable information on economic conditions in the Soviet Union during the war offer the scholar archival documentation for this broad field of research.

The following is a selected list of titles dealing with events and problems mentioned above:

OUTBREAK OF THE WAR:

Beck, Józef. *Dernier rapport: Politique polonaise, 1926–1939* (Neuchâtel, 1951).

Lipski, Józef. *Diplomat in Berlin, 1933–1939* (New York, 1970).

Łukasiewicz, Juljusz. *Diplomat in Paris* (New York, 1970).

Raczyński, Edward. *W sojuszniczym Londynie: Dziennik ambasadora* (London, 1960).

———. *In Allied London* (London, 1962).
Szembek, Jan. *Journal, 1933—1939* (Paris, 1952); and the extended Polish version: *Diariusz i teki Jana Szembeka, 1935—1945*, 4v. (London, 1964—1972).

THE 1939 CAMPAIGN IN POLAND:
Bortnowski, Władysław. *Na tropach września* (Łódź, 1969).
Norwid-Neugebauer, Mieczysław. *The Defense of Poland: September 1939* (London, 1942).
Rommel, Juljusz. *Za honor i ojczyznę* (Warsaw, 1958).
Subotkin, Wacław. *"Srzydła polskie we wrześniu 1939,"* 7v. including "Fakty" (Szczecin, 1972).

THE UNDERGROUND, THE HOME ARMY, AND THE WARSAW UPRISING:
Bór-Komorowski, Tadeusz. *The Secret Army* (London, 1951); and also the Polish version, *Armia podziemna* (London, 1951).
Borkiewicz, Adam. *Powstanie warszawskie* (Warsaw, 1957).
Karski, Jan. *The Secret State* (New York, 1944).
Korboński, Stefan. *Fighting Warsaw: The Story of the Polish Underground State* (London, 1956).
Pełczyński, Tadeusz. *Armia Krajowa w dokumentach, 1939—1945*, 3v. (London, 1970—1976).

POLISH-RUSSIAN RELATIONS:
Ciechanowski, Jan. *Defeat in Victory* (Garden City, N.Y., 1947).
*Facts and Documents Concerning Polish Prisoners of War Captured by the USSR During the 1939 Campaign* (London, 1946).
Kot, Stanisław. *Conversations with the Kremlin and Dispatches from Russia* (London, 1963).
———. *Listy z Rosji do Generała Sikorskiego* (London, 1956).
London, Instytut Historyczny imienia Generała Sikorskiego. *Documents on Polish-Soviet Relations, 1939—1945*, 2v. (London, 1961).
Mikołajczyk, Stanisław. *The Rape of Poland: Pattern of Soviet Aggression* (New York, 1948).
Poland. Ministerstwo Spraw Zagranichznych. *Stosunki polsko-sowieckie od września 1939 roku do kwietnia 1943 roku: Zbiór dokumentów* (London, 1943).
Poland. Rządowe Centrum Informacyjne, New York. *Polish-Soviet Relations, 1918—1943: Documents* (New York, 1943).
U.S. Congress. House of Representatives. Select Committee on the Katyn Forest Massacre. *The Katyn Forest Massacre*, 7v. (Washington, D.C., 1952).

POLISH ARMED FORCES:

Anders, Władysław. *An Army in Exile* (London, 1959); and the Polish version, *Bez ostatniego rozdziału* (London, 1949).

Kopański, Stanisław. *Wspomnienia wojenne, 1939–1946* (London, 1963).

Maczek, Stanisław. *Od podwody do czołga* (Edinburgh, 1961); and the French version, *Avec mes blindés: Pologne, France, Belgique, Hollande, Allemagne* (Paris, 1967).

*Polskie siły zbrojne w drugiej wojnie światowej*, 7v. (London, 1959– 1975).

Sosnkowski, Kazimierz. *Materjały historyczne* (London, 1966).

GERMAN WAR CRIMES IN POLAND:

Apenszlak, Jacob, ed. *The Black Book of Polish Jewry* (New York, 1943).

Poland. Główna Komisja Badania Zbrodni Hitlerowskich w Polsce. *Biuletyn*, 22v. (Poznań, 1947–1977).

Poland. Ministerstwo Informacji. *The Black Book of Poland* (New York, 1942).

THE POLISH COMMITTEE OF NATIONAL LIBERATION
AND THE PEOPLE'S ARMY:

Błagowieszczański, Igor, ed. *Ludowe wojsko polskie, 1943–1945* (Warsaw, 1973).

Kersten, Krystyna. *Polski Komitet Wyzwolenia Narodowego, lipiec 22– grudzień 31, 1944* (Lublin, 1963).

Malinowski, Marian. *Polska Partia Robotnicza: Kronika I.1942–V.1945* (Warsaw, 1962).

Pawłowicz, Jerzy. *Z dziejów konspiracyjnej KRN, 1943–1944* (Warsaw, 1961).

Poland. Laws, statutes, etc. *Zbiór najważniejszych przepisów prawnych z uwzględnieniem zmian i uzupełnień wydanych w okresie od lipca 1944 r. przez Krajową Radę Narodową i Polski Komitet Wyzwolenia Narodowego* (Kraków, 1945).

Poterański, Wacław, ed. *Dowództwo Główne GL i AL: Zbiór dokumentów (Warsaw, 1967)*.

The scholar interested in events leading to the creation of the Union of Polish Patriots in Moscow, the National Council, the Polish Committee of National Liberation, and the Polish People's Army should search in the Hoover catalog for the titles of writings by Bolesław Bierut, Władysław Gomułka, Piotr Jaroszewicz, Stefan Jędrychowski, Alfred Lampe, Aleksander Zawadzki, and other prominent participants in these events.

## THE POLISH PEOPLE'S REPUBLIC

Following the conclusion of World War II, great changes took place in the territorial, political, economic, and social status of Poland. This entire period of communist rule of the country is excellently covered in the Polish Collection by government documents, memoirs, eyewitness reports of Communists and their opponents, and related materials. Practically every pertinent piece published at the time and since is available. Holdings are rather weak for the newspapers of the early postwar period, however.

Since 1952 and the adoption of a new constitution modeled after Stalin's Soviet constitution of 1936, the Communists have been in full control of the country. The "thaw" in 1956 and a short period thereafter are well covered. The documentation of developments in Poland since complete communist domination has grown slowly so that it now constitutes the largest part of the Hoover Institution collection on Poland. As the Communist Party of Poland (PZPR) plays the leading role in these developments, the material on the party, its organizational features and activities, its political and economic planning, and every aspect of its work are carefully followed and collected. Holdings of its official organ, the daily *Trybuna ludu* (Warsaw), are nearly complete since 1949.

The other existing parties—tolerated by the PZPR—are not neglected, but they issue only a few publications. The organ of the Democratic Party (Stronnictwo Demokratyczne) is the most vociferous among them. Its weekly *Polityka* (Warsaw) is a sounding board for problems which the Communist party organs prefer not to touch.

Special attention is given to the publications of the independent Catholics grouped around the periodical *Znak*. Holdings of the unofficial organ of the Catholic hierarchy, the weekly *Tygodnik powszechy* (Kraków), are sporadic for the years 1950−1955 and complete since 1963. In addition, the publications of the Pax group, a communist-supported organization that tries to lead Polish Catholics, are well covered in the holdings.

Materials on economic changes and developments, foreign policy with special attention to Polish-Soviet and Polish-U.S. relations, military affairs, demographic problems, ethnic and religious minorities, and penal as well as civil legislation and codes have been systematically collected with a view to their research value. The perennial peasant problem in Poland, the changing emphasis of collectivization of the land, the migration of the village population to cities and new industrial centers, the relations between the peasants and the Communist party are especially well covered by government documents, monographs, and statistical publications.

The Polish Collection in the Hoover Institution is well equipped to support any major research project on political, economic, and social changes in Poland since World War II, both from a topical and from a historical aspect. Below are listed some of the major and pertinent publications of this period. The interested scholar, however, is referred for detailed information to the Hoover catalog published by G. K. Hall. Both parts, listing monographs as well as serials and newspapers, should be consulted.

## Government Documents

The most important sources are two official serials containing legislative decisions and executive decrees of the government of the Polish People's Republic published from 1944 to the present. The first is the *Dziennik ustaw Polskiej Rzeczpospolitej Ludowej* (actually a continuation of the prewar publication of the same title). The second is the official gazette, *Monitor polski: Dziennik urzędowy Polskiej Rzeczpospolitej Ludowej* (also a continuation of a prewar item). Renewed in 1946, it appears irregularly and contains mainly the executive orders and resolutions of the Council of State (Rada Państwa) and the Council of Ministers (Rada Ministrów), as well as full texts of speeches by prominent state officials.

Both of the above sources are supplemented in Hoover holdings by cumulative volumes of Polish legislation and a number of gazettes, including:

Poland. Laws, statutes, etc. *Legislation of Poland: Laws, Decrees, Ordinances,* 6v. (Warsaw, 1954–1959).

————. ————. *Legislation of Poland: Statutes, Laws, Decrees, Ordinances, Official Regulations and Excerpts from Motivations and Speeches,* 2v. (Warsaw, 1949–1953).

————. ————. *Ustawodawstwo Polski Ludowej: Zbiór przepisów prawnych, ogłoszonych w Dzienniku Ustaw w latach 1955–1956; 1957 i 1958,* vols. 6 and 7 (Warsaw, 1964, 1968).

## Parliamentary Records

The records of the early Krajowa Rada Narodowa and of the Sejm are contained in:

*Skorowidz do sprawozdań stenograficznych Sejmu Ustawodawczego Rzeczypospolitej Polskiej,* 3v. (Warsaw, 1949).

*Sprawozdanie stenograficzne z posiedzeń Krajowej Rady Narodowej* (Warsaw, 1944–1947).

*Sprawozdanie stenograficzne z posiedzeń Sejmu Ustawodawczego,* 6v. (Warsaw, 1947–1952).

The stenographic records of the Sejm since 1952 have not been available by subscription and have been received only irregularly.

## Statistics

All statistical yearbooks published by the Central Statistical Office since 1945 are available in the collection, as are nearly complete sets of specialized statistics, such as foreign trade, education, industry, transportation, and similar serials.

## Party Publications

The holdings of the collection contain all published records of party congresses, plenums, and special commissions of the PZPR. Holdings of the ideological periodical, *Nowe drogi* (Warsaw), are complete since its beginning in 1947, as are holdings of the organ of the Central Committee, *Trybuna ludu* (Warsaw), since 1949. Furthermore, all party publications on specialized subjects, particularly on economic planning and performance, are in the holdings. Special care is taken to acquire everything that documents the activities of the PZPR.

## Economy

All important serials and monographs on Poland's economy are in the collection. Holdings of the informative quarterly *Ekonomista* (Warsaw) and the monthly *Gospodarka planowa* (Warsaw) are nearly complete since 1947 and 1946, respectively. Publications on the economy of particular regions are also well represented. Particular attention is given to collectivization, agricultural cooperatives, and the land and peasant problem in general.

## Legal Problems and the Judiciary

The Hoover Institution, through an understanding with the Law Library of Stanford University, covers the entire field of legislation and the judiciary in Poland. Hence, all publications concerning constitutional, civil, penal, military, industrial, commercial, and family law, as well as publications concerning the judiciary, are currently acquired. Holdings of the law periodicals *Państwo i prawo* (Warsaw) and *Nowe prawo* (Warsaw) are nearly complete since 1946 and 1949, respectively.

## Learned Societies

Publications of the Polish Academy of Sciences within the collecting scope of the institution are systematically acquired, particularly publications dealing with history and political science. Periodical publications and monographs issued by the Instytut Zachodni in Poznań are in the holdings.

## Trade Unions

The state-controlled labor unions publish a wealth of monographs, pamphlets, and serials. Particular attention is given to publications on health conditions in factories and mines. This field is fairly well covered in the holdings.

## Armed Forces

As in other communist-dominated countries, publications appearing in Poland on its armed forces are scarce. The publishing house of the Ministry of National Defense has produced a wealth of historical monographs, but produces little on current organizational and technical problems. The quarterly review *Wojskowy przegląd historyczny* limits itself to military history, giving obvious priority to the popularization of the campaigns of the People's Army, formed during World War II in the Soviet Union, and its participation in the last phase of the war.

## Speeches, Memoirs, and Personal Accounts

Following the models set by the Soviets, Polish communist leaders often give long speeches and addresses, which are then issued in multivolume collections. This was done for Bierut and Gomułka in the past, but Gierek's speeches have so far been published only as pamphlets. These collections and speeches are being acquired and are available in the collection. A large number of memoirs of members of the pre-1938 Communist Party of Poland, many of whom were jailed in prewar Poland, have appeared describing the activities of the party while illegal. These include the memoirs of members of the Polish unit who fought during the Spanish Civil War on the side of the "loyalists."

## CLANDESTINE PUBLICATIONS

In recent years a number of clandestine publications have begun to appear in Poland. These publications are somewhat similar to "samizdat" publications in the Soviet Union, but differ in their method of origin. After being written in Poland, many are sent abroad, especially to England, France, and Sweden, where they are printed or photoduplicated and then brought back into Poland for distribution.

None of these publications would be published by the official, government controlled presses. In content, the publications range from official statements of dissident organizations to art and poetry. For the most part they appear as irregular serials issued by dissident organizations, such as Komitet Obrony Robotników (KOR), Ruch Obrony Praw Człowieka i Obywatela, (ROPCiO), Komitet Samoobrony Społecznej (KSS), Komitet Wolnych Związków Zawodowych (KWZZ), and Polska Partia Niepodległościowa (PPN); by student organizations, such as Studencki Komitet Solidarności Wyższych Uczelni (SKSWU); or by religious groups, such as Ruch Młodych Katolików (RMK).

The Hoover Institution is making a concerted effort to collect all possible materials of this type. The project is still in its beginnings, but already a number of such items are included in the holdings. Representative titles of clandestine publications are:

*Biuletyn informacyjny: Organ KOR-u*
*Głos: Organ ruchu demokratycznego*
*Gospodarz: Pismo w obronie praw chłopskiej gospodarki rodzinnej*
*Indeks: Niezależne pismo studenckie*
*Opinia: Pismo ruchu obrony praw człowieka*
*Poradnik społeczny: Pismo PPN*
*Spotkania: Niezależne pismo młodych katolików*

## POLES ABROAD

To the approximately seven million Poles living in foreign countries before World War II have been added some 400,000 more who left their country during the war and did not return to a communist-dominated Poland. Many of them are former officers and soldiers of the Polish armed forces abroad. The remainder are former state officials, members of the professions, scholars, and others. Their number grows each year by about 2,000 individuals, who come out of Poland by various means and do not return.

A large, new Polish settlement exists in Great Britain (about 150,000). Smaller groups live in Australia and New Zealand, where former Polish displaced persons from Germany have been admitted. The remainder settled in the United States, Canada, France, Argentina, Brazil, and even in some parts of Africa.

Poles abroad publish many books, periodicals, and newspapers in their countries of residence. Of particular importance for the study of the political and cultural activities of the Polish emigration around the world are the weekly *Wiadomości* (London, 1940−) and the monthly *Kultura* (Paris, 1946−). Holdings of both periodicals are complete. A broad selection of books, pamphlets, and other periodicals is also available.

## SERIALS COLLECTION

An important part of the Polish Collection is the great number of serial publications. These serials include more than 270 files of newspapers and some

1,500 periodical titles. Most of these titles have originated within Poland, but many have been produced outside the country as well.

The serials listed below are a selective list of the hundreds of titles held by the Institution. Only the most important, largest, and most complete runs are given.

In many cases, particularly for the earlier periods, these titles are held in broken and incomplete files. Inclusive dates of holdings, therefore, should not be considered to indicate complete runs. The holdings shown for the selected titles indicate relatively complete periods; more detailed information can be found in the Hoover Institution's serials catalog.

The following are samples of retrospective files of newspapers that appeared inside Poland:

> *Głos robotniczy: Organ KW i KL PZPR* (Łódź, 1962–1972)
> *Głos robotniczy: Organ Polskiej Partii Socjalistycznej (Lewicy)* (Warsaw, 1916–1918)
> *Kurier Polski: Pismo Stronnictwa Demokratycznego* (Warsaw, 1963–1967, 1969–1972)
> *Kurjer Polski* (Warsaw, 1917–1920)
> *Monitor polski: Dziennik urzędowy Rzeczypospolitej Polskiej* (Warsaw, 1918–1940, 1946–1954, 1956–, [incomplete])
> *Nowa reforma* (Kraków, 1915, 1917–1919)
> *Robotnik: Centralny organ PPS* (Warsaw, 1931–1938, 1944–1946)
> *Trybuna robotnicza: Organ KW Polskiej Zjednoczonej Partii Robotniczej* (Katowice, 1969–1975)
> *Wolność: Gazeta frontowa dla ludności Polski* (n.p., 1944–1945)

Many titles were also published in the past by émigrés outside of Poland, for example:

> *Dziennik polski i dziennik żołnierza* (London, 1940–1954, 1963)
> *Dziennik związkowy* (Chicago, 1940–1953)
> *Gazeta polska-niepodległość* (Paris, 1941–1951)
> *Narodowiec: Quotidien démocrate pour la défense des intérêts sociaux et culturels de l'immigration polonaise* (Lens, Fr. 1940, 1944–1953)
> *Polska walcząca: Kombatant polski na obczyźnie* (London, 1940–1951)
> *Robotnik polski: Oficjalny organ Polskiej Robotniczej Kasy Pomocy* (New York, 1944–1947, 1950, 1967)
> *Trybuna: Organ Centralnego Komitetu Wykonawczego Grup SDKPiL w Rosji* (Moscow, 1918)
> *Wolna Polska: Organ Związku Patriotów Polskich* (Moscow, 1943–1946)

In addition, the Hoover Institution currently receives the following ten Polish and émigré newspapers:

*Argumenty: Tygodnik społeczno-kulturalny* (Warsaw, 1972—)
*Kultura* (Warsaw, 1963—)
*Nowy Dziennik* (New York, 1977—)
*Ostatnie wiadomości* (Mannhein, Ger., 1947—)
*Polityka* (Warsaw, 1961—)
*Trybuna ludu* (Warsaw, 1949—)
*Tygodnik powszechny* (Kraków, 1963—)
*Wiadomości* (London, 1946—)
*Życie gospodarcze* (Warsaw, 1964—1965, 1972—)
*Życie Warszawy* (Warsaw, 1972—)

The 1,500-title collection of periodicals can also be divided into internal and émigré publications. From among those titles published in Poland, the Hoover Institution has particular strength in items from the time of both World War I and World War II.

A few of the titles from the World War I era are:

*Biuletyn Wileński* (Wilno, 1917—1918)
*Czerwony sztandar: Organ Socjaldemokracji Królestwa Polskiego i Litwy* (Warsaw, 1917—1918 [scattered issues])
*Do czynu: Organ Okręgu Warszawskiego Polskiej Partii Socjalistycznej* (Warsaw, 1915—1918)
*Goniec polowy legionów: Dziennik rozporządzeń komendy legionów polskich* (Piotrków, 1915—1916 [scattered issues])
*Gromada: Gazeta Komunistycznej Partii Robotniczej Polski dla ludu pracującego na roli* (Warsaw, 1918—1919)
*Jedność robotnicza* (Warsaw, 1916—1918)
*Komuna: Organ Komitetu łódzkiego Komunistycznej Partii Robotniczej Polski* (Łódź, 1918 [one issue only])
*Komunista: Organ Komitetu Zagłębia Dąbrowskiego Komunistycznej Partii Robotniczej Polski* (Dąbrowa, 1919 [scattered issues])
*Łodzianin: Organ Okręgu Łódzkiego Polskiej Partyi Socjalistycznej* (Łódź, 1915—1919)
*Robotnik: Organ Polskiej Partii Socjalistycznej* (Warsaw and Dąbrówa Gornicza, 1912, 1915—1920)
*Rząd i wojsko* (Warsaw, 1916—1920)
*Tydzień polityczny: Organ Związku Budowy Państwa Polskiego* (Warsaw, 1916—1918)

*Wiadomości polski* (Cieszyn and Piotrków, 1914−1919)
*Wiek nowy* (Lwów, 1914−1915, 1917 [scattered issues])

The following selection of titles from the World War II era includes mostly periodicals published clandestinely in Poland under the German occupation.

*Biuletyn informacyjny* (Warsaw, 1940−1945)
*Do broni: Organ Konfederacji Narodu* (Warsaw, 1942−1943)
*Głos ludu: Pismo Polskiej Partii Robotniczej* (Lublin, 1944−1946)
*Gwardia ludowa: Lud z armią−Armia z ludem (WRN)* (n.p., 1941−1943 [scattered issues])
*Odrodzenie* (Lublin and Kraków, 1944−1946)
*Orka: Polskie Stronnictwo Ludowe* (n.p., 1942−1944)
*Rzeczpospolita Polska* (Warsaw, 1941−1944)
*Szaniec: Dwutygodnik poświęcony sprawom Polski w niewoli* (n.p., 1940, 1942−1943)
*Wiadomości polskie* (Warsaw, 1940, 1942−1944)
*Wolność* (n.p., 1940−1944)
*Wolność, równość, niepodległość: Publikacja Polskiej Partii Socjalistycznej* (n.p., 1940−1944)
*Zielony sztandar: Naczelny organ Stronnictwa Ludowego* (Łódź and Lublin, 1944−1945)
*Żywią* (n.p., 1942−1944)

Besides the strength in these war years, the library has noteworthy titles of other periods, such as:

*Bellona: Dwumiesięcznik wojskowy* (Warsaw, 1918−1933)
*Głos więźnia: Organ więźniów X. Pawilonu Warszawskiej Cytadeli, socjalistów polskich* (Warsaw, 1879 [scattered issues])
*Myśl polska: Pismo poświęcone sprawom politycznym, społecznym . . .* (Warsaw, 1915−1916, 1926−1928)
*Na posterunku: Gazeta policji państwowej* (Warsaw, 1920−1925)
*Niepodległość: Czasopismo poświęcone najnowszym dziejom Polski* (Warsaw, 1929−1939)
*Polska informacja polityczna: Tygodniowy biuletyn informacyjny* (Warsaw, 1937−1938)
*Pracownik państwowy: Organ Związku Zawodowego Pracowników Państwowych* (Warsaw, 1946−1951)
*Prawda: Tygodnik polityczny, społeczny i literacki* (Warsaw, 1881−1886, 1910)

*Przegląd polityczny: Czasopismo poświęcone zagadnieniom polityki zagranicznej* (Warsaw, 1924–1932)
*Przegląd zachodni* (Poznań, 1945–1977)
*Przegląd polski ustawodawstwa cywilnego i kryminalnego* (Warsaw, 1928–1932)
*Sprawy narodowościowe* (Warsaw, 1927–1939)
*Zbiór orzeczeń Sądu Najwyższego: Izba pierwsza (cywilna)* (Warsaw, 1917–1924)
*Zbiór orzeczeń Sądu Najwyższego: Izba druga (karna)* (Warsaw, 1918–1924)

Periodicals published by émigrés outside of Poland and held by the Institution include:

*Bellona: Kwartalnik wojskowo-historyczny* (London, 1940–1964)
*Głos polski: Tygodnik uchodźstwa polskiego w Afryce* (Nairobi, 1945–1948)
*Myśl polska:* (London, 1945–1977)
*Na antenie: Mówi rozgłośnia polska Wolna Europa* (Munich, 1969–1974)
*Nowe widnokręgi* (Moscow and Kuibyshev, 1941–1946)
*Polonia zagraniczna* (London, 1943–1959)
*Przedświt: Organ Polskiej Partii Socjalistycznej* (Geneva and London, 1881–1899, 1901–1902, 1910)
*Robotnik: Centralny organ PPS* (London, 1940–1941, 1944–1949 [incomplete] 1950–1970)
*Skrzydła* (London, 1940–1947)
*Słowo katolickie* (Munich, 1945–1948, 1950)
*Teki historyczne* (London, 1947–1969)
*Weteran: Urzędowy organ Stowarzyszenia Weteranów Armii Polskiej w Ameryce* (New York, 1930–1937, 1940, 1945–1946)
*Wici: Organ Komitetu Obrony Narodowej* (Chicago, 1915, 1917–1919)

The Hoover Institution currently regularly receives 36 periodicals, either published in Poland or dealing with Poland. Of these 36, 6 may be considered as the Polish government's equivalent to "government documents":

Poland (1945–). Biblioteka Narodowa. *Przewodnik bibliograficzny* (Warsaw, 1946–1951, 1953–)
——. Główny Urząd Statystyczny. *Biuletyn statystyczny* (Warsaw, 1957–)
——. Laws, statutes, etc. *Monitor polski* (Warsaw, 1972–)

————. ————. *Dziennik ustaw* (Warsaw, 1918–1939, 1944–)
————. Sąd Najwyższy. Izba Cywilna oraz Izba Pracy. *Orzecznictwo* (Warsaw, 1972–)
————. ————. Izba Karna i Izba Wojskowa. *Orzecznictwo* (Warsaw, 1972–)

The remaining titles are:

*Aneks: Kwartalnik polityczny* (Uppsala, Sweden, 1973–)
*Biuletyn Żydowskiego Instytutu Historycznego* (Warsaw, 1960–)
*Dzieje najnowsze* (Warsaw, 1969–)
*Ekonomista* (Warsaw, 1914–1939, 1947–1950, 1952–)
*Gospodarka planowa* (Warsaw, 1946–)
*Handel zagraniczny* (Warsaw, 1972–)
*Kwartalnik historii ruchu zawodowego* (Warsaw, 1967–)
*Kwartalnik historyczny* (Warsaw, 1938, 1953, 1955–)
*Kultura* (Paris, 1947–)
*Myśl polska* (London, 1941–)
*Nowe drogi* (Warsaw, 1947–)
*Nowe książki* (Warsaw, 1965–1972 [incomplete], 1973–)
*Nowe prawo* (Warsaw, 1949–)
*Orzeł biały* (London, 1974–)
*Państwo i prawo* (Warsaw, 1946–1950, 1952–)
*Pokolenia* (Warsaw, 1972–)
*Polska w Europie* (Paris, 1953–)
*Przegląd historyczny* (Warsaw, 1946–1948, 1953, 1955–)
*Przegląd zachodni* (Poznań, 1945–)
*Prezentacje* (Warsaw, 1954–; note: prior to 1978 entitled *Zeszyty teo-rytyczno-polityczne)*
*Rada narodowa-gospodarka-administracja* (Warsaw, 1972–)
*Studia socjologiczne* (Warsaw, 1961–)
*Sprawy międzynarodowe* (Warsaw, 1948–)
*Studia historyczne* (Kraków, 1972–)
*Trybuna* (London, 1946–1953, 1969–)
*Wojskowy przegląd historyczny* (Warsaw, 1957–1958, 1964–1965, 1967–)
*Z pola walki* (Warsaw, 1958–)
*Zagadnienia naukoznawstwa* (Warsaw, 1965–1966 [scattered issues], 1967–)
*Zbiór dokumentów* (Warsaw, 1946–1947, 1952–)
*Życie partii* (Warsaw, 1962, 1965–)

## ARCHIVAL COLLECTIONS

Throughout this survey of the Polish Collection, mention is made of source material within the Hoover Archives. In fact, the archives possesses a large number of valuable Polish documentary collections, such as the papers of the Polish Government-in-Exile in London, 1939–1945; the papers of Prime Minister Stanisław Mikołajczyk, 1938–1966; the records of nearly a dozen Polish embassies and consulates; a collection of some 11,500 depositions of Polish prisoners of Soviet labor camps; and many others.

For more detailed information, consult the archives' recent publication, *Guide to the Hoover Institution Archives* (Stanford, 1979), by Charles G. Palm and Dale Reed.

# ROMANIA

Like most of the Hoover Institution's other area collections, the Romanian Collection had its origins during the 1919 Paris Peace Conference. Prof. Ephraim D. Adams, acting as chief of Mr. Hoover's collecting team, contacted the Romanian delegation to the peace conference and requested material on Romania's participation in World War I, which produced fairly good coverage of Romanian affairs for that period. Professor Golder visited Bucharest two years later, obtained additional material on past years, and established contact with the prominent Romanian historian Nicolae Iorga, who gave his support to library acquisitions in Bucharest. The leading Romanian book dealer, Cartea Românească, promised to send selections of current publications, but this service proved unsatisfactory. In 1939 Gardner Richardson went to Bucharest and attempted to improve book dealer services and to make arrangements for acquisition of materials for the library in case of war or other interruption of direct contact. This arrangement was successful, and after the war a considerable amount of wartime publications was obtained. Acquisitions from Romania ceased completely during the years of the cold war. Only in the mid-1960s were acquisitions and exchanges with Romania renewed.

In general terms, the Institution's coverage of material on Romania can be considered good for the years 1914–1926, fair for 1927–1932, weak for 1933–1965 (consisting mostly of post-1965 acquisitions relating to the earlier period), and improving in strength for the post-1965 period. In addition, good background material, mostly in French and German, exists for the pre-1914 period; some of it reaches back to the beginning of the reign of King Carol I (1866–1914).

A conservative estimate of the number of items in the Romanian Collection is between 11,000 and 12,000 bound volumes and pamphlets, some 375 government documents, and about 60 serial and 50 newspaper titles.

The lack of attention to acquisitions of material in the Romanian language during the interwar period was the result of the small demand for such material by

American scholars and students. Demand began to grow only in the mid-1950s when U.S. government subsidies helped to establish the teaching of Romanian in several colleges and universities and when area studies blossomed throughout the United States. Only in 1947 did the library staff include a person with a knowledge of the language and country.

The scholar and student using this survey should consult the comprehensive Hoover Institution card catalog or its printed equivalent (63v. plus supplements) under such subject headings as "Romania," "political parties," "communist party," and "agriculture."

## REFERENCE WORKS

### General Information

A dated but still useful reference work on pre-1914 Romania is *Roumania* (London, 1920), no. 22 in the series of handbooks prepared by the historical section of the British Foreign Office for its delegation to the Paris Peace Conference. A later publication, Norman L. Foster's *Roumanian Handbook* (London, 1931), includes a modest bibliography and a "who's who." For the pre-1939 period, *Politics and Political Parties in Roumania* (London, 1936), published by the International Reference Library, is useful.

For information on the war years, the communist takeover, and the first years under communist rule, the standard work is Reuben H. Markham's *Rumania Under the Soviet Yoke* (Boston, 1949).

Of the three encyclopedias published in Romania, the Hoover Institution has the post–World War II title, *Dicţionar enciclopedic romîn,* 4v. (Bucharest, 1962–1966).

The scholar and student wanting more detailed information on Romania should consult collective works on Southeast Europe and on the countries in this area. Recommended are Stephen Fischer-Galati's *Romania* (New York, 1956) and his *Eastern Europe in the 'Sixties* (New York, 1963). Several books in the German language complement the information in these volumes. The most recent volume containing an informative chapter on Romania is Richard F. Staar's *Communist Regimes in Eastern Europe*, 3rd rev. ed. (Stanford, 1977).

### Bibliographies

Only a few, recent bibliographies exist. For an older bibliography, Foster's *Roumanian Handbook* is recommended. A more recent bibliography by Stephen A. Fischer-Galati, *Romania: A Bibliographic Guide* (Washington, D.C., 1968) contains a bibliographic essay and a list of 748 titles. Another useful publication, with valuable annotations, prepared by Robert C. Carlton, is "Part V: Romania," in Paul Horecky, ed., *Southeastern Europe: A Guide to Basic Publications* (Chicago, 1969). Other useful titles are Léon Savadjian's *Bibliographie balkanique, 1920–1939*, 8v. (Paris, 1931–1939); and his *Südosteuropa-Bibliographie 1945–1960*, 3v. (Munich, 1956–1964). In 1970 the Romanian Academy began a serial publication of specialized bibliographies, *Bibliografia istorică a României*, which is available in the collection. Extensive bibliographic information on the Communist Party of Romania is available in each volume of the *Yearbook on International Communist Affairs* (Stanford, 1966–1979), published by the Hoover Institution.

## Biographies

No comprehensive biographical dictionary for Romania has ever been published. Biographic sections in two pre-1939 books, listing politicians and diplomats (Foster's *Roumanian Handbook* and *Politics and Political Parties in Roumania)*, are based on haphazard selection and are incomplete. A more useful guide is *Who's Who in Central and East Europe, 1933/34–1935/36*, 2v. (Zurich, 1935–1937), which includes prominent Romanians of the period.

For the post–1945 period, good biographies of leading Communist party members and personalities in the state administration are contained in several volumes of the *Yearbook on International Communist Affairs*.

## Ethnographic Atlases

Before World War II Romania included large concentrations of national minorities: Hungarians, Germans, Ukrainians, Bulgarians, and Jews. Two ethnographic atlases presenting the territorial distribution of these minorities are N. M. Petresco-Comene's *Rumania Through the Ages: An Historical, Political and Ethnographic Atlas* (Lausanne, 1919), prepared for the Paris Peace Conference and intended to document Romanian claims to those portions of Hungary, Austria, and Bulgaria in which a large number of Romanians lived; and Marcel Guillemont's *L'Unité roumaine, avec une carte ethnographique* (Paris, 1919), which was published for the same purpose. A later publication, *Rumänien: Ethnographischer Atlas* (Bucharest, 1936), presented the locations of nationalities in Romania after the Paris Peace Conference.

## GOVERNMENT DOCUMENTS

### The Legislature and Official Journals

The government documents part of the collection is strong for the 1913–1926 period, becomes weaker for subsequent years, is much improved for the period after the communist takeover in 1948, and is particularly strong after 1956. The basis for the 1913–1926 documentation is stenographic records of both houses of parliament (*Adunarea Deputaţilor: Desbaterile* and *Senatul: Desbaterile*) and the official gazette *Monitorul oficial* (1918–1920). To these have been added extensive holdings of publications of ministries and special agencies (see below). The new official journal, *Buletinul oficial,* is held for the years 1957–1958, 1965–1973, and 1976 to the present. Its two series include decrees of the Council of Ministers and other enacted laws and decrees since 1956, with certain gaps.

## Publications of Ministries and Governmental Agencies

Publications of the Ministry of Foreign Affairs for the years up to 1940 are well covered by collections of diplomatic documents, documentary monographs on particular problems, and relations with particular countries, including such subjects as the 1905 conflict with Greece, the Balkan wars, the German occupation during World War I, the Paris Peace Conference of 1919–1920, the Bessarabian question, the Little Entente, the Balkan conferences, and relations with Hungary (particularly minority conflicts), Czechoslovakia, and Poland.

Among the major collections of diplomatic documents is the three-volume *Condica tratatelor şi altor legăminte ale României, 1354–1941* (Bucharest, 1938–1942), edited for the ministry by Frederic Nano. Romania's part in the Balkan Wars is dealt with in *Documents diplomatiques: Les événements de la péninsule Balcanique. L'Action de la Roumanie, septembre 1912–août 1913* (Bucharest, 1913).

## STATISTICS

The principal source for statistics on Romania is the *Anuarul statistic al României,* for which Hoover holdings begin with 1912. Although called an "annual," only three volumes appeared between 1912 and 1922. Volumes were published each year between 1923 and 1926, but after 1926 it was again published irregularly. It has been continued since 1957 by the *Anuarul statistic al RPR.* The Hoover Library has an almost complete set of these yearbooks. The last volume available is for 1976. An important source for current statistical data is the serial *Revista de statistică* (1956–).

Results of the 1930 population census are covered in the Hoover collection only by a pamphlet published in 1931. However, the census of 1956 is well documented in several volumes.

Statistical information published by various ministries on agriculture, the oil industry, commerce, and finance for the years 1919–1940 are fairly well represented in the collection.

## THE TWENTIETH CENTURY UP TO WORLD WAR I

Romania under King Carol I was a constitutional monarchy, with the government responsible to the parliament. The conflict with Greece in 1905 was peacefully settled, and publications of the Romanian Ministry of Foreign Affairs, held in the collection, document this agreement.

### Peasant Riots in 1907

For many years these disturbances were poorly covered in Romanian and foreign writings. Only after the country had been taken over by the Communists in 1948 did these events begin to be treated as an uprising heralding the development of the Romanian working class. The well-known Romanian historian Andrei Oțetea published the most objective history of the riots, *Marea răscoală a țăranilor din 1907* (Bucharest, 1967). Gheorghe Matei's *Răsunetul internațional al răscoalei țăranilor din 1907* (Bucharest, 1957) is somewhat less objective. Several items on the same subject printed in Moscow and Kishinev also view the 1907 local riots as a major social upheaval. Examples include V. N. Vinogradov's *Krestîânskoe vosstanie 1907 goda v Rumynii* (Moscow, 1958), E. I. Spivakovskiĭ's *Podem revoliûtsionnogo dvizheniîa v Rumynii v nachale XX veka* (Moscow, 1958), and A. E. Novak's *Pervaîa russkaîa burzhuazno-demokraticheskaîa revoliûtsiîa i dvizhenie v Rumynii 1905–1907 gg.* (Kishinev, 1966).

### The Balkan Wars

Romania's participation in the Balkan Wars of 1912–1913 is documented in the collection by a single official publication of the Foreign Affairs Ministry of Romania, *Documents diplomatiques: Les événements de la péninsule Balcanique. L'Action de la Roumanie, septembre 1912–août 1913* (Bucharest, 1913). Other secondary sources on this subject in the collection are less informative.

## WORLD WAR I

During the first two years of the war, Romania remained neutral, even though the two major political parties were divided in their sympathies between the Allies and the Austro-German camp. The stronger Liberal party, led by Ion Brătianu, was faithful to its traditional connections with France and hoped that in case of an Allied victory, Romania could obtain areas of Austria and Hungary with strong concentrations of Romanian inhabitants. The Conservative party under Alexandru Marghiloman, supported by King Carol I, a Hohenzollern prince sympathetic toward Germany, advocated entry into the war on the side of the Central Powers.

After the death of Carol I late in 1914 and the accession to the throne of his son Ferdinand I (who was married to a British princess), Brătianu was able to negotiate a secret treaty with the Allies that promised in the event of Romania's entry into the war on the Allied side to cede Transylvania, the Banat, and Bukovina to Romania. On August 27, 1916, Romania entered the war against Austria-Hungary.

Documentation on Romania's role in the war is well represented in the collection. The writings of Marghiloman deal with the political cleavage during the first months of the war. Romanian, German, and Russian sources on the military campaigns are abundant. Descriptions of campaigns in Romania can be found in the memoirs of the commanding German (von Falkenhayn and von Mackensen) and Austrian (Conrad von Hötzendorf) generals.

The occupation of Romanian territory by the Germans and its economic exploitation is well documented by Romanian and German authors (Grigory Antipa, Constantin J. Băicoianu, Alexander Berindey, George D. Creangă, Franz D. Enders, Gerhard Velburg, and others).

After the collapse of the Russian army following the 1917 revolution, Romania was forced to conclude a humiliating peace treaty with Germany, Austria, and Bulgaria (Bucharest, May 7, 1918), but in November of the same year, Romania broke this treaty and resumed hostilities against Austria and Germany. After the collapse of the Central Powers, the Paris peace treaties ceded Transylvania, the Banat, and Bukovina to Romania, as promised in the agreement with the Allies. Romania also obtained Dobrudja, which in the 1918 Bucharest treaty had been given to Bulgaria.

Documentation on these events in the collection is very good. Works on the subject include Constantin Kiritescu's *Istoria războiului pentru întegrirea României, 1916–1919*, 2v. (Bucharest, 1927), and its abbreviated French edition, *La Roumanie dans la guerre mondiale, 1916–1919* (Paris, 1923); Mircea Djuvara's *La Guerre roumaine, 1916–1918* (Paris, 1919); and, perhaps the best presentation in English, Charles U. Clark's *United Roumania* (New York, 1952).

Other important titles on this subject are *Tsarskaîa Rossiîa v mirovoĭ voĭne* (Leningrad, 1925), D. Iancovici's *La Paix de Bucharest* (Paris, 1918), and a more recent Soviet publication, *Bukarestskiĭ mir 1918* (Moscow, 1959). The best work on the German occupation of Romanian territory is a volume in the series of the Carnegie Endowment for International Peace by Grigorie Antipa, *L'Occupation ennemie de la Roumanie et ses conséquences économiques et sociales* (Paris, 1929). The collection includes sixteen issues of *Bulletin d'informations roumaines* which appeared in Paris during the latter part of the war and a few issues of the same publication in English. The Romanian delegation to the Paris Peace Conference published much material on its country, which can be found in the Hoover catalog under the subject heading "Paris Peace Conference 1919, Romania."

## THE INTERWAR PERIOD

For Romania, the interwar period lasted from November 1918 until June 1941, when it joined Nazi Germany in the war against the Soviet Union. During the latter part of this period, the country suffered from unfortunate experiences with its monarchs. Ferdinand I, who reigned between 1914 and 1927, was followed by his teenaged grandson Michael (b. 1921), on whose behalf a regency council performed the functions of government. On June 30, 1930, Michael's father returned from banishment, was immediately recognized by parliament as King Carol II, and sent his son to be educated in England. But in September 1940, after several short-lived cabinets were unable to quell pro-Nazi and anti-Semitic riots and assassinations, King Carol fled the country. Michael again returned and remained on the throne until his abdication under communist pressure on December 30, 1947.

Monographs on the interwar period are well represented in the collection. The following general works are particularly informative:

Clark, Charles U. *United Romania* (New York, 1932).
Markham, Henry L. *Roumania Under the Soviet Yoke* (Boston, 1949), especially chapters 2–12.
Pătrăşcanu, Lucreţiu. *Sub trei dictaturi* (Bucharest, 1945).
Roberts, Henry L. *Roumania, Political Problems of an Agrarian State* (New Haven, Conn., 1951).
Seton-Watson, Robert F. *A History of the Roumanians, from Roman Times to the Completion of Unity* (Cambridge, Eng., 1934; reprinted 1963).

The monarchical problems that played a considerable role in the shaping of Romania's destinies during this period are discussed in:

Bolitho, Hector. *Roumania Under King Carol* (New York, 1940).
Deroyer, Michelle. *Au pays de Carol II, roi de Roumanie* (Paris, 1939).
Easterman, Alexander L. *King Carol, Hitler and Lupescu* (London, 1942).
Hillgruber, Andreas. *Hitler, König Carol und Marschall Antonescu: Die deutsch-rumänischen Beziehungen, 1938–1944* (Wiesbaden, 1954).
Lambrino, Jeanne M. V. *Mon mari, le roi Carol* (Paris, 1950).
Wolbe, Eugen. *Ferdinand I, der Begründer Grossrumäniens: Ein Lebensbild* (Locarno, 1938).

The archives of the Hoover Institution hold the papers of Jeanne Lambrino and a few letters of Queen Mary of Romania.

## Political Parties

Before World War II, Romania had well-established political parties. The two most important ones were the Partidul Naţional-Liberal, whose leader, Ion Brătianu, was prime minister in several cabinets of the period; and the Partidul Naţional-Ţărănesc, which emerged in October 1926 from a fusion of the pre-1914 Peasant party of "old" Romania under the leadership of Mihalake, a prominent politician of peasant origin, and the Partidul Naţional under the leadership of Iuliu Maniu and Vaida Voevod in Transylvania and Banat.

The previously mentioned volume, *Politics and Political Parties in Roumania* contains short essays on 26 political parties in Romania before 1935. In addition, Take Ionescu's Partidul Conservativ, General Averescu's Partidul Poporului, and the Partidul Naţional-Democrat, founded by Prof. Nicolae Iorga, each became ruling parties for brief periods. Other parties were small and frequently merged or changed names. The radical nationalist Iron Guard, organized by Corneliu Codreanu, was an imitation of the German Nazi party. During the interwar period, the insignificant Communist Party of Romania operated underground and under assumed names of front organizations.

The Hoover Institution has exceptionally good coverage of materials on these political parties. A few of the more important items are:

Herjeu, N. *Istoria partidului Naţional-Liberal de la origine până în zilele noastre* (Bucharest, 1915).

Marghiloman, Alexandru. *Note politice, 1897−1924,* 5v. (Bucharest, 1915).

Savu, Al. *Dictatură regală, 1938−1940* (Bucharest, 1970).

Smogorzewski, Kazimierz. *La Roumanie à un tournant de son histoire: Le cabinet Maniu* (Paris, 1929).

Ţuţui, Gheorghe. *Zdrobiţi de popor: Falimentul partidelor burghezo-moşiereşti, 1944−1947* (Bucharest, 1959).

Important titles on the Iron Guard and Romania under fascist rule include:

Antonescu, Ion. *Zum Aufbau des Legionären Rumäniens: Aufrufe, Ansprachen und Weisungen* (Bucharest, 1940).

———. *Câtră ţară* (Bucharest, 1941).

Antonescu, Mihail. *Im Dienste des Vaterlandes: Die Verwirklichungen der Regierung des Marschalls Ion Antonescu in Rumänien, 6 September 1940−4 September 1942* (Bucharest, 1942).

Codreanu, Corneliu Z. *Pentru legionari,* 3rd ed. (Bucharest, 1940), also available in German, French, and Spanish editions.

The volume *Politics and Political Parties in Roumania* contains biographies of about 1,300 Romanians prominent in politics in the interwar years. Twenty essays on the political press, both Romanian and minority, are a valuable addition to this volume.

## Land Reform

The most objective work on the agrarian problem was published in a volume sponsored by the Carnegie Endowment for International Peace, *The Land and the Peasant in Rumania: The War and Agrarian Reform, 1917–1921* (London, 1930). Additional pamphlets on the subject are available in the collection.

## New Constitution and Electoral Law

The constitution of March 27, 1923, modified the old constitution along modern, democratic principles. It provided for equal treatment of all citizens in the greatly enlarged kingdom, abolished the three-class voting system, and introduced the direct, secret ballot. The English text of this document is available in all major compilations of modern constitutions. This Romanian constitution was repeatedly violated and suspended during the turbulent late 1930s. This subject is well covered in the collection.

## Bessarabia

The Bessarabian problem, including unification with Romania, actions at the Paris Peace Conference, the Soviet attitude toward this problem, Romanian resistance to Soviet pressures, and the ultimate Soviet seizure of the province with German acquiescence, is well covered in the collection.

A few of the more important titles are:

Arbure, Zamfir. *Besarabia în secolul XIX* (Bucharest, 1898).
Bereznikov, N. V. *Bor'ba trudîashchikhsîa Bessarabii protiv interventov v 1917–1920* (Kishinev, 1957).
*Dicţionarul statistic al Besarabiei: Ediţie oficială* (Chişinău, 1923).
Kroupensky, N. A. *Bessarabie et Roumanie* (Paris, 1919).
*Mémoire sur la situation de la Bessarabie* (Paris, 1919).
Miliukov, Pavel. *The Case for Bessarabia: A Collection of Documents on the Rumanian Occupation* (London, 1919).

The Hoover Archives also holds the papers and a collection of materials (1918–1935) assembled by N. A. Kroupensky, Bessarabian delegate to the Paris

Peace Conference, relating to the Bessarabian question, to relations between Russia, Romania, and Bessarabia, to the reunification of Bessarabia with Romania (1918), and to the Paris Peace Conference.

## Foreign Relations

Internal developments, as well as the foreign policy of Romania during these interwar years, are well covered in the holdings of the collection. The more important works include:

Campus, Eliza. *Înțelegerea balcanică* (Bucharest, 1972).

Desfeuilles, Paul. *Les Français et la Roumanie* (Bucharest, 1937).

Djuvara, Trandafir. *Mes missions diplomatiques: Belgrad, Sofia, Constantinople* (Paris, 1930).

*L'Entente balcanique, du 9 février 1939 au 8 février 1940* (Bucharest, 1940).

Gafencu, Grigore. *Prelude to the Russian Campaign: From the Moscow Pact (August 21, 1939) to the Opening of Hostilities in Russia (June 22, 1941)* (London, 1945).

————. *Last Days of Europe: A Diplomatic Journey in 1939* (New Haven, Conn., 1948).

Geshoff, Theodore I. *Balkan Union* (New York, 1940).

Godresco, Florin. *La Petite entente,* 2v. (Paris, 1931).

Institutul Social Român, București. *Politica externă a României: 19 prelegeri publice* (Bucharest, 1926).

Iorga, Nicolae. *Polonais et Roumains: Rélations politiques, économiques et culturelles* (Bucharest, 1921).

Kerner, Robert, and Howard, Harry N. *The Balkan Conference and the Balkan Entente, 1930–1935* (Berkeley, 1936).

Lambrino, Jeanne M. V. *Mon mari, le roi Carol* (Paris, 1950).

Lukasik, Stanislaw. *Pologne et Roumanie: Aux confins des deux peuples et des deux langues* (Paris, 1938).

Machray, Robert. *Little Entente* (London, 1929).

————. *Struggle for the Danube and the Little Entente* (London, 1939).

Macovescu, George, ed. *Nicolae Titulescu: Documente diplomatice* (Bucharest, 1967).

Marie, Queen of Romania. *The Story of My Life,* 3v. (New York, 1934–1935).

Oprea, Ion M. *Nicolae Titulescu* (Bucharest, 1966); and its English translation, *Nicolae Titulescu's Diplomatic Activities* (Bucharest, 1968).

Savu, Al. *Dictatură regală, 1938–1940* (Bucharest, 1970).

Titulescu, Nicolae. *Discursuri, studii, texte alese şi adnotări* (Bucharest, 1967).

Vladesco, O. A. *L'Entente balcanique* (n.p., 1939).

The Hoover Archives holds the manuscripts of reminiscenses of I. Duca, the private papers of Nicolae Titulescu and of Jeanne Marie Lambrino, and other Romanian material on this subject and period.

## WORLD WAR II

This episode in Romania's history is well covered by Romanian, Soviet, and German sources. A few of the more important titles are:

*Contribuţia României la victoria asupra fascismului* (Bucharest, 1965).

Gheorghe, Vasili, ed. *Armata română în războiul antihitlerist: Culegere de articole* (Bucharest, 1965).

Mitchievici, Victor. *Rumänien 1943* (Bucharest, 1943).

*România în războiul antihitlerist: 23 August 1944 – 9 Mai 1945* (Bucharest, 1966).

Antonescu, Mihail, comp. *Rumänien's heiliger Krieg im Spiegel der deutschen Presse* (Bucharest, 1942).

## UNDER COMMUNIST RULE

After Romania's surrender, several months passed before a government responsible to King Michael could be established. The small Communist party organized a National Democratic Front allegedly representing the people. Its pressure, combined with that of Soviet occupation authorities, forced the king to appoint Petru Groza, head of the Plowman's Front, a communist front organization in Transylvania, as prime minister. This government consisted predominantly of National Democratic Front members, with a few noncommunists added at the request of French and British representatives to the Inter-Allied Control Commission.

Elections held in November 1946 secured a majority for the government. The peace treaty signed in Paris on February 10, 1947, returned Transylvania to Romania, but levied heavy reparations for the USSR. Under pressure from Soviet Foreign Minister Andreĭ Vishinskiĭ, King Michael abdicated on December 30 and left the country. Romania became a satellite of the USSR. A new Soviet-style constitution was adopted (April 1948), and Romania became a people's republic.

## ROMANIAN COMMUNIST PARTY

The first communist cells in Romania were founded in 1918 when the bolshevized Russian army still occupied the eastern part of the country. Only in 1925 were these cells united into the Communist Party of Romania (Partidul Communist din România). The party operated underground until the occupation of the country by the Soviet army in 1944. In February 1948, at its first congress, the party adopted the name Romanian Workers' Party (Partidul Municitoresc Român) and absorbed the insignificant Partidul Social Democrat. In July 1965 at the ninth congress of the Romanian Workers' Party, the party adopted the name Romanian Communist Party (Partidul Communist Român; PCR).

Early pre-1944 publications of the party are extremely rare. Reprints are available in several volumes of the history of the party and the workers' movement in Romania published by the Institute of Historical and Social-Political Studies of the PCR's Central Committee in Bucharest. Particularly important is the volume *Documente din istoria Partidului Communist şi a mişcării muncitoreşti-revoluţionare din România, Mai 1921−August 1924* (Bucharest, 1970). Other volumes cover the years between 1910 and 1921 and deal with various leftist organizations, which communist authors present as "ancestors" of the Romanian communist movement.

The coverage of material published by and about the PCR is good for the years 1945−1960 (first to third congresses of the party), weak for the years 1961−1965, and again good after 1965. Reports, speeches, and writings (many in official English translations) by the two general secretaries of the party, Gheorghe Gheorghiu-Dej, who died in 1965, and his successor, Nicolae Ceauşescu, are almost complete. Speeches and reports of the general secretary are the most important primary sources for the study of Romanian foreign policy, planned economy, education, internal affairs, and so forth. Monographs on these subjects are rather scarce.

A few samples of these publications are:

Babici, Ion. *Solidaritate militantă antifascistă, 1933−1939* (Bucharest, 1972).

*Basic Principles of Romania's Foreign Policy: Joint Meeting of the CC of the RCP, the State Council and the Romanian Government, August 21, 1968. Special Session of the Grand National Assembly of the Socialist Republic of Romania, August 22, 1968* (Bucharest, 1968).

Ceauşescu, Nicolae. *România pe drumul desăvîrşirii construcţii socialiste: Rapoarte, cuvîntari, articole,* v.1−5, 12−13 (Bucharest, 1969−1977).

――――. *Romania on the Way of Completing Socialist Construction: Reports, Speeches, Articles,* 10v. (Bucharest, 1969−1977).

*Documente ale Partidului Communist Român: Culegere sintetică* (Bucharest, n.d.).
Gheorghiu-Dej, Gheorghe. *Articole şi cuvîntări,* 3v. (Bucharest, 1960–1962).
*Politica internaţionalistă a PCR* (Bucharest, 1972).
*The Rules of the Romanian Communist Party: Endorsed by the Eleventh Congress of the RCP* (Bucharest, 1975).
*Statutul PCR* (Bucharest, 1969).

For current developments in the PCR, consult the *Yearbook on International Communist Affairs.*

## ROMANIANS ABROAD

During and after World War II, particularly after the takeover of the country by a communist government, many former government officials, noncommunist politicians, army officers, and intellectuals of various professions left the country and settled in Germany, France, Spain, Argentina, Canada, and the United States. This new Romanian emigration issues newspapers and periodicals and has established a few publishing houses that produce books and pamphlets. The Hoover Institution attempts to collect this rather fugitive and hard to obtain material. The most informative book on this subject is Alexandre Creţianu's *Romania: A Decade of Soviet Rule* (New York, 1956).

## NEWSPAPERS AND PERIODICALS

Holdings of newspapers from the interwar period are weak. Important titles are found in the collection, but their runs are for short periods:

*Universul* (Bucharest, 1925–1927)
*Dimineaţa* (Bucharest, 1927)
*Kronstadter Zeitung* (Kronstadt, 1936–1939)
*Siebenbürgisch-Deutsches Tagblatt* (Sibiu, 1936–1939)

Since Romania came under communist rule, the Hoover Institution's coverage of the press has improved considerably. The library currently receives six newspaper titles, either from Romania or dealing with Romania:

*Cuvântul Românesc*
*Munca*

*Scînteia*
*România liberă*
*A hét* (published for the Hungarian minority)
*Die Woche* (published for the German minority)

Furthermore, the library regularly receives 30 periodical titles and three documentary serials, including

*Biserica Ortodoxă Română*
*Era socialistă*
*Lumea*
*Magazin istoric*
*Munca de partid*
*Partidul Muncitoresc Român: Anale de istorie*
*Revista de statistică*
*Revista economică*
*Revista română de drept*
*Romanian Review*
*Viaţa militară*

The documentary government serials are *Colecţia de legi şi Decrete şi Colecţia de Hotărîri ale Consiliului de Ministri şi Alte Acte Normative; Romania: Buletinul oficial al Republicii Socialiste Românei* (all parts); and *Romania: Documents-Events*.

## ARCHIVAL SOURCES

The Hoover Archives possesses a number of manuscript collections that serve as resources for the study of recent Romanian history. A few of the larger and more important collections are:

*Dumitru Danielopol Collection on Romania,* research files, 1940–1953 (7 manuscript boxes).
*George I. Duca* (diplomat, 1928–1946, executive director of the Federation of French Alliances, New York, 1961–1975), 1919–1975 (60 manuscript boxes).
*Ion G. Duca* (minister of education, 1914–1918; agriculture, 1919–1920; foreign affairs, 1922–1926; Interior, 1927–1928; and prime minister, 1933), 1914–1926 (4 manuscript boxes).
*Radu Irimescu* (minister of air and navy, 1932–1938; ambassador to the United States 1938–1940), 1918–1940 (4 manuscript boxes).

*Jeanne Marie Lambrino* (wife of Prince Carol of Romania, 1918–1919), 1916–1956 (2 manuscript boxes).

*Paris Peace Conference, 1919, Commission on Romanian and Yugoslav Affairs,* microfilm of minutes and meetings, 1919 (1 microfilm reel).

*Dimitri G. Popescu* (private secretary to the undersecretary of state for foreign affairs of Romania), 1940–1946 (6 manuscript boxes).

*Romanian National Committee,* Washington, D.C., records, 1946–1975 (20 manuscript boxes).

*Nicolae Titulescu* (minister of finance, 1920–1922, and minister of foreign affairs, 1927–1928, 1932–1934), 1923–1938 (16 manuscript boxes).

*Constantin Visoianu* (minister of foreign affairs, 1945–1946), 1940–1960 (2 manuscript boxes).

# RUSSIA AND

# THE SOVIET UNION

The collecting of materials on Russia for the Hoover Library began in 1919 when on Herbert Hoover's initiative, Prof. E. D. Adams from the history department at Stanford University went to Paris to collect documentation on the peace conference. The first material on Russia came from members of the Russian Political Conference. In September 1920, Prof. Frank Golder, a specialist on Russian history who had lived in Russia before and during World War I, was sent to Eastern Europe as a roving acquisitions agent for the library. He obtained large quantities of material (books, pamphlets, periodicals, newspapers, and archival collections) from Russia and from its former provinces of Estonia, Finland, Latvia, Lithuania, and Poland. A trip to the then independent Caucasian states produced additional documentation.

The largest amount of material on Russia was obtained by Golder when he participated in the American Relief Administration mission to Soviet Russia organized by Hoover from late 1921 to the middle of 1923. Golder acquired more than 40,000 valuable items with funds provided by Hoover and with the help of an old Russian student friend, Anatolii Lunacharskiĭ, who after the bolshevik overthrow of the Provisional Government became people's commissar for culture. With the documentation collected earlier, the Golder acquisitions from Soviet Russia became a solid foundation for the further development of the collection in the Hoover Library. The early appointment of area specialists as curators for particular area collections guaranteed good selection and organization of the material on a high scholarly level. In 1924 Dimitry M. Krassovsky, who had been trained as a lawyer in Russia and then completed his library education at Berkeley, became the first curator of the collection. Former Gen. N. N. Golovine became acquisitions agent in Europe. Both men, particularly

Krassovsky (1924—1947), contributed substantially to the growth and quality of the collection.

During the past six decades, the collection on Russia has been systematically expanded. Gaps that emerged during World War II and in the late Stalin period, when acquisitions from the Soviet Union were limited, were filled in later with original material or microfilms. For the period since the Great Reforms, which started in 1861, and in the areas of history, politics, military affairs, and related subjects, the Hoover Institution's collection on modern Russia, supplemented by extensive archival holdings, is one of the richest in the Western world and a unique source for advanced research. The collection has grown more than fivefold in the years since 1954 when it was last surveyed.

The collection on Russia consists predominantly of materials in the Russian language printed in Russia itself and abroad, as well as works in some fifteen European and Asiatic languages dealing with Russian affairs. It includes material pertaining to Imperial Russia, Russia under the short-lived Provisional Government, and under communist rule. The Civil War period that followed the overthrow of the Provisional Government is excellently covered. Publications of the Russian political and revolutionary emigration in Western Europe before the revolution of March 1917 and those of the various emigrations after 1918, 1945, and in recent years are well represented.

The Soviet Russian Collection also contains publications in the languages of the various national minorities within the confines of the present Soviet Union. Separate chapters of this survey cover material pertaining to the Baltic States and the Ukraine. Materials in the languages of the Caucasian and Central Asian nationalities (Armenians, Georgians, Uzbeks, and others) are treated in this survey as an integral part of the Russian Collection because of their close relation to Russian affairs.

The Russian Collection covers a much broader range of topics and a longer time span than most of the other area collections of the Hoover Institution. In addition to printed materials and manuscripts documenting politically significant developments in Russia since the latter part of the nineteenth century, the collection contains certain background materials concerning even earlier times. The holdings pertaining to the period immediately following the 1917 revolutions include materials dealing with some subjects (philosophy, education, religion, and similar subjects) not included in most other collections of the library because in the communist state politics pervades many areas.

Another extension of the collection resulted from the fact that after the November Revolution of 1917 Russia became the center of the world communist movement. Consequently, part of the Russian-language material that appeared after 1917 touches directly or indirectly on global political, social, economic, and other problems. It deals with the Comintern, the Cominform, communist youth, trade, and other organizations that, although international in appearance, have actually been extensions of the Communist Party of the Soviet Union.

In principle, works dealing with science and technology, geography, fiction, poetry, drama, and music are not collected by the Hoover Library. These materials and works covering the earlier periods of Russian history are to be found in Stanford University's Green Library. Only literary works dealing with the Russian revolutionary movement, Russia's participation in wars, modern dissident movements, or other politically significant events are procured for the Hoover Library.

Due to the organization of materials in the library, it is impossible to give an exact numerical evaluation of the collection on Russia. A conservative estimate of the present number of books and pamphlets (including government documents and society publications) is:

| Language | Total Number of Titles |
| --- | --- |
| Russian | 220,000 |
| Other Languages | 43,000 |
| Total | 263,000 |

The serial holdings in the Russian Collection include an estimated 3,500 periodical titles, containing approximately 110,000 issues. The newspaper collection includes some 650 files of varying lengths. The file of *Izvestiîa* alone, covering 60 years, includes well over 20,000 issues. Furthermore, there are about 950 archival units, which vary in size from a few documents to 90,000 (Okhrana Archives), several thousand posters, and hundreds of maps.

Because of repeated political purges in the Soviet Union and changes in the political line of the ruling Communist party, many publications have been withdrawn from circulation in the USSR. These publications are available only outside the Soviet Union, and when lost they are practically irreplaceable. Moreover, because of the elimination of the private book trade in the Soviet Union, earlier books are difficult or impossible to obtain. These circumstances have forced the Hoover Library to restrict the use of a sizable number of books in the Russian Collection to the library building. This restriction also applies to the interlibrary loan service. (Microfilm copies of noncirculating materials can be purchased from the Hoover Institution.)

In several places this survey mentions manuscripts and special collections that have been deposited by their owners in the Hoover Institution's Archives for safekeeping and use. They may be consulted only in the reading room of the archives under conditions specified by the depositors and under supervision of archival personnel.

This survey of the Russian Collection has seven distinct parts. The first evaluates general reference works on Russia, regardless of period of publication. The second discusses other material produced during and pertaining to the tsarist period (up to March 14, 1917). The third covers the eight months of the Provisional Government (up to November 7, 1917). The fourth includes material on the Civil War and Allied intervention in Russia. Part five covers the Soviet period, from the overthrow of the Provisional Government to the present, chronologically subdivided. Part six covers the three waves of emigration and exile from the Soviet Union. Part seven deals with the Comintern, Cominform, and other international communist organizations.

## REFERENCE WORKS

Reference material on Russia in the library includes practically all pertinent Russian- and Western-language publications listed in Karol Maichel's *Guide to Russian Reference Books*, v.1−2 (Stanford, 1962−1964); and Paul Horecky's *Basic Russian Publications* (Chicago, 1962).

### Encyclopedias, Almanacs, and Dictionaries

The collection contains all standard Russian encyclopedias from the 1870s to the present, for example:

PREREVOLUTIONARY ENCYCLOPEDIAS:

*Bol'shaîà entsiklopediîà: Slovar' obshchedostupnykh svedeniĭ po vsem otraslîàm znaniîà*, S. N. Îùzhakova. 22v. (St. Petersburg, 1900−1909).

*Entsiklopedicheskiĭ slovar'*, F. A. Brokgauz and I. A. Efron. 41v. (St. Petersburg, 1890−1907).

*Entsiklopedicheskiĭ slovar' Russkogo bibliograficheskogo instituta Granat*, 58v. (Moscow and Paris, 1910−1948 [Hoover set nearly complete]).

*Novyĭ entsiklopedicheskiĭ slovar'*, Brokgauz-Efron. (St. Petersburg, 1911−1916 [only 29 of projected 48 volumes published; Hoover has v.1−12]).

*Voennaîà entsiklopediîà* 18v. (Moscow, 1911−1915).

SOVIET ENCYCLOPEDIAS:

*Bol' shaîà sovetskaîà entsiklopediîà*, 65v. (Moscow, 1926−1947).

――――, 2d ed., 51v. (Moscow, 1950−1958).

――――, 3rd ed., 30v. (Moscow, 1969−1978).

*Great Soviet Encyclopedia*, 30v. projected (New York, 1973−  ). An English translation of the preceding entry.

*Malaı̐a sovetskaı̐a entsiklopediı̐a,* 10v. (Moscow, 1929–1931).
————, 2d ed., 11v. (Moscow, 1933–1940, 1947).
————,3rd ed., 10v. (Moscow, 1958–1961).
*Sibirskaı̐a sovetskaı̐a entsiklopediı̐a,* 3v. (Novosibirsk, 1929–1933).

In addition, the library has virtually all regional encyclopedias published for the various republics and such subject-oriented encyclopedias as *Sovetskaı̐a voennaı̐a entsiklopediı̐a, Sovetskaı̐a istoricheskaı̐a entsiklopediı̐a, Kratkaı̐a geograficheskaı̐a entsiklopediı̐a, Literaturnaı̐a entsiklopediı̐a,* and *Diplomaticheskiı̆ slovar'*.

Most almanacs, yearbooks, dictionaries, and other similar reference aids published before and after the 1917 revolutions are held by the Hoover Library. An attempt is made to acquire all current reference material of this nature as it becomes available. The large collection of Russian-language dictionaries includes: Dal', Vladimir I. *Tolkovyı̆ slovar' zhivogo velikorusskogo ı̐azyka,* 4v. (Moscow, 1955); Ushakov, D.N. *Tolkovyı̆ slovar' russkogo ı̐azyka,* 4v. (Moscow, 1935–1940); and Akademiı̐a nauk SSR. Institut Russkogo ı̆Azyka. *Slovar' sovremennogo russkogo literaturnogo ı̐azyka,* 17v. (Moscow, 1950–1965).

## Bibliographies

The library has the standard Russian bibliographies: the now weekly serial, *Knizhnaı̐a letopis'* (Moscow, 1907– ); the monthly *Sovetskaı̐a kniga* (Moscow, 1946–1953); and the annual *Ezhegodnik knigi SSSR* (Moscow, 1925– ). The file of *Knizhaı̐a letopis'* has some gaps, but total coverage of the title is assured on campus by using the files of the Hoover Institution and the Green Library together.

The several thousand specialized bibliographies and bibliographies of bibliographies in the collection are too numerous to list. Some of these are mentioned in the later parts of this survey.

Periodicals are well covered by major bibliographies, starting with the comprehensive prerevolutionary listings by N. Lisovskiı̆ and L. Belı̐aeva and continued by the major Soviet bibliographies.

Bibliographies of periodical and newspaper articles are extensive. Two retrospective ones should be mentioned: Popov, Vladimir A. *Sistematicheskiı̆ ukazatel' . . . stateı̆ s 1830 po 1884 god* (St. Petersburg, 1885); and Ulı̐anov, N. A. *Ukazatel' zhurnal'noı̆ literatury,* 2v. (Moscow, 1911), an index to articles in the "thick journals" for the years 1899–1910. The library has all standard Soviet bibliographic publications relevant to the scope of its collection.

The collection includes a number of union lists of books, journals, and newspapers pertinent to Russian area studies in the libraries of the United States and

Europe. *The Cyrillic Union Catalog of the Library of Congress* (New York: Readex Microprint, 1963) gives the holdings of monographs in Cyrillic script in 185 U.S. libraries as of 1956. Post-1956 entries are recorded in the *National Union Catalog*. The catalogs of the New York Public Library Slavonic Collection (2d ed., 1947), the International Institute for Social History in Amsterdam, and the Johann Gottfried Herder Institute in Marburg are included in the library's reference collection. In addition to the generally known union lists of Soviet serials and newspapers issued by the Library of Congress, several other compilations are based on the holdings of individual libraries in the United States and Europe. Peter Bruhn's *Gesamtverzeichnis russischer und sowjetischer Periodika und Serienwerke in Bibliotheken der Bundesrepublik Deutschland und West Berlins*, 4v. (Wiesbaden, 1962−1973), besides being a union list of Russian periodicals and series publications in West German libraries, is also a dependable source of bibliographical information.

## Biographies

*Russkiĭ biograficheskiĭ slovar'*, 25v. (Moscow and St. Petersburg, 1896− 1918 [never completed]) and *Russkiĭ biograficheskiĭ slovar'* . . . *Vsesoiûznoe obshchestvo politicheskikh katorzhan* . . . *Deiateli revoliûtsionnogo dvizheniiâ v Rossii*, 4v. (Moscow, 1927−1934) are among the major retrospective biographical works in the library's collection. Additional biographical information is found in the general encyclopedias. D. M. Krassovsky's manuscript, "Biographical Index of Slavic Men and Women" (1943−1945), is helpful for biographical data that appeared in periodicals and newspapers. A great majority of those listed in Krassovsky's biography were persons who emigrated from Russia and were not included in customary biographical sources. Erik Amburger's *Geschichte der Behordenorganisation Russlands von Peter dem Grossen bis 1917* (Leiden, 1966) contains a list of higher officials who served Russia during that period, with birth and death dates among other data. The biographical directories, *Who's Who in the USSR* (New York and London, 1962, 1966); *Who Was Who in the USSR* (Metuchen, N.J., 1972); *Prominent Personalities in the USSR* (Metuchen, N.J., 1968); the semiannual cumulative guide, *Current Soviet Leaders* (Oakville, Ontario, 1976−); and Boris Levytsky's *The Soviet Political Elite*, 2v. (Stanford, 1970) are supplemented and updated by Boris Levytsky and Julius Stroynowski's *Who's Who in the Socialist Countries* (Munich, 1978). Current Soviet Communist party officials are covered by *Sowjetunion Intern* (Frankfurt-am-Main, 1978−). Isaak M. Kaufman's bibliography, *Russkie biograficheskie i bibliograficheski slovari* (Moscow, 1950), serves as a source for identifying biographical reference works that have appeared in print over a period of more than 200 years.

## General Works

After 1917 a steadily growing number of general reference works on the Soviet Union as a whole and its republics and regions appeared in Russian, English, and other languages. They describe the country, its people, government, economic and social conditions, education, and other matters. Practically all important publications are in the library and are complimented by large files of periodicals of the same character. The directory *Vsı͡a Rossiı͡a: Torgovo— promyschlennyĭ adreskalendar' Rossiĭskoĭ Imperii* (St. Petersburg, 1895, 1899, 1903, 1911−1912, 1913, 1923 [additional volumes available in Green Library]) contains information on all government agencies, communications, finance, trade, industry, agriculture, population, legal system, and public health. *Spravochnaı͡a i adresnaı͡a kniga "Vsı͡a Rossiı͡a" na 1923* (Moscow, 1923) is a directory of officials and employees.

## Maps and Atlases

A good collection of Russian geographical atlases and maps is included in the library's holdings. Among them are the large atlas of the Asiatic territories of Russia, *Aziatskaı͡a Rossiı͡a*, 3v. (St. Petersburg, 1914), and *Bol'shoĭ sovetskiĭ atlas mira*, 2v. (Moscow, 1937−1939), of which the Hoover Library has the first volume only. (The Branner Geological Library of Stanford University has the rare second volume.) Another rare work in the library's collection is Oskar von Niedermayer's *Wehrgeographischer Atlas der Union der Sozialistischen Sowjetrepubliken* (Berlin, 1941), produced by the Germans for military operations in the Soviet Union.

## THE TSARIST PERIOD

The research collection on Russia in the Hoover Library and Archives starts with the period of Great Reforms under Alexander II in the early 1860s, for which extensive documentation is available. Since a Slavic Collection, centered on Russia, was started at the Green Library in the 1960s, a large amount of material on earlier centuries, including the famous Letopis' series and publications of the Imperial Archeological Commission, has been transferred there from the Hoover Library.

The rise of political parties in the 1870s and their later development in Russia and abroad are represented by primary sources hardly matched by any library outside the Soviet Union. All aspects of political, social, and economic development, education and ethnography, the police system and military affairs, and the critical years of World War I that led to the overthrow of the tsarist regime are excellently covered. Government documents and publications, thick journals (those of a literary or general nature are held in the Green Library), memoirs of contemporaries, monographs, and ephemeral pamphlets form a solid base for research on a wide range of topics. Rich archival and manuscript resources contribute to the unique strength of this collection.

## Government Documents

Series of official records include historical and juridical documents, collections of laws, archives, and serial publications of various government institutions.

*Public Archives.*   Outstanding among public archives are the voluminous archives of the State Council (Gosudarstvennyĭ Sovet) and a large collection of reports on the activities of this council. These sources contain reprints of important state papers relating to the years 1768–1910 and cover a wide range of subjects that came under the consideration of this body. Equally important are the archives of the Governing Senate, Russia. Pravitel'stvuĭûshchiĭ Senat. *Senatskiĭ arkhiv*, 15v. (St. Petersburg, 1889–1910), of which the library has v.2, 11–12, and 14. These volumes contain various documents of historical importance and acts not included in *Polnoe sobranie zakonov*. (See the section Laws, Statutes, and Official Gazettes below for the full bibliographical citation.)

After the revolution of 1917, the Soviet government published additional documents on the reign of Nicholas II. Among these is the well-known series on the foreign policy of the imperial government, *Mezhdunarodnye otnosheniiā v epokhu imperializma,* in German and Russian.

*Laws, Statutes, Official Gazettes.*   The holdings of the library contain ample materials for research on juridical matters and legislation in Imperial Russia. These materials cover Russian laws from the time of Vladimir up to the day of the overthrow of the Romanovs and include the following fundamental works and series:

> Russia. Laws, statutes, etc. *Ukazatel' rossiĭskikh zakonov*, 10v. (Moscow, 1803–1812). This work contains a condensation of and excerpts from all laws issued in Russia from the time of Vladimir in the tenth century to 1781.
>
> ———.   ———. *Polnoe sobranie zakonov Rossiĭskoĭ Imperii*, 236v. (St. Petersburg, 1830–1913), which contains all laws issued in Russia from 1649 to 1913.
>
> ———.   ———. *Sobranie uzakoneniĭ i rasporîazheniĭ privitel'stva* (St. Petersburg, 1914–1917), which covers the period from January 1, 1914 to February 28, 1917 (Julian calendar dates), that is, up to the overthrow of the tsar.

————. ————. *Svod zakonov Rossiĭskoĭ Imperii, 1857—1915* (St. Petersburg, 1857), which covers in four series the entire legislation of the empire.

Sources on the areas under Russian imperial rule include the two large sets on Poland and Finland:

Poland. Laws, statutes, etc. *Dziennik praw: Dnevnik zakonov*, 70v. (Warsaw, 1816—1870), with text in Polish, Russian, and French.
Finland, Laws, statutes, etc. *Sbornik postanovleniĭ Velikago Knĭazhestva Finlĭandskogo za 1860—1916*, 57v. (Helsinki, 1860—1917).

For the Baltic provinces, the library has Russia. Laws, statutes, etc. *Svod grazhdanskikh uzakoneniĭ guberniĭ Pribaltiĭskikh*, 2v. (Riga, 1914).

In addition to these basic sets, the library has a considerable number of law handbooks, monographs on particular aspects and problems of Russian law, and a fairly good collection of law journals of the 1900s.

*Publications of Ministries and Special Committees.* The library has the records of the Committee of Ministries, Russia. Komitet Ministrov. *Zhurnaly Komiteta Ministrov*, for the years 1802—1812, and a complete set of the records of the Council of Ministers, Russia. Sovĭet Ministrov. *Osobyĭ zhurnal*, for the years 1906—1917. The last part of this journal also includes the rare records of the secret meetings of the council. In addition, the collection includes a considerable number of official gazettes, monographs, and miscellaneous publications of the ministries of Agriculture, Education, Finances, Foreign Affairs, Justice, Trade, War, and others. Most of these were published between 1908 and 1916. This material is complemented by records and documents of various special committees appointed by the government, including a set of records of the committee that prepared the Decree of 1861 abolishing serfdom and providing for the regulation of peasant affairs. (For complete citation of the set, see the section Land and Peasant Question.) Another important work of a special committee is a work on the planned reorganization of the state police, *Proekt reformy politsii*, 11v. (St. Petersburg, 1911), published by the Interior Ministry. The coverage of individual ministries and committees is quite uneven. An important addition to the original official publications of the tsarist period are several series and monographic reprints published after the November Revolution by the Soviet government. The titles of these reprints are mentioned in the appropriate subject sections of this survey.

*Histories of Ministries and Other Official Institutions.* In commemoration of the centennial of the creation of the ministries by Alexander I, a number of special publications presenting the development and activities of the Committee of Ministers and some of the individual ministries between 1802 and 1902 appeared.

The library has the following of these anniversary publications: *Ministerstvo finansov 1802—1902, Ministerstvo vnutrennikh del, 1802—1902, Stoletie voennago ministerstva, 1802—1902, Istoricheskiĭ obzor deĭatel'nosti komiteta ministrov, 1802—1902,* and *Istoriĭa pravitel'stvuĭushchago senata za dvesti let, 1711—1911.*

*Legislative Bodies.* The library has a complete set of the stenographic records of the Duma, Russia. Gosudarstvennaĭa Duma (1—4: 1906—1917). *Stenograficheskie otchety,* and the majority of the stenographic records of the State Council, Russia. Gosudarstvennyĭ Sovet. *Stenograficheskie otchety (1906— 1917),* including the records of the last session, comprising about 200 volumes. The set contains documentary appendexes to the records, printed material originating with various committees (including the Finance Committee), and the state budgets. In addition, the library has many diaries and other writings of Duma and State Council members and publications of various political parties and writers relating to the activities of both houses.

*Statistics.* Statistical publications for the tsarist period are well represented in the library for the years 1908 to 1916 only. Publications concerning earlier years are rather scattered. However, the library has a comprehensive set of publications containing the results of the first general census in 1897, *Pervaĭa vseobshchaĭa perepis' naseleniĭa Rossiĭskoĭ imperii,* 5v. (St. Petersburg, 1899— 1900), and the land tenure statistics resulting from this census, Russia. Otdel Sel'skoĭ Ekonomii i Sel'skokhoziaĭstvennoĭ Statistiki. *Svod statisticheskikh svedeniĭ po sel'skokhoziaĭstvennoĭ Rossii k kontsu XIX veka,* 2v. (St. Petersburg, 1903). The statistical yearbook *Statisticheskiĭ ezhegodnik Rossii* and the statistical publications of the ministries of Commerce and Industry, and Finance and of the Central Land Office are available for similar periods. In evaluating these holdings in the collection, the user should remember that regular publication of detailed Russian statistics began only in the first years of the present century.

## Books, Pamphlets, and Archival Material

In this survey of the collection on Russia, a compromise has been made between a strictly chronological and a topical approach to the material in order to emphasize particular topics that are especially well documented in the collection and offer prime opportunities for research. The selection of a limited number of topics in each period by no means indicates the entire coverage of the library holdings on the given period. This selection attempts merely to draw attention to the more important topics. The materials contained in the collection (contemporary original prints and microfilms and reprints of rare originals) cover all aspects of political, social, economic, military, and related problems of modern

Russia. The periodicals pertaining to the tsarist period are surveyed generally in a later section. In the discussion of certain topics, attention is drawn to periodicals and newspapers containing especially useful material on the topic under consideration. Pertinent archives, manuscripts, and special collections are also mentioned.

*The Decembrist Revolt.* The political background of the Decembrist revolt is represented by numerous pre-1917 publications as well as later ones. These include memoirs and writings of some of the participants in the revolt, a few biographical studies, and a number of monographs. The Russian periodicals of the pre-1917 period, the thick journals, contain many articles dealing with the Union of Salvation (Soiûz Spaseniîa Rossii), the Union of Welfare (Soiûz Blagodeĭstviîa), and other groups that began the movement leading to the revolt, as well as articles on the revolt itself and its repercussions. A few works on the subject are available in Western languages.

*Slavophiles and Westernizers.* The controversy between the Slavophiles and the Westernizers, which developed in Russia around the middle of the nineteenth century, is much better covered in the library than is the Decembrist revolt. The material on the Westernizers is, however, more complete than that on the Slavophiles. The writings of Herzen, Belinskiĭ, Kavelin, Solov'ev, Cherny-shevskiĭ, and Dobroliûbov represent both the earlier and later Westernizers' views. As for Slavophile writers, the library has all of Kireevskiĭ's and some of Samarin's works, but lacks most of the writings of Komiâkov, Cherkasskiĭ, the Aksakov brothers, and others. The collection includes biographies of the main participants in this controversy and monographs on both movements. A wealth of material on the subject is contained in contemporary and later thick journals, which are abundant in the Hoover Collection, including *Sovremennik* (St. Petersburg, 1851−1862 and 1912−1913 [new series]) and *Vîestnik Evropy* (St. Petersburg, 1866−1918) for the Westernizers' views; *Russkiĭ arkhiv* (Moscow, 1863−1915) and *Russkaîa starina* (St. Petersburg, 1870−1918) for the Slavophiles; and *Zhurnal Ministerstva narodnogo prosveshcheniîa* (St. Petersburg, 1834−1917) and others for materials on both.

*The Rise of Political Parties and the Revolutionary Movement.* The rise of liberalism and radicalism that preceded the beginnings of the revolutionary movements in Russia is well documented by contemporary memoirs and writings published in these early times and later. Thick journals of the period, starting in the 1850s and published both in Russia and abroad, such as Herzen's *Kolokol* (London and Geneva, 1857−1866), *Russkaîa starina* (St. Petersburg, 1870−1918), *Russkiĭ arkhiv* (Moscow, 1863−1915), *Russkiĭ vîestnik* (Moscow, 1856−1906), *Sovremennik* (St. Petersburg, 1851−1862 and 1912−1913), and *Vîestnik Evropy* (St. Petersburg, 1866−1918), provide valuable source material for this early period.

The Populist Movement (Narodniki), which was initiated by the radical intelligentsia in the 1870s, is thoroughly documented by contemporary writings (pamphlets and periodicals published in Russia and abroad), reprints of contemporary material published in later years, diaries, biographies, trial records, monographs, and finally by a wealth of articles in the thick journals. The journals *Narodnaîa volîa* (Paris, 1879–1885) and *Vîestnik narodnoĭ voli* (Geneva, 1883–1886) are valuable sources on these movements. Soviet publications of police records and other contemporary government materials on the Narodniki are valuable additions to this group of materials. The collection contains equally good source material on the earliest Marxist groups in Russia and abroad.

*Land and Peasant Question.*    The land problem and the peasant question are excellently covered at the Hoover Library. Holdings include collections of pertinent laws, statistics on land tenure and land use (of which the basic work was cited earlier in the section on statistics), monographs and special studies, and a large number of articles in Russian periodicals. Publications of various official bodies include the basic set of records of the special commission that prepared the drafts of laws on the abolition of serfdom in 1861, Russia. Redaktsionnyîa Komissii dlîa Sostavleniîa Polozheniîa o Krest'îanakh. *Materialy redaktsionnykh kommissiĭ dlîa sostavleniîa polozheniîa o krest'îanakh vykhodîashchikh iz krepostnoĭ zavisimosti,* 18v. (St. Petersburg, 1859–1860), and other documentary material on the peasant question. The material increases in volume after 1906, when the Duma and the political parties gave special attention to this problem. Stolypin's attempts to solve the peasant and land problem are well documented.

*Economic Development and Territorial Expansion.*    Although the library has a considerable amount of material on these and related subjects, the coverage is only fair. The material on natural resources and their industrial exploitation is rather weak. Holdings of statistics on industrial production, investments, and related topics are good only for the years after 1908. For earlier years only scattered sources are available; however, monographs provide ample information on industrialization since 1880. Commerce is covered much better; there are more statistics and monographs on this subject, and they cover a longer time span. The material on the beginning of the cooperative movement is fair. Economic aspects of agriculture are well covered by statistics, monographs, and many government publications. Although the holdings in this field are not extensive, they represent a valuable section of the collection, as material of this kind is scarce outside Russia.

*Annexed Areas in Europe.*    Russia's territorial expansion in the eighteenth and nineteenth centuries in Finland, the Baltic countries, and Poland added to the empire large areas with non-Russian populations. Until 1917, Finland enjoyed a changing degree of autonomy, and material on the Russian administration of Finland is quite extensive. It includes a complete set of laws for the period 1860–1917: *Sbornik postanovlenĭi Velikago Kniâzhestva Finliândskago za 1860–1916* and other administrative material (see the section "Laws, Statutes, Official Gazettes"). The Baltic countries, incorporated into Russia in the eighteenth century, were administered as Russian provinces (gubernii), and their documentation is discussed above. (For details, see the chapter Baltic States.)

Documentation on Poland in the Hoover Institution Library and Archives begins with the period of the kingdom, created at the Vienna Congress in 1815, and is particularly strong for the period after the 1830 uprising when Russian administration was imposed on the country. The documentation of this later period of Russian occupation is excellent. (For details, see the chapter Poland.)

*Asiatic Russia and Its Colonization.* The library has sizable holdings dealing with Russian Asia published before 1917. They contain descriptions of the various areas (Siberia and Central Asia mainly), climatic conditions, population, economic conditions, and similar topics. The migration of settlers into Siberia and Turkestan (Central Asia) and the planning of this movement (especially in Stolypin's time) are fairly well covered. The collection includes reports of scientific expeditions and special commissions concerned with the colonization of Russian Asia; for example, Russia. Pereselencheskoe Upravlenie. *Aziatskaiâ Rossiiâ*, 3v. (St. Petersburg, 1914), published by the Colonization Office, which serves as a basic source and includes an atlas. The material on Russian Asia, including specialized periodicals, in general is quite abundant.

*The Church.* The history of the orthodox church, its organization, and its role in the development of state and society are well covered in the collection. The library has the basic Russian works and numerous monographs on these topics, including the publications of the synod (under Russia. Sviâtîeĭshiĭ Pravitel'stvuiûshchiĭ Sinod) and other religious authorities.

*Political Parties, 1898–1917.* The collection covers all the early and post-1905 parties and their factions and includes party publications, periodicals, polemical writings, memoirs and biographies of leading politicians, monographs on the parties and their particular activities, and a considerable amount of archival material. Perhaps the weakest spot in this outstanding collection is the paucity of party newspapers of the period. This gap, to a large degree, is filled by extensive holdings of periodicals of the parties and their factions.

The Russian Social-Democratic Workers' Party is perhaps best covered. The extensive Boris I. Nicolaevsky Collection of documents (1827–1966) can be found in the Institution's archives. Besides a remarkable collection of rare handbills, leaflets, and circulars printed for party members, the library has the records of all its congresses and conferences, both before the split in 1903 and after, when the bolshevik and menshevik factions acted independently. A considerable number of party publications, many reprints of rare works, and the writings of prominent party leaders are a valuable resource for research. The material on this party includes well over one thousand catalog entries, such as the periodicals *Iskra* (Geneva, 1900–1905), *Dnevnik sotsialdemokrata* (St. Petersburg and Geneva, 1905–1911), *Proletariĭ* (Geneva and Paris, 1905–1909, *Rabochee delo* (Geneva, 1899–1902), and *Sotsialdemokrat* (Vilna, Paris, and Geneva, 1909–1916).

The Socialist-Revolutionary party is not as well covered, but the material in the Hoover holdings may be evaluated as excellent. It includes the records of congresses and conferences of the party (except the second congress), party publications, periodicals, and similar primary sources. Holdings of the party's journals, *Byloe* (London and Paris, 1903–1913), *Revoliûtsionnaia Rossiia* (Geneva, London, and Paris, 1900–1905), and *Viestnik russkoĭ revoliûtsii* (Geneva, 1901–1905), are incomplete. Memoirs and writings of leaders and monographs on the party and its activities are well represented.

The holdings dealing with the Constitutional-Democratic party are less extensive. Although they include some party publications and the most important writings of its leaders, the material as a whole should be evaluated only as good. The library has the weekly *Viestnik partii narodnoĭ svobody* (1906, 1917, incomplete).

Material on other political parties in Russia before 1917 is rather fragmentary. The complete records of the Duma and State Council and independent periodicals are a valuable source for the study of party positions and attitudes in contemporary politics.

*The Okhrana.* A peculiar but nonetheless important source for the study of political parties in Russia is the voluminous archive of the Paris office of the imperial Russian secret police, the "Okhrana." It includes a large amount of printed and duplicated material originating in the main office in St. Petersburg and the entire files and records of the Paris office for the period 1883–1917. The purpose of the Paris office was surveillance of Russian émigrés abroad. Besides the agents' reports, the files contain political surveys and reports on activities of all political parties from the farthest left to the center. Information on the rightist groups is less detailed. The secret police gave particular attention to terrorist cells and organizations, both in Russia itself and abroad.

*The Russo-Japanese War.* The period of the Russo-Japanese War is well covered. The library has a considerable number of personal accounts, official descriptions of land and sea engagements, and monographs dealing with the war. Periodicals printed abroad at this time treat the political aspects of the period. The rare *Letopis' voĭny s Îâponieĭ* (St. Petersburg, 1904 [nos.1–40, incomplete]) contains an official account of the war. Finally, the unpublished archives of

General Bazarov and other manuscript materials constitute a valuable addition to the holdings on this period.

*Local Self-Government.* The organs of land and city self-government, the so-called "zemstva," are well covered in the holdings. Collections of laws and ordinances regulating their operation, records of their congresses, their addresses to the tsar and the government, memoirs of their leading members, and monographs on existing institutions of self-government and projects for their reorganization, are quite well represented. The thick journals provide additional material. Within the Hoover Library the holdings of yearly reports for most local provincial zemstva are very irregular, with the exception of that from the Moscow zemstvo, and there are few official gazettes. The Green Library, however, possesses nearly all of these local records on microfiche. Hoover holds an important set of administrative orders for the city government of Moscow, *Prikazy po moskovskomu gradonachal'stvu i stolichnoĭ politsii,* covering the years 1881–1914.

*The First World War.* The material on Imperial Russia's participation in World War I is abundant and excellent. It includes all official publications on the war and personal accounts of officers of various ranks, politicians, and others, both in the form of printed items and archival holdings, which are too numerous to be listed here. Records of special state and self-governing bodies connected with the war effort, discussions of the attitudes of political parties toward the war published as separate items or as articles in wartime, and later periodicals issued in Russia and by émigrés provide a broad source of documentation.

The complete set of stenographic records of the Duma and the State Council, as well as contemporary newspapers, contain reflections of public opinion on the war effort and military operations. Monographs and memoirs written by participants in the war and by diplomats and scholarly works written by Russians and foreigners alike provide substantial background material for new studies.

A new addition to this material is the archive of the Russian Expeditionary Corps in France (January 1915–1918), which is part of the Gen. Peter Wrangel Military Papers, recently made available for research. The existence of this vast body of archival material became known only recently. The archives of the Russian embassy in Washington, especially the papers of Sergeĭ A. Ughet (1910–1930), the Russian financial attaché, should also be mentioned here. Ughet directed and later liquidated the activities of a purchasing commission that ordered war supplies in the United States for the Russian army.

*Foreign Policy.* This field is well covered by primary and secondary materials, especially for the period after 1890. The library has Russian treaty collections, many publications by the Ministry of Foreign Affairs, the Russian "colored books," consular reports, and other similar materials, including

Russia. Ministerstvo Inostrannykh Del. *Sbornik konsul'skikh donesenii*, 18v. (St. Petersburg, 1898 – 1904); and Russia. Treaties, etc. *Recueil des traités et conventions conclus par la Russie avec les puissances étrangères*, 15v. (St. Petersburg, 1874 – 1909).

These sources are substantially augmented by several Soviet publications of documents relating to the foreign policy of the imperial government. In addition to the voluminous publication entitled *Mezhdunarodnye otnosheniia v epokhu imperializma: Dokumenty iz arkhivov tsarskogo i vremennogo pravitel'stv, 1878 – 1917 gg.* (Moscow, 1931 – 1940), the library has separate volumes of documents on relations with specific European and Asiatic countries published by the Soviet government. Memoirs of statesmen of this period, published before and after 1917, supplement the primary sources. Documents and writings on the background of World War I are an important part of these holdings.

*The Attitude of the Russian Socialists toward the War.*　The material dealing with the attitudes of the bolsheviks and mensheviks in Russia and abroad, mainly in Switzerland and France, is especially important as background material on the bolshevik revolution and the withdrawal of Russia from the war. This material includes abundant data on bolshevik attitudes and activities in Russia, including party propaganda, recollections of participants, monographs, and other primary and secondary sources. The writings and actions of the mensheviks in wartime Russia, in originals and microfilm copies, are also fairly well covered.

*Family Histories and Genealogy.*　The library has a large amount of material on the history of the Romanov family and several other prominent aristocratic families. There are, in addition, biographies of members of the imperial family and a voluminous work on the imperial entourage, as well as several genealogical works on the Russian nobility. A few books belonging to the private libraries of the tsar, the empress, and other members of the imperial family, in luxurious bindings and with bookplates, are available in the collection, but they are mostly outside the field of interest of the library.

*Art Collection.*　Although fine arts are outside the scope of the Hoover Library, literature on Russian art was acquired along with other material and is now a special attraction in the Hoover Institution. Although fragmentary, it is quantitatively and qualitatively one of the outstanding collections in the United States. The collection consists of about 800 volumes, some truly rare, and is particularly rich in monographs and periodicals on ancient, medieval, and seventeenth to nineteenth century architecture. It contains a large number of drawings, colored plates, and photographs pertaining to church and civic architecture, as well as books, periodicals, colored plates, and photographs pertaining to iconography, religious art objects, painting, sculpture, applied arts, peasant handicrafts, numismatics, the theater, and ballet. A number of recent books and brochures reflect Soviet architectural and artistic activities.

*Periodicals.* Periodicals from the imperial era, published in Russia and abroad, form a remarkable part of the collection. Besides weekly, fortnightly, monthly, and quarterly publications, there are yearbooks, which were especially numerous in Russia during the pre-1917 period. Holdings of periodicals in the Russian language start with the 1830s. Some files of prerevolutionary serials cover as long a period as eighty years. Twenty-nine titles run for a period of over five years, and some 120 titles cover shorter periods. Holdings of some short-lived periodicals, however, are very important and very rare. The library has many such periodicals, mostly published in Russia during the eventful years 1905–1907, including:

> *Chernoe znamĭà* (Geneva, 1905)
> *Dnevnik sotsial'domokrata* (St. Petersburg and Geneva, 1905–1911)
> *Listki "Khlĭeb i volĭà"* (London, 1906–1907)
> *Listok gruppy beznachalie* (Paris, 1905)
> *Listok osvobozhdeniĭà* (Stuttgart and Paris, 1904–1905)
> *Na ocheredi* (St. Petersburg, 1906–1907)
> *Nasha tribuna* (Vilna, 1906–1907)
> *Nashe delo* (Moscow, 1906)
> *Nevskiĭ vĭestnik* (St. Petersburg, 1906)
> *Nevskiĭ sbornik* (St. Petersburg, 1906)
> *Osvobozhdenĭe* (Stuttgart, 1902–1905)
> *Professional'nyĭ soĭuz* (St. Petersburg, 1905–1906)
> *Proletarskoe dĭelo* (Geneva, 1905)
> *Vĭestnik partii narodnoĭ svobody* (St. Petersburg, 1906–1907)
> *Zemlĭà i volĭà* (Paris, 1905–1907)

The library has an outstanding collection of rare Russian-language periodicals published outside of Russia before the 1917 revolution. Most of these periodicals had short lives, and the number of ephemeral single issues is large. The prerevolutionary periodicals are predominantly historical and political. Besides containing articles on history, literature, politics, agriculture, and other matters, the thick journals broadly mirror intellectual trends and provide an important primary source on pre-1917 Russia. Some of the files have been completed by microfilm purchases.

*Newspapers.* The library has a considerable number of newspapers from Russia for the pre-1917 years, but most of these files are short and fragmentary. Exceptions are *Russkiĭà Vĭedomosti* (Moscow, 1895, 1899–1918) and *Novoe*

*Vremĩa* (St. Petersburg, 1882−1917) in originals and on microfilm. The war years, 1914−1917, are much better covered than the prewar period. The library has a rare set of digests and reprints of the Russian press during World War I, which were prepared by the British War Office for official use and, being in English, are most useful for any research on wartime Russia: Great Britain. War Office. General Staff. *Daily Review of the Foreign Press* (London, 1915−1919). Two French sources also cover the Russian press: France. Office Franco-Russe de Renseignement, Leningrad. *Bulletin de la presse* (September 19, 1917− February 14, 1918); and *Bulletin périodique de la presse russe* (Paris, March 1916−April 1940).

Newspapers published before 1917 by the Russian political emigration abroad are well covered in the holdings. Issued by various revolutionary groups, they include complete sets of the originals of such rare items as *Kolokol* and *Iskra*. For more detailed information about the newspaper holdings, see Karol Maichel's *Soviet and Russian Newspapers at the Hoover Institution: A Catalog* (Stanford, 1966). Another useful reference tool is *Russkaĩa periodicheskaĩa pechat'* (1895−1917), an annotated list that covers both journals and newspapers.

## THE PERIOD OF THE PROVISIONAL GOVERNMENT

### The March Revolution of 1917

For more than forty years, Russian revolutionary factions and parties worked to subvert the tsarist empire and overthrow the regime. But when in March 1917 demonstrations by a war-weary and hungry populace in Petrograd sparked a mutiny of the local garrison, none of the revolutionaries was prepared to lead the masses. In fact, leadership during ensuing disturbances passed into the hands of patriotic liberals who planned to replace the autocratic regime with a democratic one.

Lenin, in a public speech in Switzerland a few days before the Petrograd riots, expressed doubts that a revolution would take place in Russia during his lifetime. A group of prominent members of the Duma was able to pacify the mobs and temporarily control the mutinous soldiers. The abdication of Nicholas II occurred as unexpectedly as the revolution itself, and a provisional government assumed power.

The Hoover Institution's holdings on these events are excellent and include original primary sources and reprints issued in the West and the Soviet Union, memoirs, personal accounts, and a number of newspapers that appeared during the March Revolution. The following small selection of titles serves as an example of the richness of this material:

> Bunyan, James, and Fisher, H. H. comps. *The Bolshevik Revolution, 1917−1918: Documents and Materials* (Stanford, 1934).

*Izvestiiâ soveta rabochikh deputatov* (Moscow, 1917).
*The Letters of the Tsar to the Tsaritsa, 1914—1917* (London, 1923, and other editions).
*Padenie tsarskogo rezhima,* 7v. (Leningrad and Moscow, 1924—1927). A collection of documents of the special investigatory committee appointed by the Provisional Government.
*Pervyĭ legal'nyĭ peterburgskiĭ komitet bol'shevikov v 1917 g.: Sbornik materialov i protokolov zasedaniĭ peterburgskogo komiteta RSDRP(B) i ego ispolnitel'noĭ komissii za 1917 g.* (Moscow, 1927).
*Pervyĭ vserossiĭskiĭ s''ezd sovetov rabochikh i soldatskikh deputatov* (Moscow, 1930—1931). Documents and materials.
*Revoliûtsiiâ 1917 goda,* 6v. (Moscow, 1923—1930). A chronicle of events.
*1917 god v saratovskoĭ gubernii: Sbornik dokumentov, fevral' 1917—dekabr' 1918 gg.* (Saratov, 1957). A collection of documents.

Original primary sources include the following archival collections:

Balk, A. "Poslednie pîat' dneĭ tsarskogo Petrograda: 23—28 fev. 1917 g." (The last part of Balk's diary as the mayor of Petrograd).
Breshkovskaîâ, Catherine. A manuscript of her memoirs as a Russian revolutionary and other documents.
De Basily, Nicholas. Papers (1900—1917), including documents on the events that led to the abdication of Nicholas II and the drafts of the abdication itself. De Basily's recently published memoirs are entitled *Diplomat of Imperial Russia, 1903—1917* (Stanford, 1973).
Garvi, Peter A. A manuscript of his memoirs as a member of the Social Democratic Workers' Party (1906—1921).
Martynow, A. P. Memoirs of the chief of the Okhrana office in Moscow, 1912—1917, giving a chronological view of the Okhrana during the years 1906—1917.

The following newspapers (files of some are incomplete) detail events of the time:

*Izvestiiâ revoliûtsionnoĭ nedeli* (Petrograd, 1917)
*Pravda* (Petrograd and Moscow, 1917— )
*Birzhevyîâ viêdomosti* (Petrograd, 1914—1917)
*Diêlo naroda* (Petrograd and Moscow, 1917—1919)
*Den'* (Petrograd, 1913—1918)
*Novoe vremîâ* (Petrograd, 1876—1917)
*Riêch'* (Petrograd, 1913—1917)

*Russkoe slovo* (Moscow, 1914–1917)
*Russkaîa volîa* (Petrograd, 1916–1917)
*Russkiîa vîedomosti* (Moscow, 1890–1918)
*Vlast' naroda* (Moscow, 1917)
*Volîa naroda* (Petrograd, 1917)

## General Characteristics of the Material

The eight months in 1917 of Provisional Government rule were too short to enable Russian scholars, writers, and politicians to produce fundamental works on political, social, and economic changes in this period, as a search of the official bibliography, *Knizhnaîa letopis'*, covering these months shows. During this time, however, an extraordinarily large number of pamphlets was published in Russia. The government, political parties, newly created organizations, and individual writers used the pamphlet as the main means of conveying their ideas and plans for changing Russia from a despotic autocracy into a liberal democracy. Freedom of the press, unrestricted for the first and only time in Russian history, permitted periodicals and newspapers to become true vehicles of public opinion. Thus, certain important developments not covered by official documentation, such as the Pre-Parliament, are excellently reported. Due to collecting difficulties, Russian newspapers and periodicals from this period were, as a rule, poorly represented in American libraries. Substantial microfilming and reprinting projects have improved this situation considerably.

In Witold Sworakowski's *The Hoover Library Collection on Russia* (Stanford, 1954), the author drew attention to the importance and research qualities of the Hoover Institution's collection on this short period:

The lack of a sizable number of books published in this period and the general scarcity of pamphlets, periodicals, and newspapers from Russia under the L'vov and Kerenskiĭ governments have produced the general belief that the source material on this period in American libraries is too poor and inadequate to support larger research projects. A survey of the holdings of the Hoover Library appears to suggest that a revision of the above belief is in order. The library has an exceptionally good body of official documentation on this period, a limited number of books, a comparatively large number of pamphlets, and nearly complete sets of the most important periodicals and newspapers. Besides this material originating in Russia, the library has many writings on this period contained in publications of the post-1917 Russian emigration: memoirs of prominent leaders of all political shades, and of the high-ranking military; personal accounts of participants in important events and local developments; and reprints of documents of general and local importance. In addition to this, the library has a considerable number of manuscripts and private collections relating to this period.

Although the scholar consulting these materials will often find gaps and deficiencies, nevertheless, the resources of the library seem to be adequate for the undertaking of studies on Russia's democratic potential revealed during the short period of the Provisional Government.

Most of the material on this period was acquired by Prof. Frank A. Golder during a visit to Russia between 1920 and 1923. Before 1925, much of the missing material was ordered through commercial channels or exchanges. Under Stalin's rule, acquisitions in the Soviet Union were practically prohibited. Only after Stalin's death did acquisitions slowly return to normal. Starting in the early 1960s, the resumption of exchanges, microfilming, and acquisitions made it possible to fill remaining gaps. Particularly before and during the "Kerensky Project" (which in 1968 resulted in the publication of the monumental three-volume collection of documents entitled *The Russian Provisional Government, 1917,* selected and edited by Robert P. Browder and Alexander F. Kerensky [Stanford, 1961]), a great effort was made to obtain missing material. When .Aleksandr Solzhenitsyn, preparing to write a book on 1917, visited the Hoover Institution, he stated he had found more material than was available to him in Moscow libraries.

### Government Documents

The Provisional Government, in order to publicize its activities, produced a variety of journals and numbered publications. The preparation for the elections to the Constituent Assembly and for land reform motivated other special publications. The Petrograd Soviet of Workers' and Soldiers' Deputies, an outgrowth of the March 1917 revolution, and similar bodies throughout the country assumed a semigovernmental status, and their publications are included in this section.

*Laws, Statutes, Official Gazettes.* The library has a complete set of laws published by the Provisional Government, contained in the official gazette for the entire period: Russia. Laws, Statutes, etc. *Sobranie uzakoneniĭ i razporĭazheniĭ pravitel'stva,* 8v. (Petrograd, 1914–1917); from no. 54 of March 6 to no. 286 of November 18, 1917); and in the collection of laws, *Sbornik ukazov i posta-novleniĭ Vremennago pravitel'stva,* 2v. (Petrograd, 1917–1918; the period covering February 27 to July 24, 1917). The more important decrees of the government were also published in its official daily newspaper, *Vi̇estnik Vremennago pravitel'stva* (Petrograd, March 5–October 26, 1917). The government's legislative activity is dealt with in many official pamphlets, as well as in publications by political parties and individual writers.

*Publications of Ministries and Special Commissions.* Useful for the study of activities of the Provisional Government are two collections of the minutes of its meetings: Russia. (1917. Provisional Government). *Zhurnaly zasedaniĭ Vre-mennago pravitel'stva* (Petrograd, March 4–October 3, 1917, about one-third missing); and *Osobyĭ zhurnal zasedaniĭ Vremennago pravitel'stva* (Petrograd, April—September 1917, a few issues missing). These minutes are supplemented by detailed reports on the meetings published in *Vĭestnik Vremennago pravitel'stva*.

The official publications of particular ministries include an almost complete collection of drafts of laws and regulations presented by them for action by the Council of Ministers. These publications cover the period up to July or August 1917. The official gazettes of particular ministries are not well represented in the holdings. The collection of circulars of the Ministry of the Interior, Russia. Ministerstvo Vnutrennikh Dĭel. *Sbornik tsirkulĭarov Ministerstva vnutrennikh dĭel* (Petrograd, March—June 1917), is the best of them. The publications of the special commissions appointed by the Provisional Government to prepare the elections to the Constituent Assembly and land reform are much better covered and include:

> Russia (1917. Provisional Government). Osoboe Soveshchanie dlĭa Izgotovleniĭa. . . . *Izvestiĭa Osobago Soveshchaniĭa dlĭa izgotovleniĭa proekta polozheniĭa o vyborakh v Uchreditel'noe Sobranie,* nos. 1—100 (Petrograd, May 25—November 10, 1917).
>
>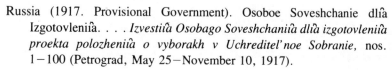
> ———. ———. *Stenograficheskiĭ otchet Osobago Soveshchaniĭa dlĭa izgotovleniĭa proekta polozheniĭa o vyborakh v Uchreditel'noe Sobranie* (Petrograd, sessions 1—5, May 1—15, June 25, 1917).
>
> ———. Vserossiĭskaĭa Kommissiĭa po Dĭelam. . . . *Izvestiĭa Vserossiĭskoĭ komissii po dĭelam o vyborakh v Uchreditel'noe Sobranie komissii,* nos. 1—23 (Petrograd, September 6—December 4, 1917).
>
> ———. Glavnyĭ Zemel'nyĭ Komitet. *Izvestiĭa Glavnago zemel'nago komiteta* (Petrograd, July 15—October 1, 1917).
>
> ———. *Trudy komissii po podgotovke zemel'noĭ reformy,* 5v. (Petrograd, 1917—1918).

The voluminous stenographic records of the special commission, Chrezvy-chainaĭa Sledstvennaĭa Komissiĭa, appointed to investigate the tsarist wartime government, *Padenie tsarskogo rezhima,* 7v. (Leningrad and Moscow, 1924—27), were published after the overthrow of the Provisional Government by the bolsheviks. Some important records and files of other ministries of the Provisional Government were later published by the Soviet government. In addition, the library has some monographs and memoirs, printed in Soviet Russia and abroad, that deal with the changes in Russian legislation under the Provisional Government.

*Pre-Parliament.* No official records of the Democratic Conference (September 27—October 3, 1917) and its creation, the Pre-Parliament (October 20—

November 7, 1917), were ever published. Contemporary newspapers, however, which are well represented in the library, contain a fair record of the proceedings and extensive reprints of important speeches made in these bodies.

*The Soviets.* The proceedings and publications of the Petrograd Soviet of Workers' and Soldiers' Deputies are excellently covered in the library, but the Moscow Soviet is less well covered. Only scattered items of publications of the Peasants' Soviet and of regional and local soviets are in the holdings. The library has a complete set of the daily of the Petrograd Soviet, *Izvestiĩa Petrogradskago soveta rabochikh i soldatskikh deputatov* (after August 1, 1917, the title was changed to *Izvestiĩa tsentral'nago ispolnitel'nago komiteta i Petrogradskago soveta rabochikh i soldatskikh deputatov*), with a few rare special editions. The All-Russian Congress of Soviets (Vserossiĩskiĩ S''ezd Sovetov), which took place in June and July 1917, is adequately covered in the holdings. Besides contemporary publications, the library has a considerable number of monographs dealing with the soviets and memoirs of members of soviets in various places. The literature on the soldiers' soviets in the army is well represented.

## Books, Pamphlets, and Manuscripts

*Overthrow of the Tsarist Regime.* Practically all publications on the tumultuous March days in Petrograd, which brought about the overthrow of tsardom, are available in the library. Many articles in Soviet, as well as Russian émigré, periodicals supplement this material. Besides printed diaries, eyewitness reports of participants, and narratives of close observers of the Petrograd events, there are several manuscripts in the collection containing additional information; among them, Gen. A. Balk's description of the last five days of tsarist Petrograd is the most detailed. The library also has most monographs dealing with the motives and the developments of the March coup.

The memoirs and correspondence of Nicholas II, the empress, and members of the imperial family, in addition to the previously mentioned records of the special inquiry commission appointed by the Provisional Government to investigate the last imperial government are particularly valuable. Most of these sources were published by the Soviet government and are in the collection.

*Political Parties.* The granting of full civil liberties by the Provisional Government brought about a mushrooming of political party life. Not only did more than a dozen Russian parties start their legal activities during this period, but most minority nationalities followed the Russian example. The material published by and on the Russian parties of this period is well represented in the library, but the parties of the non-Russian nationalities are rather poorly covered.

Among the Russian party publications in the collection, those of the bolsheviks alone are outstanding. In the early 1920s when the library acquired the material in Russia, all other parties were outlawed, and their publications were difficult to obtain. The library has the proceedings of the May Conference and the August Congress of the Bolshevik party, and propaganda publications, pamphlets, periodicals, and newspapers published by the party between March and October 1917. The publications of the Menshevik, the various factions of the Socialist-Revolutionary, and the Constitutional-Democratic parties are less well covered in the holdings, but the material is substantial. The Labor party (Trudovaîa Narodno-Sotsialisticheskaîa Partiîa) and the Jewish Bund are only fairly represented. Holdings of materials published by other and less important parties are weak. Later writings about the parties during this period, published in Soviet Russia and by Russian émigrés, are well represented.

*Civic Education.* The swift transformation of Russia from autocracy to liberal democracy under the Provisional Government led to efforts to explain this change to the masses. During its eight months, a great number of popular pamphlets discussing and explaining such concepts as universal suffrage, democratic forms of government, the Constituent Assembly, and uni- and bicameral systems of parliament appeared. These pamphlets, which were reprinted in various cities in 1917 and circulated in large numbers, became the vehicle for political education for the broad masses of Russia's population. They are important for the study of advancement toward democracy and are well represented in the library in the Russian Mass Education Collection.

*Nationalities and Movements for Autonomy.* The abolition of all political and cultural restrictions on the non-Russian nationalities of the empire brought about the creation of many new political, cultural, and other organizations that advocated self-determination and autonomy. Publications dealing with various aspects of the national-autonomous life of these areas appeared in considerable number, in Russian as well as in the languages of the particular nationalities. The library's coverage of these publications is fair, especially those concerning the Ukraine, Finland, and the Caucasus; most of this material is in the Russian language, the material published in local languages is less well represented. The collection also contains monographs, diaries, and collections of documents concerning these events in non-Russian areas that were published in later years.

*Foreign Relations.* The foreign policy of the Provisional Government, particularly its relations with the Allies, is well documented in official publications and statements of the government, in diaries of Russian and foreign participants, in material on diplomatic negotiations, and in a Soviet collection of documents pertaining to the foreign policy of the Provisional Government: Russia (1923-USSR). Komissiîa po Izdaniîu Dokumentov Epokhi Imperializma. *Mezhdunarodnye otnosheniîa v epokhu imperializma: Dokumenty iz arkhivov tsarskogo i Vremennogo provitel'stv, 1878–1917 gg.*, 16v. (Moscow and Leningrad, 1931–1940).

*Internal Affairs.* Internal developments, such as the drafting of a plan for land reform, the preparations for elections to the All-Russian Constituent Assembly, the abolition of various restrictions of civil rights, the July riots, and the Kornilov affair are well covered in the collection by publications of the government and its many agencies.

*Army and Military Affairs.* The Provisional Government's attempt to continue the war on the side of the Allies and its struggle with the Soviets over control of the army are well documented in the holdings. Besides the material contained in contemporary Russian sources and in diaries, documents, and monographs published by American, French, and British authors, several groups of manuscripts in the archives deal with this subject.

The situation in the army and navy following the famous Order No. 1 of the Petrograd Soviet to the Petrograd population ("K naseleniiu Petrograda i Rossii" in the February 28, 1917 issue of *Izvestiia*) and the progressive disintegration of the armed forces at the front are well covered in the collection by personal accounts in periodicals and monographs published in the post-1917 period. Later publications of Soviet authors disclose the part played by the Bolshevik party in this disintegration of the armed forces. An important work is *Razlozhnie armii v 1917 godu* (Moscow, 1923).

*Periodicals and Newspapers.* The newspapers for this eight-month period are excellently represented by nearly complete runs of the papers of all important political parties that were issued in Petrograd, as well as a few in Moscow and in other cities, during these crucial days of Russian history, including:

*Birzhevyia viedomosti* (Petrograd)
*Dielo naroda* (Petrograd)
*Den'* (Petrograd)
*Izvestiia revoliutsionnoi nedeli* (Petrograd)
*Izvestiia* (Petrograd and Moscow)
*Journal de Petrograd* (Petrograd [in French])
*L'Entente* (Petrograd [in French])
*Novaia zhizn'* (Petrograd)
*Novoe vremia* (Petrograd)
*Petrograder Togblat* (Petrograd [in Yiddish])
*Pravda* (Petrograd)
*Rabochaia gazeta* (Petrograd)
*Rech'* (Petrograd)
*Russian Daily News* (Petrograd [in English])

*Russkaiâ voliâ* (Petrograd)
*Russkiiâ viêdomosti* (Moscow)
*Russkoe slovo* (Moscow)
*Vlast' naroda* (Moscow)

For additional information on newspapers in the Hoover Institution's newspaper collection, see Karol Maichel's *Soviet and Russian Newspapers at the
Hoover Institution* (Stanford, 1966). Periodicals of this period include continua-
tions of titles published during the tsarist period.


## THE CIVIL WAR

### Introduction and
### General Characteristics of the Material

Following the November overthrow of the Provisional Government and the
disbanding of the Constituent Assembly in January 1918, civilian and military
opposition against communist domination created a chaotic situation. In the
Baltic provinces, the Ukraine, the Caucasian countries, Central Asia, and
Siberia, national groups formed state organizations and declared their autonomy
or independence. In north and south Russia, Generals ÎUdenich and Alexeev
organized volunteer armies that began military operations against the communist
republic proclaimed by Lenin and his bolshevik followers. In Siberia, a government under Admiral Kolchak and local guerrilla bands (Ataman Semenov and
others) were quite successful in the beginning in their struggle against Red Army
units. These antibolshevik forces, known as the White armies, opposed with
faltering strength the imposition of bolshevik rule on Russia. This entire period is
known as the Civil War in Russia, 1918–1921.

At the time of the first survey of the Russian Collection, primary source
material on the Civil War in Russia and its particular fronts was scarce outside the
Soviet Union, and archival sources in the USSR were unavailable to Western
scholars. Beyond the military archives of the ÎUdenich army in the north and
west, available at the Hoover Institution, and fragmentary documentary material
on the Far East (Admiral Kolchak's army) and the Russian armies in southern
Russia (Volunteer Army, Deniken army, Wrangel army), only the memoirs of
statesmen, diplomats, and participants in the fighting on these fronts published in
books and articles in Soviet and émigré peiodicals served as the basis for research
on this broad topic. Soviet publications have used some documentary material
captured after the disintegration of the Civil War fronts, but this material was
never made available to Western scholars. Monographs on this subject published
in the West were based on this fragmentary documentary material. The Hoover

Institution, however, possesses a large archive received in the 1930s as a closed deposit of Gen. Peter Wrangel, covering the years 1916–1923. This archive was opened only recently, after the restriction period expired, and the papers became the property of the Hoover Institution. The 352 folders contain the archives of the first Volunteer Army organized in southern Russia by Gens. M. V. A. Alekseev and L. G. Kornilov and of the Russian Army in southern Russia under the command of General Denikin and later of General Wrangel until its collapse and evacuation to Turkey. Later, General Wrangel obtained and added to his military papers the archives of several other Russian institutions and agencies abroad (see below). It has not yet been possible to review the contents of the 352 folders. Only the military organizations, institutions, and agencies are listed, and the material will be made available to scholars after processing. The Hoover Institution now has much better primary source material on the White armies in the Civil War in the south of Russia than is available in Soviet archives.

Among this material is a vast archive of the Russian Expeditionary Corps that had been dispatched to France in 1916 and shortly thereafter subverted by bolshevik propaganda and which therefore never went to the front. Files of the military judiciary authority that investigated this affair are included. Additional material on this matter can be found in the Okhrana archives.

Holdings of printed material on the Civil War are strong. Memoirs and monographs, published in Russian and other languges, are substantially represented in the collection, including multivolume publications issued on the subject in the Soviet Union and by exiled Russian participants and scholars. The following major works are examples of valuable memoirs in the Civil War Collection:

> Alekseev, S. A. *Revoliûtsiîa i grazhdanskaîa voîna v opisaniîakh belogvardeĭtsev*, 6v. (Moscow, 1926–1930).
> Denikin, A. I. *Ocherki russkoĭ smuty*, 5v. (Paris, 1921–1926).
> Miliûkov, Pavel N. *Rossiîa na perelome*, 2v. (Paris, 1927).
> Trotskiĭ, Lev D. *Kak vooruzhalas' revoliûtsiîa*, 3v. (Moscow, 1923–1925).
> Wrangel, Peter N. *The Memoirs of General Wrangel* (New York, 1930).

## The Northwestern Front

After the peace treaty of Brest-Litovsk in March 1918, parts of the Russian army opposing the Germans in the Baltic area formed an antibolshevik volunteer army under the command of Gen. Nikolaĭ N. Îudenich. This group later included a local volunteer corps under Gen. Pavel M. Bermondt-Avalov. After an advance to the outskirts of Petrograd, Îudenich was defeated by the new Red Army. The Bermondt units were liquidated by the governments of the Baltic states, which, in the meantime, had declared their independence. Documents on the "Bermondt affair" are in the Thomas J. Orbison Archival Collection (1919–1920), along with a large amount of memoirs and monographs on these armies. In addition, the military papers of the ÎUdenich army (1919–1920) are in the Hoover Institution.

## The Southern Front

The Russian Volunteer Army in southern Russia was organized shortly after the collapse of the Provisional Government by Gens. Mikhail V. Alexeev and Lavr G. Kornilov. It grew quite rapidly and command passed to Gen. Anton I. Denikin and then to Gen. Peter N. Wrangel, who eventually had to withdraw the remnants of his forces to Turkey.

The Wrangel papers contain the archives of the headquarters of these armies. Denikin and Wrangel attempted to form surrogates of a Russian state on territories under their command: hence the archives deal not only with military questions (organizational, operational, and intelligence), but also with political affairs and relations with Allied governments and military missions.

In addition, the Wrangel papers contain the archives of the following military offices and agencies:

> Board of Directors, charged with the organization of a Russian air force (up to 1919)
>
> Foreign Supplies Board, Paris and London (1918–1921)
>
> Military representative of the Supreme Regent (1919–1920)
>
> Russian military agent in Constantinople (1920–1923)
>
> Representatives of the commander in chief of Russian armies in southern Russia for military and naval affairs in Paris (up to 1922)
>
> Correspondence with Russian representatives in Czechoslovakia and Japan (1920–1922)
>
> Military representative of Russian armies with the Allied governments and General Headquarters

Finally, the voluminous archive of the Russian Expeditionary Corps, which in 1915 had been dispatched to France, should be mentioned. This subject has never been studied in detail because of the prevailing view that documentary material on the corps did not exist. Some information on the mutiny in this corps was available in the archive of the Paris office of the Okhrana. With the opening of the Wrangel papers, historical sources for this topic have become available after sixty years.

## The Siberian Front

Because the material concerning the Civil War on the Siberian front is fragmentary and often in the context of large archival collections, a selective list of archival documents instead of a general discussion of sources is given below. (For material on the Allied intervention, see the section Soviet Russia):

Beck, Stephen M. A manuscript entitled "The Coup d'état of Admiral Kolchak: The Counter-Revolution in Siberia and Eastern Russia, 1917−1918."

Chernov, Viktor Mikhailovich. "Partiĭa Sotsialistov-Revoliŭtsionerov: Tsirkulĭarno. Ko vsem partiĭnym organizatisiĭam." Text of the Socialist-Revolutionary proclamation known as the "Chernov Manifesto" and Chernov's detailed comments on the situation at that moment.

Dotsenko, P. S. "Pobeda i porazhenie: Zapiski sovremennika (1917−1919)." Manuscript memoirs of a Socialist-Revolutionary on the events in Siberia during the revolution and Civil War. The author was a member of the executive committee of peasant deputies during the revolution. When the bolsheviks came to power, he was a representative of the Siberian government.

Dotsenko, P. S. Text of a speech given in New York in 1954 reflecting on the history of the Civil War in Siberia.

Far Eastern Republic. Records, 1921.

Fedichkin, Dmitrii Ivanovich. "Izhevskoe vozstanie, ot 8 avgusta po 15 oktiabriā 1918 goda." A manuscript, written by the commander of the Izhevsk insurgents.

Giers, Mikhail N. de, chief diplomatic representative of the Wrangel government, 1920. File contains many telegrams between Omsk, Washington, D.C., and several European capitals.

Graves, William S., Maj. Gen., commanding officer of the American Expeditionary Forces in Siberia, 1918−1920. Papers.

Harris, Ernest L., U.S. consul at Irkutsk, 1918−1921. Papers.

"The B. A. Kriukov Collection, in the Hoover War Library." Materials relating to events in Siberia and especially in the Russian Far East during the Civil War; official documents, intelligence reports, letters and manuscripts, newspapers, periodicals, broadcasts, etc., mostly of the White armies, 1917−1923.

Maklakov, Vasilii A. Papers include a manuscript copy of memoirs on the Omsk government by I. I. Sukin, an adviser to General Kolchak.

Melgunov, Sergeĭ P. Files contain a memorandum by K. I. Morozov, head of the cooperatives, which deals with the Siberian uprising against the bolsheviks in May-June 1918 and the organization of the Siberian government.

Moravsky, Valerian I., member of the first and second antibolshevik Siberian governments, 1918, 1922. A large collection of papers.

Nicolaevsky, Boris I. Archives containing the minutes of the Provisional

Government of Siberia: Vremennoe Pravitel'stvo Avtonomnoĭ Sibiri (Pravitel'stvo P. Derbera). *Protokoly Dal'nevostochnoĭ delegatsii Vremennogo pravitel'stva Avtonomnoĭ Sibiri, iiŭl'-avgust, 1918.*

Serebrennikov, I. I. *Vospominaniiâ (1917—1922).* Memoirs of a conservative regionalist, member of the Siberian and later of the Kolchak government.

Sychev, E. An unpublished report entitled "Vozstanie v Irkutsk" on the uprising in Irkutsk and liquidation of the rule of Admiral Kolchak, December 23, 1919—January 5, 1920.

Ungern-Shternberg, Baron Roman F. Unpublished memoirs and reminiscences about him by several contemporaries relating to the Civil War in Siberia and Mongolia. Parts of the reminiscences have been translated into English.

Published sources contain many memoirs on the Civil War in Siberia by participants, mostly Soviet authors. Among printed sources is the testimony of Kolchak, entitled *Dopros Kolchaka: Protokoly zasedaniĭ Chrezvychaĭnoĭ sledstvennoĭ komissii v Irkutske. Stenograficheskiĭ otchet.* It was published in English by the Hoover Institution in 1935.

## Serials

The following Russian-language serials are particularly valuable sources of materials regarding the events in Siberia and the Russian Far East:

*Arkhiv grazhdanskoĭ voĭny,* an irregular historical journal published in Berlin in 1922 (only two numbers appeared).

*Arkhiv russkoĭ revoliûtsii,* an irregular historical journal, first published in Berlin in 1921 (22 volumes containing memoirs and other valuable historical material appeared).

*Bîeloe diêlo: Letopis' bîeloĭ borby,* a collection of historical materials on the White armies, published in Berlin, 1926—1928 (seven numbers appeared).

*Bîelyĭ arkhiv,* a serial dealing with the history and literature of war, revolution, bolshevism, the White movement, etc., published in Paris, 1926—1928 (only three issues appeared).

*Byloe,* an irregular journal dedicated to the history of the revolutionary movement in Russia in the early 1900s; first issued in London and Paris, then in St. Petersburg, 1906—1907, when it was officially closed. It continued under the titles *Nasha strana* and *Minuvshie gody* until 1909, resumed publication in Petrograd in 1917, and ceased publication in 1927.

*Byloe Sibiri,* a journal containing early records of the Civil War, published by the Historical Commission of the Tomsk Gubernia Committee of the All-Russian Communist Party at Tomsk in 1923 (only three issues appeared).

*Krasnyĭ arkhiv*, a bimonthly historical journal, published by the Central Archive of the RSFSR in Moscow, 1922–1941. It contains papers and documents on prerevolutionary events, as well as on the revolution and Civil War.

*Sibirskiĭ arkhiv*, an irregular historical journal, published in Prague by the Society of Siberians in Czechoslovakia, 1929–1935 (five numbers containing articles and documentary materials appeared).

*Vestnik Man'chzhurii*, a monthly journal published by the Economic Department of the Chinese Eastern Railway Administration at Harbin, 1924–1933. In 1923 and 1924 it appeared as a weekly newspaper.

*Voliâ Rossii*, a bimonthly journal of politics and culture; organ of the émigré Socialist-Revolutionary circles, mostly of the right and center; published in Prague, 1922–1932. It had the format of a newspaper for the first year.

*Volnaıa Sibir'*, an irregular historical and political journal published in Prague by the Society of Siberians in Czechoslovakia, 1926–1930.

## Newspapers

Of the Siberian and Far Eastern papers in the collection, the following are representative of different political currents:

*Dalekaıâ Okraina* (Vladivostok, 1917–1918), antibolshevik, liberal
*Dal'nevostochnaıâ zhizn'* (Vladivostok, 1921), Yakushev's liberal group
*Dıêlo naroda* (Blagoveshchensk, 1921–1922), Socialist-Revolutionary
*Dıêlo Rossii* (Tokyo, 1920), conservative
*Golos Primorıâ* (Vladivostok, 1917–1918), progressive-conservative, antibolshevik
*Golos rodiny* (Vladivostok, 1919), liberal, antibolshevik, anti-interventionist
*Izvestııâ Vladivostokskogo Soveta rabochikh i soldatskikh deputatov* (Vladivostok, 1917), pro-Soviet and bolshevik
*Izvestııâ Ulan-Bator-Khoto* (Urga, 1924–1928), official Soviet organ
*Nasha zarıâ* (Omsk, 1919) Kolchak's supporters
*Otechestvennyıâ vıêdomosti* (Ekaterinburg, 1919), conservative, nationalist
*Rabochiĭ put'* (Omsk, 1922), labor
*Russkaıâ armııâ* (Omsk, 1919), monarchist
*Sibirskaıâ rıêch'* (Omsk, 1919), Constitutional-Democrat
*Sibirskaıâ zhizn'* (Tomsk, 1897–1916), Siberian regionalist

*Svobodnaĭa Sibir'* (Krasnoĭarsk, 1919), moderate, liberal
*Svobodnyĭ kraĭ* (Irkutsk, 1919), moderate, liberal
*Vĭestnik Vremennago pravitel' stva Avtonomnoĭ Sibiri* (Vladivostok, 1918),
    Derber group
*Vĭestnik Vremennago pravitel' stva* (Vladivostok, 1917), antibolshevik
*Volĭa* (Vladivostok, 1920–21), Socialist-Revolutionary.

Russian-language newspapers and journals published by émigré groups in
Western Europe and in the Orient often contain articles of interest and value on
the period considered. Among those of particular importance are:

*Dni* (Paris, 1922–1928), liberal
*Obshchee delo–La Cause commune* (Paris, 1918–1930), conservative,
    antibolshevik
*Posledniĭa novosti* (Paris, 1920–1940), liberal, antibolshevik
*Pour la Russie* (Paris, 1919–1920), moderate Socialist-Revolutionary
*Rul'* (Berlin, 1920–1931), democratic
*Sotsialisticheskiĭ vestnik* (Berlin and Paris, 1921–1965), menshevik
*Volĭa Rossii* (Prague, 1920–1921), right and center Socialist-Revolutionary
*Vozrozhdenie* (Paris, 1925–1940), conservative

The Hoover holdings include some runs of these émigré titles.


## SOVIET RUSSIA

### General Characteristics of the Material

An earlier survey of the Russian Collection, published in 1954 during the cold
war with the Soviet Union, was compiled when acquisitions from the Soviet
Union were most difficult. At that time considerable gaps in material covering
World War II and the last years of the Stalin regime greatly affected the quality of
the collection for the years 1939 to 1954. Shortly after the publication of that first
survey, however, acquisition conditions in the USSR changed dramatically.
Renewal of old exchanges with Soviet learned institutions and libraries and the
increase of microfilming of library material permitted the curator of the Eastern
European Collection to start a broad program of filling gaps, with a reconstruction program realized at a cost of over $1 million during the 1950s and 1960s.
This program resulted in the firm establishment of the Hoover Institution as one
of the world's leading centers of documentation on Russia and on the USSR in
particular, outside of the Soviet Union itself.

Holdings on the USSR cover practically all aspects of political, economic, and social change. Due to the pervading influence of communism and the Soviet state into such fields as philosophy, education, indoctrination of youth, and practically all aspects of daily life, documentation had to be expanded beyond normal coverage for other countries so that scholars would have an opportunity to study the totalitarian state comprehensively. The strength of the collection is illustrated by the fact that the library has a nearly perfect file of the important daily newspapers *Pravda* and *Izvestiĭa*, from number one in 1917 up to the current issues, in originals, and the minutes and protocols of all available congresses and conferences of the ruling Communist Party of the Soviet Union, predominantly in originals.

The material on the Soviet Union can be evaluated by periods as follows:

*1917–1925:* The material is excellent. It covers the early years of "war communism," the New Economic Policy (NEP) until its abolition by Stalin, the beginning of the collectivization of agriculture with its liquidation of the kulaks, and local opposition to communism (material on the Tambov uprising is outstanding). Primary sources, particularly government documents and periodicals, are well covered. Emigré publications on this period are abundant.

*1926–1936:* The material is excellent, although coverage of certain subjects is less complete. In this period when Stalin consolidated his personal rule and liquidated the old bolsheviks and suspected opponents, some periodicals disappeared and were replaced by others. Former gaps in this material have been almost entirely filled by microfilming. Coverage of the first analytical monographs on the Soviet Union published in the West is good. Holdings of emigré material published during this period are excellent.

*1937–1941:* This period is excellently covered. Former gaps, produced by export difficulties, were filled by renewed exchanges and microfilming in the 1960s. Emigré material, particularly following the outbreak of World War II, is meager.

*1941–1945:* Export of library material from the USSR during this period broke down nearly completely. Material had to be acquired after the war in the 1950s and later, but this has been completed to a large degree. Material on the "Great Patriotic War" is extremely broad, including some extremely rare publications. Holdings of the important periodicals for this period are complete. The weakest part in this period is in emigré material, which was difficult to obtain.

*1945–1956:* With Stalin's dictatorship at its peak, the struggle for succession, and the cold war followed by the first "thaw," acquisitions of material from the Soviet Union during this period were limited, and contemporary coverage became very weak. It has been subsequently much improved, and the scholar will find practically all important sources in the collection.

*1956—* : Acquisitions in the Soviet Union during this period slowly returned to normal. A broad exchange program with the Lenin Library in Moscow was established. This resulted in obtaining certain publications from the outlying areas that were not readily available to other American libraries. Budgetary difficulties of the Institution during the years 1956—1960 considerably reduced all acquisitions for the Institution's library, but they have been overcome since 1960, and acquisitions from the Soviet Union are maintained at a high level. Hence, the entire coverage of the Russian Collection after 1957 is excellent.

## Government Documents

*Laws, Statutes, Official Gazettes.*  The official gazettes of the Russian republic (RSFSR), *Sobranie zakonov i razporíazheniĭ Raboche-Krest' íanskago pravitel' stva RSFSR,* and of the USSR, *Sobranie zakonov i razporíazheniĭ Raboche-Krest' íanskago pravitel' stva SSSR,* are well represented in the collection. These are collections of laws and enactments. Before July 4, 1924, acts were promulgated in *Sobranie uzakoneniĭ i rasporíazheniĭ.* The file of the official gazette of the RSFSR covers the years 1917—1939 and 1946—1949; the file for the USSR covers the years 1924—1928, 1932—1939, 1946—1949, and 1957—1958 (the last two periods refer to the gazette of the Council of Ministers of the USSR). The library also has the early Soviet collection of decrees, *Sbornik dekretov,* for the years 1917—1919 (this serial reprinted important laws from the official gazettes), and a similar collection, *Sistematicheskiĭ sbornik vazhneĭshikh dekretov,* compiled by subject for the years 1917—1920. Reprints of all decrees, legislative acts, and resolutions from October 24, 1917 to May 1920 have been issued in the collection: Russia (1917-RSFSR). Laws, statutes, etc. *Dekrety sovetskoĭ vlasti* (Moscow, 1957—1976). The library has a complete set.

A complete set of the official gazette of the Supreme Soviet, *Vedomosti Verkhovnogo Soveta SSSR* (April 1938—  ), and a collection of its laws, Russia (1923-USSR). Laws, statutes, etc. *Sbornik zakonov SSSR i ukazov Prezidiuma Verkhovnogo soveta SSSR,* covering the years 1938 to the present, are in the library.

Holdings of the official gazettes of particular ministries (formerly commissariats), containing ordinances and regulations for various branches of administration, are fairly well represented for the period up to 1925, but are much weaker for later periods.

The library also has the rare official bulletin of the Executive Committee of the Soviets of the Far Eastern Region, *Biulletin' Dal' nevostochnogo Revoliutsionnogo Komiteta,* for the years 1920—1925.

The texts of all constitutions of the USSR and those of most constituent republics, autonomous republics, and other areas are available in the library, many in English translations. Monographs on Soviet constitutional law, by Soviet and foreign writers, are well represented.

The collection of Soviet law codes (many of the later editions in English) is not complete, but contains a large and representative sampling. The best coverage is in codes issued in the periods before 1925 and after 1945.

The library also has many monographs on Soviet legal problems, written by Soviet and foreign scholars. These are supplemented by four Soviet law journals: *Biulleten' verkhovnogo suda* (1957– ), *Sotsialisticheskaia zakonnost'* (1937– ), *Sovetskoe gosudarstvo i pravo* (1933– ), and *Sovetskoe pravo* (1922–1928).

*Publications of Ministries.* The publications of ministries are unevenly covered. Some branches of the Soviet government are well represented (foreign relations, national economy, foreign trade, internal affairs during the earlier period, and nationality problems), but coverage of others can be rated only fair or even poor.

The activities of the Soviet of People's Commissars of the RSFSR are well covered in the holdings for the years 1924–1929 (no earlier material was published). The publications of the Ministry of Foreign Affairs are well represented for the entire period. Included are collections of diplomatic correspondence, "red books," treaties, reprints of speeches on foreign relations by leading Soviet statesmen, and similar source material. The collection of documents, *Vneshniaia politika Sovetskogo Soiuza,* published in three series, covers the years 1941–1975. In addition, the library has several collections of documents concerning relations with the Soviet Union published by other governments. Monographs on Soviet foreign policy include the most important Soviet as well as foreign publications and are well covered in the holdings.

The publications of various Soviet government agencies concerned with the national economy are well represented for the period up to the early 1930s, when the publications of these agencies were gradually replaced by party publications containing more general information. The records and publications by and on the Council of National Economy (Vyshii Sovet Narodnogo Khoziaistva) are well covered. The library has the serial *Sotsialisticheskoe khoziaistvo* (1918–1930) and *Planovoe khoziaistvo* (1925– ). The records of the congresses of the All-Russian Communist Party of the late 1920s and the early 1930s contain much additional documentary material on economic problems. Especially well covered are the various publications of the Ministry of Finance. The library has several long runs of its periodicals, *Finansovye problemy* (1922–1928, 1929–1930), *Finansy i sotsialisticheskoe khoziaistvo* (1927–1933), and *Sovetskie finansy* (1940–1947), and its newspaper, *Finansovaia gazeta* (1918–1940). The library has copies of the budgets of the RSFSR for the years 1918, 1919, 1922, and 1924−1926, and of the USSR for the years 1924−1928. In addition, there are many publications on the budget and its administration for almost all periods. Monographs on budget laws and budget operations in the Soviet Union are well represented.

Publications of the Ministry for Foreign Trade are quite fragmentary and consist of the official gazette, *Vestnik Komissariata Vneshneĭ Torgovli* (1921−1922), statistics for the period 1924−1937, and scattered issues of other publications. There is, however, a good set of the ministry's periodical, *Vneshniai̊ȃ torgovlia*, from 1923 to the present. Russian and foreign monographs on Soviet trade are fairly well represented in the collection.

The ministries of Justice, Interior, and Social Security (formerly Health) are well covered. The library has many of their publications, as well as periodicals and monographs concerning their activities. The erstwhile Commissariat for Nationality Affairs (1917−1924) and its very few and scarce publications are quite well represented in the collection. The library has a set of the commissariat's rare press organ, *Zhizn' natsional' nosteĭ* (1918−1924). Several reports on the activities of the commissariat and a few of its foreign-language publications are available.

*Congress of Soviets and the Supreme Soviet.* The library has an almost complete set of minutes and records of the All-Union (formerly All-Russian) Congress of Soviets, Russia (1917 RSFSR). *S''ezd Sovetov* (Petrograd and Moscow, 1918−1935). These are supplemented by numerous reports presented to the congress and published separately. The Supreme Soviet, which replaced this congress, is also well covered. The library has the records of its sessions to date with some gaps. In addition, it has the collection of laws and the official gazette of the Supreme Soviet (see the section Government Documents). A few monographs on both bodies, published by Russian and foreign authors, are also in the holdings. Although the records of the Petrograd Soviet of Workers' and Soldiers' Deputies are well covered for the years 1917−1920, the material on the Moscow Soviet is rather weak.

*Statistics.* The census of industrial enterprises of 1918, the incomplete general census of 1920, the census of cities of 1923, the general census of 1926, and the subsequent censuses are well represented in the library holdings. Statistics on economic subjects (trade, industry, employment, agriculture) are well covered for the 1920s, rather fragmentary for the 1930s and 1940s, and excellently covered from the mid-1950s to the present. The library has a complete set of the bulletin of the Soviet Central Statistical Office, Russia (1923−USSR). Tsentral'noe Statisticheskoe Upravlenie. *Biulleten'* (Moscow, 1919−1926), and its series of monographs, *Trudy,* for the years 1920−1928. For the 1930s and 1940s, the statistical periodicals and series are incomplete. After the middle

1930s, Soviet statistics became practically unavailable until publication of the statistical yearbooks *Narodnoe khoziaĭstvo* and *SSSR v tsifrakh* began in the late 1950s. A *Narodnoe khoziaĭstvo* series is also published for each Soviet republic.

## Books, Pamphlets, and Manuscripts

*The November Revolution.* Primary and secondary material on the November Revolution (in Soviet terminology the October Revolution) is excellently represented in Hoover Library holdings. There is an abundance of documents, personal narratives, descriptions of street fights and military engagements, and monographs on all aspects of the events that ended with the overthrow of the Provisional Government. Of this material, special reference should be made to publications of the Central Executive Committee of the All-Russian Communist Party (Bolsheviks), which dedicated its work exclusively to the revolution and to the party's struggle for power. Manuscripts in the Hoover Archives contain additional material on this subject.

*The Civil War.* Material on the Civil War in Russia originates from three sources: Soviet, White, and neutral. Publications from the first two contain abundant primary source material; the last is limited to monographs. The material covers all fronts of the Civil War (Generals Alekseev, Kornilov, ĬUdenich, Denikin, Wrangel, Admiral Kolchak, and others) and includes several special Soviet periodicals dedicated to the Civil War, including *Proletarskaia revoliutsiia* (Moscow, 1921–1941) and *Krasnaia letopis'* (Moscow and Leningrad, 1922–1936). The considerable number of monographs on the subject originate in rather equal parts with Soviet, White, and non-Russian authors. The rare standard Soviet work on the Civil War, *Grazhdanskaia voĭna, 1918–1921,* 3v. (Moscow, 1928), which was later "purged" by the Soviet authorities, is available in the library.

To the period of the Civil War belong the materials concerning relations between the Volunteer Army (General Denikin's) on the one hand and the Georgian Socialist (menshevik) government (1919–1920) and the Ukrainian People's Republic (Petliura's) on the other. Printed materials are supplemented by manuscripts on the Civil War. The relations of Kolchak, Denikin, and Wrangel with the Allies are another aspect of the Civil War period that is well documented in the library. British and French series of diplomatic correspondence, published in recent years, contain abundant documentation on this subject.

*War Communism, 1918–1921.* The library has an excellent body of material on the period of war communism, during which the Soviet government attempted to transform Russia into a communist state and at the same time sought to carry its political ideologies into Central Europe. This period began with the disbanding of the Constituent Assembly and ended with the failure of the Red Army to break the resistance of the newly established republics on the former western borderlands of Russia. Internal developments are covered by excellent documentation of the one-day session of the Constituent Assembly, the struggle against the old political parties that refused to submit to the nationalization of land and the food levy, the execution of the imperial family, the rise of the Cheka and the Red Terror, and the Kronstadt mutiny, which occurred on the last day of this period. Military developments are excellently documented, including the creation of the Red Army, the failure of the Finnish operations, the war and peace with the Baltic States and Poland, victorious campaigns of the Civil War, and the elimination of Allied intervention.

Among international developments during the period of war communism, the peace treaty of Brest-Litovsk and the founding of the Third International are excellently covered in the holdings. The famine that occurred during this time is documented by the voluminous archives of the American Relief Administration, which are a part of the Herbert Hoover papers. On-the-spot reports prepared by units of the American Red Cross on conditions in European Russia and Siberia preceding and during the famine were also deposited in the archives. The library has all decrees and laws issued during this period by the Soviet government, an abundance of other publications of the government and its various agencies, numerous monographs and memoirs on this period published in Russia and abroad, and many manuscripts and private collections containing additional material.

*The Red Terror and Forced Labor.*   Out of the terror of the Cheka and its successors developed the Soviet forced labor camps, which ·grew both in the number of camps and in the number of inmates to excessive proportions (about ten million inmates during the Beria period in the 1940s). Among the documentary material on the Soviet forced labor system are the General Anders Archives, which include about 47,000 personal identification cards of former Polish inmates and over 11,000 personal accounts of these inmates prepared after their release on the basis of the Sikorski-Maĭskiĭ agreement of 1941, which included an amnesty for these Polish deportees. These and other materials constitute a unique source for the study of the Soviet forced labor system.

*Antireligious Action.*   Antireligious action, which was inaugurated by the decree of December 17, 1917 that confiscated all church property, is quite well covered in the holdings. Propaganda pamphlets and posters, extensive files of the serial *Bezbozhnik* (Moscow, 1924–1941), and of other periodicals, together with related materials, are available.

*The Allied Intervention.*   All major collections of documents issued by the Soviet and Allied governments concerning the intervention are held. A number of manuscripts dealing with the intervention are an important addition; the Serebrennikov papers on the Siberian government and a large manuscript by Fritz R. Epstein on the intervention deserve special attention. The library has practically all important monographs dealing with the intervention, with Soviet resistance, and with the Czech, Polish, and other forces in Siberia. Soviet and émigré periodicals provide further information (see the section on the Civil War above).

*Separatist Movements and the Nationality Question.* The collection contains material documenting the separatist movements in the Ukraine, the Baltic States, the Caucasian republics, and the Don Republic. Although the material is not complete, it is valuable because of its rarity. The collection of documents and papers presented by delegations from these areas and by pressure groups working in their favor at the Paris Peace Conference in 1919—1920 is excellent. The separatist movement is reflected in the ephemeral periodical *Bulletin of the Nationalities of Russia* (Bern, 1916—1917), of which the library has an incomplete file.

Besides the publications of the previously mentioned Commissariat for Nationality Affairs, Soviet monographs and pamphlets and a fair file of the periodical *Revoliutsiia i natsional'nosti* (Moscow, 1933—1937) are available. The collection contains publications of émigré former leaders of nationalities in Russia who did not succeed in defending their short-lived independence, as well as a long file of the French-language periodical *Promethée* (Paris, 1926—1938).

*Relations with Border States.* The Russian Collection (as well as the other area collections concerned) contains a great amount of documentation relating to the events that brought about the creation of independent states in the former Russian borderlands of Finland, Estonia, Latvia, Lithuania, and Poland. The material on the Bessarabian question deals with similar matters. These publications, originating during the early bolshevik period and the Civil War, have regained significance since most of the areas concerned were either reincorporated into the Soviet Union during World War II or became satellites of that country. Material on events in those regions between 1918 and 1920 is well represented in the library by contemporary publications and monographs published in later years. The files of the American Relief Administration concerning these areas contain additional, valuable information. These materials now form an important body of background material for developments in these areas in 1939 and later times. Material on the Polish-Soviet war of 1919—1920, originating from Soviet publications put out by the general staff and high-ranking officers of the Red Army, is particularly valuable.

The library has good documentation of recent developments regarding Soviet nationalities. The most significant part of it is found within the samizdat collection, which consists of clandestinely circulated antigovernment writings sent abroad and collected for distribution by the Samizdat Archive Association in

Munich. Among these documents are many issued by the national, civil rights, and religious movements in the Ukraine, the Baltic States, Georgia, and Armenia. English-language translations of some of them are available. Similar material is published with increasing frequency in books and serials, of which the library has a good collection.

*The NEP Period, 1921–1927.*   The NEP period is quite well covered as a whole, with some specific problems (foreign and domestic trade and the peasant question) excellently documented. The earlier part of the period (up to 1925) is much better covered than the later years. Monographs published later on the economic and internal political aspects of this period are well represented in the collection.

*Peasant Question and Collectivization.*   The early Soviet decrees that directly concerned the situation of the Russian peasantry (the Land Decree of November 8, 1917, the Decree on Nationalization of Land of February 19, 1918, and the Decree on the Food Levy of December 14, 1920), with the subsequent regulations concerning forcible requisition of agricultural products, are excellently covered in the collection. The ensuing resistance of the peasants and the liquidation of this resistance by Soviet authorities are adequately documented. In addition to printed materials, several manuscripts in the library pertain to these early events. Soon after launching the First Five-Year Plan (October 1, 1928), collectivization of agriculture began and precipitated a new cycle of peasant resistance and reprisals. The library has all laws and regulations concerning the collectivization that began in 1929 and a few monographs on the subject, but these holdings must be qualified as fair. Later developments of this policy are better covered because of an increase in the number of articles in periodicals. The material on more recent developments, such as the creation of "agricultural cities" and Khrushchev's new policies toward the peasants, are quite well represented by articles in current newspapers and periodicals. Post-Khrushchev developments are well covered in currently received materials.

*Planned Economy.*   This vast subject is excellently documented by Hoover Library holdings. The publications of the Economic Soviet (Russia 1917-RSFSR, Vysshiĭ Sovet Narodnogo Khoziaĭstva) include an abundance of primary sources on economic planning and industrialization. Beginning with the Third Five-Year Plan, additional material is contained in the records of the Supreme Soviet of the USSR. Statistics in practically every field are abundant up to the year 1936, when a policy of publishing only indices was initiated. Periodicals on planning and the economy are excellently represented for the whole period and contain ample information on the consecutive five-year plans. Valuable information on conditions in Russia during the First Five-Year Plan is contained in a collection of personal accounts (in the archives) of a group of American engineers who worked in Russia during this time. The latest stages of the planned economy and recent developments (legislation, decrees, statistics, monographs) are excellently covered in material currently received from the Soviet Union.

*Education and Learned Societies.* The collection has ample material documenting the Soviet government's struggle against backwardness and illiteracy in the country, including a unique collection of popular pamphlets used to promote mass education. These pamphlets deal with almost every phase of peasant life (health problems, child care, agriculture and cattle raising, cooking, and other matters) and are an unusual body of documentation on the struggle against backwardness in the countryside. (These pamphlets are listed in the library catalog under Russian Mass Education Collection.)

The progress of education in schools is also well documented in the collection, particularly for the 1920s and 1930s and after 1945. Teaching programs for schools of various levels, reports on educational projects, publications of the Pedagogical Academy and the Ministry (formerly Commissariat) of Education, and education statistics illuminate past and current educational problems. The collection also contains many monographs and articles in specialized periodicals on various fields of education, dealing with the Soviet Union as a whole as well as with specific regions. The material also focuses attention on political indoctrination in schools of all levels.

The Hoover Institution has almost complete sets of publications of the leading Soviet learned societies whose activities are closely related to the Institution's field of interest, including the Academy of Sciences of the USSR and its affiliates, as well as the Marx-Engels-Lenin Institute. In addition, the library has scattered publications of learned societies from various non-Russian republics.

*The Russian Communist Party.* Publications of and about the Communist Party of the Soviet Union (formerly All-Russian or All-Union Communist Party) and all its organs and special bodies form a substantial part of the holdings of this period. Included are well over 4,000 catalog entries, a considerable number of them in languages other than Russian.

The library has a large number of contemporary editions of Lenin's earliest writings and other publications of the bolshevik faction of the Russian Social-Democratic Workers' Party from 1903 to 1919. The early newspapers issued abroad by Lenin, *Iskra* (Geneva, 1900–1905) and *Proletariĭ* (Paris, 1905–1909), are also in the holdings.

The history of the party from its very beginnings up to the most recent developments is well covered by documentary reprints, diaries, monographs, periodical articles, stenographic minutes of party congresses, and other publications concerning congresses and party conferences. The collection also includes publications by and about the Central Committee, local and regional committees (Moscow, Leningrad, Siberia, Caucasus, Central Asia, and others), the two

special commissions on the history of the revolution (see Russia [1917 Provisional Government], Chrezvychaĭnaĭa Sledstvennaĭa Komissiĭa and Russia
[1923-USSR], Komissiĭa po Izdaniĭu Dokumentov Epokhi Imperializma), various party schools, and several other, less important bodies. There are also
collections of resolutions of various party bodies. The library has a 68-reel
microfilm collection of the records of the All-Union (Russian) Communist
Party, Smolensk district, covering the years 1917–1941: Kommunisticheskaĭa
Partiĭa Sovetskogo Soĭuza. Smolenskiĭ Oblastnoĭ Komitet. Partiĭnyĭ Arkhiv.
*Records*. . . .

Additional source material on the Bolshevik party can be found in the
voluminous collected works of Lenin, Trotsky, Bukharin, Stalin, and other
bolshevik leaders. Before Stalin's death, the official Moscow publication of his
collected works had reached volume thirteen, covering the years up to 1934. At
that time publication ceased. The Hoover Institution was able to initiate
collection of later material and publish (in 1967) three volumes in Russian, thus
completing the edition of Stalin's collected works. The library has the works of
bolshevik leaders in all Russian editions and, if available, in English translations.
Monographs on the party and its activities, originating with writers of all shades
of opinion and many nationalities, are numerous.

Files of the most important party periodicals and newspapers are almost
complete in the library, including the ideological monthly *Kommunist,* formerly
*Bol'shevik,* (Moscow, 1924–    [almost complete]); and *Novoe vremĭa,* formerly
*Voĭna i rabochiĭ klass,* (Moscow, 1943–    [complete]). *Novoe vremĭa* is also
available in the library in English, German, and French. Among the newspapers
are *Pravda* (published originally in Petrograd and later in Moscow, 1917–
[almost complete]), *Komsomol'skaĭa pravda* (Moscow, 1929–    [some gaps,
particularly in the war years]), and *Leningradskaĭa pravda* (Leningrad, 1918–
1925 [nearly complete]). The files of party periodicals dealing with organizational matters and propaganda are relatively weaker. The strongest of these is
the file of *Bloknot agitatora* (Moscow), covering the years 1946–1957. *Par-
tiĭnaĭa zhizn',* the journal of the Central Committee of the All-Russian Communist Party, took over the functions of *Bloknot agitatora* in 1957. The library
has a continuous subscription to this journal.

Holdings of the material published by the Communist party in the non-Russian
areas of the Soviet Union are less complete. Exceptions are the publications on
various bolshevik organizations in the Caucasus in the early years of the period,
which are fairly well represented in the collection. Monographs published later
on the growth of the party in various non-Russian areas are well covered. The
library has some publications of Polish, Czech, and Latvian Communists in
Russia during the years 1918–1920.

*Foreign Policy.*   The subject of foreign policy is excellently covered both for
pre- and post–World War II periods. Rare publications of the Commissariat of

Foreign Affairs (Russia [1917-RSFSR], Narodnyĭ Komissariat po Inostrannym Delam) before 1941 are almost complete. Also useful are the yearbook, *Ezhegodnik,* of the commissariat (Russia [1923-USSR], Narodnyĭ Komissariat po Inostrannym Delam) for the years 1925−1935 and the official and semiofficial periodicals of the commissariat, *Bĭulleten'* (1921−1929), *Vestnik* (1919−1922), and *Mezhdunarodnaĭà zhizn'* (1920−1930). Collections of diplomatic documents on particular areas and subjects, as well as monographs on Soviet foreign policy for the pre−World War II period published by Soviet and Western authors, add considerable strength to the collection on this subject.

Shortly after the Soviet Union found itself at war with Germany, the Commissariat of Foreign Affairs began publishing a collection of documents on Soviet foreign policy, *Vneshnĭàĭà politika SSSR,* 4v. (Moscow, 1944−1946), which covered the period between 1917 and June 1941. For foreign buyers, the entire last part of volume four, which contained important annotations, was deliberately eliminated by the Moscow exporter and was unavailable for many years. In 1977 the Hoover Institution was able to acquire copies of the missing part of this volume. For many years the Hoover Institution held the only copy of this set in the United States.

After World War II, the Soviet foreign office, now the Ministry of Foreign Affairs, published two more collections of foreign policy documents: *Vneshnĭàĭà politika SSR v period Otechestvennoĭ voĭny,* 3v. (Moscow, 1944−1947), covering the years 1941−1945; and *Vneshnĭàĭà politika Sovetskogo Soĭuza,* 9v. (Moscow, 1949−1953), covering the years 1945−1950. These were succeeded by *Vneshnĭàĭà politika Sovetskogo Soĭuza i mezhdunarodnye otnoshenĭà: Sbornik dokumentov* (Moscow, 1961− ) and the Ministry of Foreign Affairs series, *Dokumenty vneshneĭ politiki SSR* (Moscow, 1957− ).

During the years of the cold war, a large number of books and articles in periodicals dealing with the foreign policy of the USSR and its policymakers began to appear in the West. The Hoover Library acquired most of them.

In 1957 the Institute of World Economics and International Relations at the Academy of Sciences (Akademĭà Nauk SSSR, Institut Mirovoĭ Ekonomiki i Mezhdunarodnykh Otnoshenĭĭ) initiated the monthly journal *Mirovaĭà ekonomika i mezhdunarodnye otnoshenĭà,* which has been published continuously since then. The library has a good collection of the institute's publications. Ten years later, a special institute for the study of the United States and Canada was founded in Moscow (Akademĭà Nauk SSR, Institut Soedinennykh Shtatov Ameriki i Kanady). The Hoover Institution receives its monthly journal, *SShA,* and other publications.

In a centralized state like the USSR, foreign trade is often an adjunct to and an instrument of foreign policy. The scholar interested in this field can find essential government regulations, statistics, and monographs in the Hoover Institution collection. The current periodical *Vneshnĭàĭà torgovlĭà SSSR* (Moscow, 1933− ) strengthens this material.

*Trade Unions.*   The number of government publications, books, pamphlets, and periodicals produced in the Soviet Union for and about trade unions is large. The library has a considerable number of them, especially those originating in the 1920s. Although an incomplete file, the Central Committee of Trade Unions' daily newspaper, *Trud,* is available for the years 1921—1923, 1933—1940, and 1944—1955 (fragmentary for the earlier years). Among the most important periodicals dealing with trade union matters are *Golos rabotnika* (Moscow, 1919—1923 [fragmentary]), *Vestnik truda* (Moscow, 1920—1927 [fair]), *Organizatsiia truda* (Moscow, 1921—1922, 1925, 1935—1938 [fair]), and *Professional'nye soiuzy* (Moscow, 1938—1953 [fragmentary]).

*The Finnish War of 1939—1940.*   The library has some one hundred books and pamphlets on the military and political aspects of the Finnish war from Finnish, German, and Western European sources. Soviet material is limited to a few items. The library has a collection of Finnish official documents relating to the outbreak of the war, the documentation of the action of the League of Nations, and some less valuable propaganda publications.

*The Soviet Union's Part in World War II.*   The Soviet Union during World War II is well covered. The library was originally able to acquire only a few Soviet items dealing with military operations during the war. In later years missing material has been acquired in original or microfilm copies. Of particular value is a collection of daily reports from the front published by Red Army headquarters, Russia (1923-USSR). Sovetskoe Informatsionnoe Biuro. *Soobshcheniia sovetskogo informbiuro,* 8v. (Moscow, 1944—1945), which covers the entire war period. Soviet war fiction, personal accounts, publications on German atrocities and destruction, and propaganda pamphlets are well covered. The standard major Soviet works on the ''Great Patriotic War'' are all available in the collection. The library has a number of rare Soviet bibliographies of books and periodical and newspaper articles published in Moscow during the war years, including:

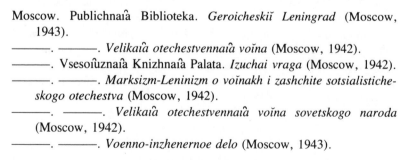

> Moscow. Publichnaia Biblioteka. *Geroicheskii Leningrad* (Moscow, 1943).
> ———. ———. *Velikaia otechestvennaia voina* (Moscow, 1942).
> ———. Vsesoiuznaia Knizhnaia Palata. *Izuchai vraga* (Moscow, 1942).
> ———. ———. *Marksizm-Leninizm o voinakh i zashchite sotsialisticheskogo otechestva* (Moscow, 1942).
> ———. ———. *Velikaia otechestvennaia voina sovetskogo naroda* (Moscow, 1942).
> ———. ———. *Voenno-inzhenernoe delo* (Moscow, 1943).

The collection contains a considerable number of German publications on the war, including operational accounts by generals commanding large German units. A few books written by other non-Russian authors serve as secondary sources. Material on Soviet partisan warfare behind German lines is abundant.

*Special Subjects Concerning Soviet Russia, 1939–1945.* The library has two large deposits containing documentation on mass deportations from Eastern Poland and the Baltic States by the Soviet Union in the early years of World War II. The deposit of the Latvian National Committee contains the records of an inquiry by local Latvian authorities during the German occupation. The General Anders records contain a large number of documents gathered from deported Polish citizens. There are also more than 11,000 firsthand reports on conditions in Soviet forced labor camps, written by persons who were released from these camps on the basis of the Polish-Soviet agreement in August 1941.

Another special subject of this period concerns General Vlassov's Russian Liberation Army and other Russian military groups sponsored by the Germans during World War II. Besides practically all publications that have appeared up to now on this subject, the library has a few unpublished items originating from German authorities. Some articles in camp papers of Russian displaced persons in Germany, published after the collapse of the Nazi regime, contain additional information on the subject.

*Postwar Internal Developments.* Complete files of the most important Soviet newspapers and periodicals and a few monographs published in the USSR since the end of the war provide the researcher with the source material currently available on numerous subjects. Among the subjects covered by the collection are postwar industrialization, major construction projects, administrative changes, recent congresses of the Communist party and ensuing organizational changes, Stalin's death and the resulting changes in the state and party leadership, and recent changes in Soviet policy concerning agricultural production and the situation of the peasants on collective farms.

*Periodicals and Newspapers.* Soviet periodicals and newspapers for the entire period since November 1917 are excellently represented in the library. As stated previously, the Soviet serial collection consists of some 3,500 titles of Russian periodicals and files of over 650 Russian newspapers, as well as 750 periodical titles and nearly 200 more files of newspapers for the non-Russian Soviet Baltic and Ukrainian areas. For the years 1926–1937, the holdings are weaker and more limited, but contain almost complete sets of the most important periodicals and newspapers. Their use is complicated by the fact that due to conditions in the Soviet Union, periodicals often changed names or were abruptly discontinued, only to be replaced by new ones. The library has collected newspapers not only intended for the Soviet reader at large, that is, *Izvestiĩa* and *Pravda*, but also those for certain sectors of the population, such as the members of labor unions, *Trud* (Moscow, 1921–1955); the peasants, *Sel'skoe khozĩaĩstvo* (Moscow, 1922, 1953–1955); youth, *Komsomol'skaĩa pravda* (Moscow,

1929– [with gaps]); the professional intellectuals, *Literaturnaia̧ gazeta* (Moscow, 1932– ); and other groups. The Communist party, besides publishing its main press organ, *Pravda* (Moscow), also issues regional dailies, such as *Pravda Ukrainy* (Kiev) and *Pravda vostoka* (Tashkent). Likewise, in addition to the All-Union Communist Party Central Committee's serial *Kommunist* (Moscow, 1924– ), the library subscribes to the monthly *Kommunist*s published in the capitals of several republics. These regional papers are acquired in order to broaden the sources of information for researchers. The library has nearly complete sets for most of these papers and runs of varying lengths for many others.

The émigré press for this period includes not only the more important publications, but also periodicals and newspapers of much smaller circulation and importance. Most of these files are almost complete. During World War II many of them were suspended or ceased publication. After 1945 some of the old newspapers and periodicals reappeared, and new titles came into being, especially in response to population movements during World War II. The following current émigré serials titles are in the library's collection:

> *Posev* (Frankfurt, 1968– )
> *Grani* (Frankfurt am Main, 1946– )
> *Khronika tekushchikh sobytiĭ* (Frankfurt am Main, 1969– )
> *Khronika zaschity prav v SSSR* (New York, 1973– )
> *Novyĭ zhurnal* (New York, 1942– )
> *Kontinent* (Berlin, 1974– )
> *Vozrozhdenie* (Paris, 1949–1974 [ceased publication in 1974])

## THE SOVIET EMIGRÉS
## AND DISSIDENT PUBLICATIONS

The present Soviet emigration abroad originated in three distinct groups. The first group was composed predominantly of Russian army and navy personnel of various ranks, former government officials, and professional intelligentsia who fled from Russia after the November 1917 bolshevik takeover, after the Civil War debacle, and during the period of the secret police (GPU) terror. They settled at first in Western and Southeastern Europe, but a considerable number later found their way to both Americas.

The second group dates back to the Second World War, when a large part of Western Russia, Ukraine, and the Baltic States were invaded by Nazi Germany. Some 300,000 Soviet citizens of various ethnic backgrounds were deported to forced labor in Germany. After the defeat of Germany, a large number (perhaps another 300,000) of Russians, Belorussians, Ukrainians, Lithuanians, Latvians, Estonians, and other ethnic groups fled into Germany before the advancing Red

Army. Finally, after the end of hostilities, there were in Germany at least four million Soviet war prisoners. The civilians were designated displaced persons (DPs) and placed in special DP camps located in the American, British, and French zones of occupation in Western Germany. Occupation authorities forced a large number of these civilians and almost all war prisoners to return to the Soviet Union. Among the multinational DPs who managed to remain in Germany, a large part were Russians who now became an addition to the Russian emigration abroad. Most of them were able to move to the Americas and Australia. The remainder stayed in Germany and France.

The third and most recent group consists above all of some 150,000 Russian Jews who received Soviet permission to emigrate to Israel. A large number of them went to various Western countries, including the United States. In their new places of settlement, some of these Jews, born and educated in Russia, consider themselves a part of the Russian cultural community abroad. To this third group belongs a small number of Russians and other non-Jewish nationals who in the past few years either fled the Soviet Union because of their political convictions or were forcibly exiled for the same reason by the government. Among the latter group are such famous names as Aleksandr Solzhenitsyn, Andreĭ Amalrik, Vladimir' Bukovskiĭ, Valeriĭ Chalidze, Aleksandr Ginzberg, Nataliĭa Gorbanevskaĭa, Vladimir' Maksimov, Zhores Medvedev, and others.

Documentation on Russian and Soviet affairs produced by these three groups is quite varied in subject matter and extent. Publications by the first group of Russian émigrés deal predominantly with the Russian past and relate to the tsarist period, to Russia's participation in World War I, the February and October 1917 (old style) revolutions, the Civil War, and the early Soviet period, including the GPU terror and the NEP experiment. These publications include a large number of books, pamphlets, periodicals, and newspapers. They appear predominantly in Germany, France, Czechoslovakia, the United States, and a few in the Far East. They are excellently covered in the Hoover Institution collection.

The following are the most valuable of the periodicals published by this group:

*Arkhiv russkoĭ revoliŭtsii* (Berlin, 1922−1937)
*Bęloe delo* (Berlin, 1926−1933)
*Novaĭa Rossiĭa* (Paris, 1936−1940)
*Sovremennyĭa zapiski* (Paris, 1920−1940)
*Zarĭa* (Berlin, 1922−1925)
*Znamĭa Rossii* (Prague, 1929−1939)
*Kavkaz* (Paris, 1934−1939)
*Novyĭ zhurnal* (New York, 1942−   )

All holdings are complete. In addition, the Hoover Institution has long runs of a large number of émigré newspapers from the 1920−1940 period, which, although incomplete, are a rare source of information, available only in part on microfilm in other libraries.

Although the second group of Russian exiles published less prolifically than their predecessors, they founded three, now defunct, scholarly institutions: the Research Program on the USSR in New York, the Chekhov Publishing House in New York, and the Institute for the Study of the History and Culture of the USSR in Munich. Memoirs, personal accounts, reference works, and monographs in Russian, English, French, and German were published by the three institutions. The Hoover Library has practically all publications that are pertinent to its subject scope. These institutions contributed greatly to the development of academic studies on the USSR in the 1950s and 1960s. Two other important publishing centers, which also began in the 1950s and have survived until the present, are the YMCA Press in Paris and the Posev Publishing firm in Frankfurt am Main. Since 1945, the latter has published the serial *Posev,* of which the library has a file from March 1948 to the present.

A number of short-lived, mimeographed "newspapers," which are now the rarest of ephemera, appeared after World War II in the DP camps. Holdings of these camp papers in the Hoover Institution's Library are fair. (See Helena Sworakowski's "List of Periodical Publications Published by Belorussian, Russian, and Ukrainian D.P.s, 1945–1951, Holdings of the Hoover Library," typescript [Stanford, 1951]).

The Vlassov movement scarcely had time to publish a few propaganda pamphlets and short runs of newspapers before the forced repatriation of its members to the USSR. These publications have been hard to obtain and are only sparsely covered in the collection. The library has a few later serials issued by those Vlassovites who stayed outside the Soviet Union and by other organizations that aspired to free Russia from communist domination, including *Informatsionnyĭ listok Tsentral'nogo biŭro SBONR e.V.* (Munich, 1960–1961), *Vlasovets* (Munich, 1950–1951), *Volîa* (Frankfurt am Main, 1949–1950), and *Vstrechi* (Frankfurt am Main, 1952–1961, 1978–   ).

The recent group of émigrés, contains many intellectuals. Already well known in the Soviet Union as writers, scientists, and other professionals, they are now publishing critical works on the Soviet Union, especially in the field of human rights. The Hoover Library has the complete works of Aleksandr Solzhenitsyn and the works of other important writers within the group. The monographs by Andreĭ Amalrik, Valeriĭ Chalidze, Zhores Medvedev, and others can be found by using the library's card catalog. The following serials, almanacs, and collections of essays in the library's collection contain the writings of the entire group: *Al'manakh Samizdata: Nepodtsenzurnaîa mysl' v SSSR* (Amsterdam, 1974– 1975); *Dvadtsatyĭ vek: Obshchestvenno-politicheskiĭ i literaturnyĭ al'manakh: Izbrannye materialy iz samizdatnogo zhurnala "XX-ĭ vek"* (London, 1976– 1977); *Khronika zashchity prav v SSSR* (New York, 1973–   ) and its English-language version, *A Chronicle of Human Rights in the USSR* (New York, 1973– ); *Kontinent* (Berlin, 1974– ), a quarterly journal of literary, social, political, and religious commentary; *Politicheskiĭ dnevnik, 1965–1970* (Amsterdam, 1972), a reprint of selected issues of an underground information bulletin of the same name that appeared in Moscow from 1964 to 1971 under the editorship of Roĭ Medvedev; and *Posev* (Frankfurt am Main, 1969– ), a sociopolitical quarterly.

Since 1972, through a distribution center in Munich, the Hoover Library has received 29 volumes of underground documents (samizdat) from the Soviet Union, entitled *Sobranie dokumentov samizdata* (Munich, 1972–78). The documents cover the period 1968–1974. A thirtieth volume contains documents connected with the Helsinki Agreement of 1975. There are two cumulative indexes to the documents, one in Russian and the other in English: *Polnyĭ spisok dokumentov s podrobnym nomernym ukazatelem* (Munich, 1977) and *Register of Documents 1977 Edition with Quick-Reference Document Locator* (Munich, 1977). In addition, up-to-date documents are regularly received twice a month, under the title *Materialy samizdata*.

On April 30, 1968, the first issue of *Khronika tekushchikh sobytiĭ* appeared in Moscow as an underground journal of an embryonic civil liberties union. Uninhibited by censorship, the chronicle illuminates aspects of Soviet life that the official press ignores, especially the nationality question, prisons, labor camps, and mental hospitals. The Hoover Library has a complete file of the chronicle, beginning with the first issue, which was distributed in New York in 1969. In 1971 an English-language version, *Chronicle of Current Events*, began appearing in London. The library has a complete file of it as well.

Many other underground journals have been circulating in the Soviet Union since the death of Stalin, mainly in Moscow and Leningrad, but none has enjoyed the longevity of *Khronika*. These journals can be found in *Sobranie dokumentov samizdata*, with the aid of the register. Of the several books published on this underground literature, the library's collection includes: Gerstenmaier, Cornelia. *Die Stimme der Stummen* (Stuttgart, 1972); Feldbrugge, Ferdinand. *Samizdat and Political Dissent in the Soviet Union* (Leiden, 1975); and Reddaway, Peter. *Uncensored Russia: Protest and Dissent in the Soviet Union* (New York, 1972). These publications deal with the history, nature, and content of the underground publications.

## INTERNATIONAL COMMUNISM

International organizations sponsored and directed by the Soviet Communist Party and the Soviet government are excellently documented in the library holdings. Since the period of war communism in Soviet Russia, these organizations have acted more or less openly as auxiliaries to Soviet foreign policy. The scholar studying the relations between the Soviet Union and certain other countries from 1918 to 1943 must consider Communist International (Comintern) material in order to understand all aspects of these relations.

## The Communist International (Comintern)

*Official Records.*    The library has a complete set of the stenographic records and minutes of all seven congresses of the Comintern (1919–1935; in Russian or German, some in English) and a considerable amount of reports, speeches, resolutions, appeals, and other material concerning these congresses. The thirteen meetings of the Central Executive Committee, the so-called "plenums," and some executive committee meetings (insofar as published) are excellently covered. This source material is supplemented by a large number of monographs in several languages dealing with the activities of the Comintern. No definitive history of the Comintern exists. The 600-page publication of the Institute of Marxism-Leninism, *Kommunisticheskii internatsional: Kratkii istoricheskii ocherk* (Moscow, 1969), gives a revised Soviet interpretation, reducing Stalin's domination of the Comintern to two modest footnotes. Western histories of this important institution are only fragmentary.

*Comintern Publications.*    The library has a complete set of the Russian edition of *Communist International* (Moscow, 1919–1943) and incomplete sets of the English, French, and German editions. The collection also includes the 1923 edition of the rare yearbook of the Comintern, *Ezhegodnik Kominterna,* containing statistics and lists of communist parties all over the world.

Another valuable source for the study of Comintern policies is its former official periodical, *World News and Views* (Berlin, Vienna, and London, 1921–1953), of which the library has a nearly complete set. The library also has practically all major works on the Comintern.

## Anti-Comintern Movements

Hoover holdings include the publications of several organizations that were active in combating and studying communism and its international organs. The oldest and largest among them before World War II was the International Anti-Communist Entente, which produced a number of publications, including the periodical, *La Vague rouge* (Geneva and Paris, 1926–1929 and 1931 [nearly complete]). Shortly before World War II, a Nazi-sponsored organization, Gesamtverband Deutscher antikommunistischer Vereinigungen (known as Anti-komintern), whose activities became exceptionally broad, arose in Germany. The library has several publications of this organization and a large part of its archives.

Since World War II, two anticommunist organizations have been active in Europe: the Antibol'shevistskiĭ Blok Narodov (Antibolshevik Bloc of Nations), under Ukrainian leadership, active among DPs from the Soviet Union residing in Germany, France, and Great Britain; and the Centre international de la lutte active contre le communism in Brussels. Periodicals and other publications of these two organizations are well represented in the library.

## Red Internationals and
## Related Organizations

Coverage of the Red International of Labor Unions (Profintern) is excellent. The eight congresses of this organization covering the years 1921 to 1931 are documented by records of sessions, resolutions, reprints of important speeches, and other material. The library has the periodical published by its Executive Committee in Russian, *Krasnyĭ international profsoĭuzov* (Moscow, 1923–1927 [incomplete]); in English, *Red International of Labour Unions Monthly Magazine* (London, 1928–1929, 1932–1933 [incomplete]); in French *L'Internationale syndícale rouge* (Paris, 1921–1927 [incomplete]); and in German, *Die rote Gewerkschafts-Internationale* (Berlin, 1921–1929 [incomplete]). Other publications of and on the Profintern are quite numerous in the holdings.

Material on the Young Communist International (YCI) is good; coverage is excellent for the years 1919 to 1928, but weaker for later years. The library has the resolutions and other publications of its first five congresses (1919–1928) and a considerable number of pamphlets on the activities of the YCI in several countries (France and Germany are the best covered.)

Holdings of material on the International Red Aid are weak and limited to pre-1930 publications. The American branch of this organization, the International Labor Defense, is much better covered. Holdings of materials on the Peasants' International, the Women's Communist International, and similar organizations are rather weak.

## Bibliography on the Comintern
## and Its Front Organizations

A full listing of books and pamphlets in the Hoover Library and 43 other American and 4 European libraries by and about the Comintern and its international front organizations was compiled by Witold S. Sworakowski and published in 1965 by the Hoover Institution under the title *The Communist International and Its Front Organizations: A Research Guide and Checklist of Holdings in American and European Libraries*. Of the 2,281 items in eighteen languages listed in this volume, the Hoover Library held 1,251 items or 54.6 percent of the total; the New York Public Library had 602 items, or 26.2 percent; and the Library of Congress 322 items, or 14.0 percent. Although this listing did not pretend to be a comprehensive bibliography, it has remained the only one on the subject to date. It also contains a partial listing of publications by anti-Comintern organizations.

## Fourth International

Although this organization is completely independent of the Communist (Third) International, it is discussed here as one of the worldwide communist organizations. The library has an excellent body of documentation on this Trotskyite movement, including the periodicals *Bulletin internationale de l'opposition communiste de gauche* (Paris, 1930–1933), *Quatrième internationale* (Paris, 1936–1939; 1942, 1944–1975 [almost complete]), *Fourth International* (London, 1964–1972), and the American counterpart, *Fourth International,* which the Socialist Workers' Party began publishing in New York in 1940. It changed its title to *International Socialist Review* in 1956 and merged with *Militant* in 1975. A large number of pamphlets published by Trotskyite organizations in various countries provide an additional source for the study of this movement.

## Cominform

The Communist Information Bureau (Cominform) was founded in September 1947 and dissolved in 1956. The material published by this organization is limited to a few records of its meetings and to the newspaper *For a Lasting Peace* (Belgrade, later Bucharest, 1947–1956). The collection includes the few items on the Cominform published by noncommunist writers.

## ARCHIVAL COLLECTIONS

Throughout this survey of the Russian Collection, references are made to many archival and manuscript holdings. In fact, the Hoover Archives has a vast amount of such Russian material. For more detailed information, consult the recent publication, *Guide to the Hoover Institution Archives* (Stanford, 1979), by Charles G. Palm and Dale Reed.

# UKRAINE

The Ukrainian Collection at the Hoover Institution originated with the materials collected by Prof. F. A. Golder in Russia and in Russia's borderlands in 1921. As an agent for the Hoover War Collection, Professor Golder's primary responsibility was to secure materials from Russia (including Ukrainian lands and the Baltic States) dealing with the revolutionary period of 1917–1921 and with the newly emerging states and their problems. Before coming to Stanford, Professor Golder had in 1919 been the expert for Ukrainian and Lithuanian affairs for the Colonel House Commission of historians preparing studies to be used by the American delegation at the Paris Peace Conference. His collecting expertise is reflected in Ukrainian materials covering the period of World War I and its aftermath, 1914–1921. In the early 1940s, the holdings on this earlier period were supplemented by the John Petrushevych Collection. This era, therefore, is the best documented historical period within the Ukrainian Collection.

Subsequently, the Ukrainian Collection was not systematically enlarged. Changes in occupying powers and territorial subdivisions, frequent armed conflicts, and the resulting different rates of cultural, political, and economic development have always complicated the gathering of a good representative collection.

Due to the Hoover Institution's interests in territorial questions, minorities, nationalist and revolutionary movements, and communism, however, the collection developed peripherally, through other major collections. It presently includes nearly 6,000 monographs, some 230 periodical titles, and files of about 80 newspapers. The Ukrainian Collection is primarily supplemented by the Russian and Polish collections and secondarily by the Austrian, Czech, Slovak, German, Hungarian, and Romanian collections. In addition, the collection is supplemented by the Stanford Green Library's holdings in archeology, bibliography, folklore, language, literature, philosophy, religion, early history (pre–twentieth century), and periodicals.

As a result, a scholar interested in Ukrainian studies can find material dealing with all relevant historical periods in or near the Hoover Library and Archives. Since 1978, there has been a concerted effort to expand the Ukrainian Collection.

This survey of the collection is divided into five major categories and subdivisions: reference tools (encyclopedias, dictionaries, bibliographies, etc.); historical sources (subdivided chronologically); economy (divided into pre-Soviet and Soviet periods); dissident materials and nationality problems; and serial publications.

## REFERENCE WORKS

Most standard reference works dealing with the Ukrainian people, territory, and recent history can be found within the Hoover Library.

### Encyclopedias and Dictionaries

The collection contains several Ukrainian encyclopedias. The standard work, *Ukraïns'ka radîans'ka entsyklopediîa*, 17v. (Kiev, 1959–1965), edited by M. P. Bazhan, is presently being superseded by a second edition of the same title. Volume one appeared in 1977, and eleven more volumes are to be published. A more concise work, also edited by Bazhan, is the three-volume *Ukraïns'kyĭ radîans'kyĭ entsyklopedychnyĭ slovnyk* (Kiev, 1966–1968).

Several encyclopedias have appeared outside the Soviet Union; for example, two edited by V. Kubijovyč, *Entsyklopediîa ukraïnoznavstva, 3v.* (Munich, 1949–1962); and *Ukraine: A Concise Encyclopedia, 2v.* (Toronto, 1963–1971). Another is ÎEvhen Onats'kyĭ's *Ukraïns'ka mala entsyklopediîa,* 16 fascicles (Buenos Aires, 1951–1967).

A few subject-oriented encyclopedias have been published as well, including: Skaba, A. D., ed. *Radîans'ka entsyklopediîa istoriï Ukraïny,* 4v. (Kiev, 1969–1972).

A large selection of Ukrainian dictionaries can be found within the collection. The most basic one is I. Bilodid's *Slovnyk ukraïns'koï movy,* 10v. (Kiev, 1970–[8v. published thus far]). Among dictionaries of Ukrainian and other languages, some of the earliest were produced under the Austro-Hungarian empire; for example, O. Partyts'kyĭ's *Nimets'ko-ruskyĭ slovar* (Lemberg, 1867) and V. Kmitsykevych's *Deutsch-ukrainisches(-ruthenisches) Wörterbuch* (Chernovtsy, 1912).

Many dictionaries of the Ukrainian and Russian languages exist. Two of the larger ones within the library are B. Hrinchenko's *Slovar ukraïns'koï movy: Ukraïns'ko-russkyĭ slovar,* 2v. (Berlin, 1924) and the Academy of Sciences' *Ukraïns'ko-russkyĭ slovar,* 6v. (Kiev, 1953–1963).

For English speakers, the most useful dictionary is C. H. Andrusyshen's *Ukrainian-English Dictionary* (Toronto, 1957). The two standard publications, M. L. Podves'ko's *Anhlo-ukraïns'kyĭ slovnyk* (Kiev, 1948) and his *Ukraïns'ko-anhliĭs'kyĭ slovnyk* (New York, 1954), are available as well.

Some specialized subject dictionaries may be useful in research, including:

> Akademiia Nauk URSR. Instytut Movoznavstva. *Slovnyk vlasnykh imen liudeĭ, ukraïns'ko-rosiĭs'kyĭ ĭ rossiĭs'ko-ukraïns'kyĭ*, 2d ed. (Kiev, 1961).
>
> Deĭ, O. I. *Slovnyk ukraïns'kykh psevdonimiv ta kryptonimiv XVI-XX st.* (Kiev, 1969).
>
> Shevela, H. H., ed. *Politychnyĭ slovnyk* (Kiev, 1971).

## Handbooks and Guides

In the twentieth century, many publications that can serve as general handbooks or guides to the study of the Ukrainian land and people have appeared. Some of the earlier works available at the Institution are:

> Guttry, A. *Galizien, Land und Leute* (Munich, 1916).
>
> Korduba, M. *Territorium und Bevölkerung der Ukraine: Ein geographisch-statistischer Beitrag* (Vienna, 1919).
>
> Krasilnikov, F. *Ukraina i ukraintsy* (Moscow, 1918).
>
> Mirchuk, I. *Handbuch der Ukraine* (Leipzig, 1941).
>
> Rudnicki, S. *Ukraina, Land und Volk* (Vienna, 1916).
>
> Ukrainskaia zhizn'. *Galichina, Bukovina, Ugorskaia Rus'* (Moscow, 1915).
>
> Wasilewki, L. *Die Ostprovinzen des alten Polenreichs* (Kraków, 1916).

After World War II, many similar works were published. As a part of the *Ukrainian Soviet Encyclopedia,* M. Bazhan's work appeared first in Ukrainian as *Ukraïns'ka Radîans'ka Sotsiîalistychna Respublyka* (Kiev, 1965), and then in English as *Soviet Ukraine* (Kiev, 1969). Other titles include:

> Dossick, J. J. *Doctoral Research on Russia and the Soviet Union, 1960–1975* (London, 1976).
>
> Shoepflin, G., ed. *The Soviet Union and Eastern Europe: A Handbook* (New York, 1970).
>
> Mirchuk, I. *Ukraine and Its People. Handbook with Maps, Statistical Tables and Diagrams* (Munich, 1949).
>
> Zamkovoĭ, V. *Ukraina: Obshchiĭ obzor* (Moscow, 1969).

## Bibliography

Bibliographical reference works dealing with Ukrainian matters specifically or as a part of the Russian empire or the Soviet Union abound. A selective list of the most important ones to be found at the Hoover Institution includes:

Akademiiâ Nauk URSR. Instytut Istoriï. *Istorychni dzherela ta ïkh vykorystannîâ,* 7v. (Kiev, 1963–1972).

———. Vsenarodnîâ Biblioteka Ukraïny. *Bibliohrafîîâ na Ukraïni* (Kiev, 1927).

Borshchak, I. *L'Ukraïne dans la littérature de l'Europe occidentale* (Dijon, 1935).

Hnatyshak, M. *Katalog der Ucrainica in der Abteilung "Ukraine im Lichte der deutschen Presse und Literatur" der Internationalen Presse-Ausstellung 1928 in Köln* (Berlin, 1928).

Horecky, P., comp. *Preliminary Check List of Russian, Ukrainian and Belorussian Newspapers Published since Jan. 1, 1917 within the Present Boundaries of the USSR and Preserved in U.S. Libraries. A Working Paper* (Washington, D.C., 1952).

———. *Russian, Ukrainian and Belorussian Newspapers, 1917–1953: A Union List* (Washington, D.C., 1953).

Hurzhiï, I., ed. *Radîâns'ki vydannîâ dokumental'nykh materiîâliv z istoriï Ukraïny (1917–1918): Bibliohrafichnyĭ pokazhchyk* (Kiev, 1970).

Knyzhkova Palata Ukraïns'koï RSR. *Ukraïns'ka radîâns'ka kul'tura za 40 rokiv, 1917–1957: Bibliohrafichnyĭ pokazhchyk literatury* (Kharkov, 1960).

Lavrynenko, ÎÛ. *Ukrainian Communism and Soviet Russian Policy Toward Ukraine: An Annotated Bibliography, 1917–1953* (New York, 1953).

Magocsi, Paul R., and Mayo, Olga K. *Carpatho-Ruthenica at Harvard: A Catalog of Holdings* (Englewood, N.J., 1977).

Pelens'kyĭ, E. *Ucrainica: Selected Bibliography on Ukraine in Western-European Languages* (Munich, 1948).

Pidhaïnyĭ, O. *The Ukrainian Republic in the Great East-European Revolution: A Bibliography,* 2v. (Toronto, 1971–1975).

Stanford University. Hoover Institution on War, Revolution and Peace. *Periodicals and Newspapers Concerning East-Central and East Europe in the Library of the Hoover Institution: A Checklist* (Stanford, 1958).

———. ———. *List of Periodical Publications Published by Belorussian, Russian and Ukrainian DP's, 1945–1951* (Stanford, 1957).

Weres, R. *Ukraine: Selected References in the English Language,* 2d ed. (Chicago, 1974).

## Biography

Biographical publications dealing solely with Ukrainian personages are not numerous in the Hoover Institution collection. Some of those available are:

Berlin. Ukraïns'kyĭ Naukovyĭ Instytut. *Prof. M. Hrushevs'kyĭ, sein Leben und sein Wirken, 1866–1934* (Berlin, 1935).

Hutsuliak, M. *Pershyĭ lystopad 1918 roku na zakhidnikh zemliakh Ukraïny, zi spohadamy ĭ zhyttiepysamy chleniv vykonavtsiv Lystopadovoho Chynu* (New York, 1973).

Kostomarov, N. *Istoriia Ukraïny v zhyttiepysakh ïï diiachiv* (L'viv, 1918).

Naukove Tovarystvo imeni Shevchenka. *Istorychni postati Halychyny XIX-XX st.* (New York, 1961).

A great many reference works dealing with Ukrainian topics, especially bibliography, biography, and statistics, are held within the Russian Collection. During the tsarist period and under the Soviet regime, many reference tools mixed Russian and Ukrainian persons and data with little differentiation. As a result, anyone researching Ukrainian topics is advised to consult the section Reference Works in the chapter Russia and the Soviet Union in this survey.

## HISTORY

Since the demise of the medieval state of Kievan Rus, the Ukrainian nation has been dominated by other powers for most of its subsequent history. Periods of independence have been few and brief. All during the nineteenth century and up to World War I, the Ukrainian ethnic territory was divided between the Austro-Hungarian and Russian empires.

After World War I and the short period of independence, the Ukrainian ethnic territory was partitioned among the Ukrainian Soviet Socialist Republic, Poland, Romania, and Czechoslovakia as follows:

1) Eastern Ukraine was incorporated into the Ukrainian Soviet Socialist Republic.
2) Eastern Galicia and western Volhynia, collectively called Western Ukraine, were incorporated into Poland.
3) Part of the province of Bessarabia, parts of the former Austrian territory of Bukovina, and part of the former Hungarian territory of Marmarosh were incorporated into Romania.
4) Carpatho-Ukraine, officially known as Sub-Carpathian Ruthenia, and the northeast corner of Slovakia were incorporated into Czechoslovakia.

As a result of the changes brought about by World War II, most territories inhabited by Ukrainians were placed within the boundaries of the Ukrainian Soviet Socialist Republic.

## General Historical Works

The Hoover Library has many of the numerous general works that have been written on the history of the Ukrainian area. A few of those works that cut across the chronological subdivisions established for this survey are:

Allen, W. E. D. *The Ukraine: A History* (New York, 1963).
Bondioli, R. *Ucraina, la storia e l'anima di un grande popolo* (Rome, 1939).
Borshchak, I., ed. *La Légende historique de l'Ukraine* (Paris, 1940).
Chamberlain, W. H. *The Ukraine: A Submerged Nation* (New York, 1944).
Dikiĭ, A. *Neizvrashchennaiā istoriiā Ukraïny-Rusy*, 2v. (New York, 1960–1961).
Doroshenko, D. *History of the Ukraine* (Edmonton, Alberta, 1939).
————. *Ohliâd ukraïns'koï istoriohrafiï* (Prague, 1923).
Hrushevs'kyĭ, M. *A History of Ukraine* (New Haven, Conn., 1941).
————. *Istoriiā Ukraïny-Rusy*, 10v. (New York, 1954–1958).
Kholms'kyĭ, I. *Istoriiā Ukraïny* (Munich, 1949).
Krypiâkevych, I. *Istoriiā Ukraïny* (L'viv, 1941).
Manning, C. *The Story of Ukraine* (New York, 1947).
Nahaiêvs'kyĭ, I. *History of Ukraine* (Philadelphia, 1962).
Onats'kyĭ, IÊ. *Studi di storia e di cultura ucraina* (Rome, 1939).

## Pre-1914 Period

For the period prior to World War I, the library (in conjunction with the Green Library) has a reasonably strong collection. Most titles dealing with medieval and early Ukrainian history (before the late 1800s) are housed in the Green Library, although some may be found at Hoover. Since these publications fall outside the focus of the Institution's interest, they are not mentioned here.

Examples of the library's holdings for the late 1800s and up to the First World War are:

Akademiiā Nauk URSR. Instytut Istoriï. *Otmena Krepostnogo prava na Ukraine* (Kiev, 1961).
Arkas, N. N. *Istoriiā Ukraïny*, 3rd ed. (Kiev, 1913).
Franko, I. *Beiträge zur Geschichte und Kultur der Ukraine: Ausgewählte deutsche Schriften des Revolutionären Demokraten 1882–1915* (Berlin, 1963).

Hrushevs'kyĭ, M. *Iz polsko-ukrainskikh otnosheniĭ Galitsii* (St. Petersburg, 1907).

————. *Nasha polityka* (Lvov, 1911).

Kieniewicz, S. *Galicja w dobie autonomicznej, 1850–1914* (Wrocław, 1952).

Kiev. Instytut Istoriĭ Partiĭ. *Bil'shovyts'ki orhanizatsiĭ na Ukraïni v period pershoï rosiïs'koï revolîutsiĭ, 1905–1907* (Kiev, 1955).

Krupnitzky, B. *Geschichte der Ukraine von den Anfängen bis zum Jahre 1917, 3rd ed. (Munich, 1963).*

Perényi, J. *Iz istorii zakarpatskikh ukraintsev, 1849–1914* (Budapest, 1957).

Smiñan, P. *Revolîutsyĭnyĭ ta natsional'no-vyzvol'nyĭ rukh na Zakarpatti kintsîa XIX–pochatku XX st.* (L'viv, 1968).

Svistun, F. I. *Prikarpatskaîa Rus' pod vladîeniem Avstrii,* reprint of 2d ed. (Trumbull, Conn., 1970).

Ukraine. Arkhivne Upravlinnîa. *Revolîutsiîa 1905–1907 gg. na Ukraine,* 2v. (Kiev, 1955).

## WORLD WAR I, REVOLUTION, INDEPENDENCE, PARIS PEACE CONFERENCE, ETC., 1914–1921

The eight short years between 1914 and 1921 saw a catastrophic series of events fall upon the Ukrainian people and their country. Probably more occurred during these years than during any other short period in Ukrainian history. As stated before, this is coincidentally the best documented part of Ukrainian history in the Hoover Library.

### World War I

Because of the Hoover Institution's excellent coverage of World War I in general, a great deal of material touches peripherally on the war in the Ukrainian area. A few titles dealing specifically with World War I in Ukraine are:

Borowsky, P. *Deutsche Ukrainepolitik 1918* (Lübeck, 1970).

Central Powers (1914–1918). Treaties, etc. *Treaty of Peace Signed at Brest-Litovsk Between the Central Powers and the Ukrainian People's Republic* (London, 1918).

*Die deutsche Okkupation der Ukraine: Geheimdokumente* (Strasbourg, 1937).

Doroshenko, D. *Z istoriĭ ukraïns'koï politychnoï dumky za chasiv Svitovoï viĭny* (Prague, 1936).

Mints, I. I., ed. *Dokumenty o razgrome germanskikh okkupantov na Ukraine v 1918 godu* (Moscow, 1942).

Shulgin, O. *L'Ukraïne, la Russie et les puissances de l'entente* (Bern, 1918).

Sydorchuk, M. *Bil'shovyky Ukraïny v period Pershoï Svitovoï Viïny ï Liûtnevoï revoliûtsiï, 1914—liûtyï 1917* (L'viv, 1966).

Tsehel's'kyï, L. *Der Kreig, die Ukraina und die Balkanstaaten* (Vienna, 1915).

## Paris Peace Conference

At the Paris Peace Conference in 1919, the Ukrainians fielded a delegation that made claims for Ukrainian independence. The attempt, however, was unsuccessful since the representatives of the leading powers had little knowledge of the historical side of the Ukrainian question. For various reasons, the major powers supported the positions of Poland and Russia.

The Hoover Institution is well known for its outstanding holdings concerning the Paris Peace Conference. Part of these holdings deal with Ukrainian claims, including:

Butler, R. *The New Eastern Europe* (London, 1919).

*Delegation Propaganda: Carpatho-Russians. Documents Distributed to the Peace Conference. 3538—3555, Nos. 1—8* (Paris, 1919).

*Delegation Propaganda: Ukraine. Documents Presented to the Peace Conference, Nos. 1—2* (Paris, 1919).

Dnistrïans'kyï, S. *Ukraina and the Peace Conference, 1919* (Paris, 1919).

Evain, E. *Le Problème de l'indépendance de l'Ukraïne et la France* (Paris, 1931).

Kataisov, A. *Ukraina* (Copenhagen, 1918). Includes text of Treaty of Brest-Litovsk.

Paris. Peace Conference. Ukraine. *Mémoire sur l'indépendance de l'Ukraïne présenté à la Conférence de la paix par la délégation de la Republique ukrainienne* (Paris, 1919).

## Revolution and Civil War

After the overthrow of the tsar in March 1917, while the Kerensky government was in power in Petrograd, the de facto government in the Ukraine was the Central Rada, under the leadership of Mykaïlo Hrushevs'kyï. On November 20, 1917, following the bolshevik takeover in Petrograd, the Rada proclaimed the Ukraine a ''people's republic'' (Ukraïns'ka Narodna Respublika). Until 1921, the land was torn by a multisided civil war. Besides the bolsheviks and Russian White forces, there were Poles and several factions of Ukrainians, and all sides were fighting each other. Documentation on the revolution and the civil war in the Ukraine is abundant. The Ukrainian Collection is extremely rich, both in material published by pro-independence forces and by the pro-Soviet faction. Particularly useful are:

Adams, A. E. *Bolsheviks in the Ukraine: The Second Campaign, 1918– 1919* (New Haven, Conn., 1963).

*Arkhiv grazhdanskoĭ voĭny*, 2v. (Berlin, 1922).

Doroshenko, D. *Istoriı̈a Ukraïny 1917–1923* rr. (Uzhgorod, 1932).

Dotsenko, O. *Litopys ukrains'koï revoliûtsiï*, 2v. (L'viv, 1923–1924).

Fedyshyn, O. *Germany's Drive to the East and the Ukrainian Revolution* (Newark, N.J., 1971).

Hunchak, T. ed. *The Ukraine, 1917–1921: A Study in Revolution* (Cambridge, Mass., 1977).

Kapustıâns'kyĭ, M. *Pokhid ukraïns' kykh armiĭ na Kyïv-Odesu v 1919 rotsi*, 2d ed., 2v. (Munich, 1946).

Khrystıûk, P. *Zamitky ĭ materiıâly do istoriï ukraïns'koï revoliûtsiï 1917– 1920 rr.* (Vienna, 1921).

Kossak-Szczucka, Z. *The Blaze: Reminiscences of Volhynia, 1917–1919* (London, 1927).

Kostiv, K. *Konstytutsiĭni akty vidnovlenniıâ Ukraïns'koï Derzhavy 1917– 1919 rokiv i ïkhniıâ politychno-derzhavna ıûakist'* (Toronto, 1964).

Markus, V. *L'Ukraïne soviétique dans les relations internationales et son statut en droit international, 1918–1923* (Paris, 1959).

Martovych, O. *Ukrainian Liberation Movement in Modern Times* (Edinburgh, 1951).

Nazaruk, O. *Rik na Velykiĭ Ukraïni: Konspekt spomyniv z ukraïns'koï revoliûtsiï* (Vienna, 1920).

Reshetar, J. *The Ukrainian Revolution, 1917–1920* (Princeton, N.J., 1952).

Shandruk, P. *Arms of Valor* (New York, 1959).

Shankovs'kyĭ, L. *Ukraïns'ka armiıâ v borot'bi za derzhavnist'* (Munich, 1958).

Shulgin, O. *L'Ukraïne contre Moscou, 1917* (Paris, 1935).

Stakhiv, M. *Ukraïna v dobi Dyrektoriï UNR, 7v.* (Scranton, Pa., 1962– 1966).

―――. *Ukraine and Russia: An Outline of History of Political and Military Relations, Dec. 1917–Apr. 1918* (New York, 1967).

―――. *Ukraine and the European Turmoil, 1917–1918* (New York, 1973).

Ukraine. Laws, statutes, etc. *Vistnyk derzhavnykh zakoniv dliâ vsikh zemel' Ukraïns' koï Narodnoï Respublyky, vyp. 1—39, 18 sich.—31 zhovt. 1919* (Kamenets Podolski, 1919).

―――. *Memorandum to the Government of the United States on the Recognition of the Ukrainian People's Republic* (Washington, D.C., 1920).

―――. Mission Diplomatique Extraordinaire en Roumanie, 1919. *Memoriu asupră chestiunei ucraine* (Bucharest, 1920).

―――. Presova Sluzhba. *The Ukrainian Problems*, 5v. (Vienna, 1919).

―――. Special Diplomatic Mission in London. *Ukrainian problems: A Collection of Notes and Memoirs, etc., Presented by the Ukrainian Special Diplomatic Mission in London to the British Foreign Office* (London, 1919).

Ukraïns'ke Informatsiïne Biûro, Munich. *Materials Concerning Ukrainian-Jewish Relations During the Years of the Revolution, 1917—1921* (Munich, 1956).

Vynnychenko, V. K. *Vidrodzhenniâ natsiï*, 3v. (Kiev and Vienna, 1920).

As numerous as the publications of the pro-independence Ukrainian faction were, they were nearly equaled by pro-Soviet Ukrainian publications. Most of these procommunist titles were published in later years in the Soviet-dominated Ukrainian SSR. A short selection of this type of literature in the Hoover Library includes:

Akademiiâ Nauk URSR. Instytut Istoriï. *Moriâki v bor' be za vlast' sovetov na Ukraine, noiâbr' 1917—1920 gg.* (Kiev, 1963).

―――. Sektor Derzhavy ï Prava. *Ukraïns'ka RSR na mizhnarodnïï areni: Zbirnyk dokumentiv, 1917—1923 rr.* (Kiev, 1966).

*Bol'shevistskie organizatsii Ukrainy v period podgotovki Velikoï Oktiâbr'skoï Revoliûtsii* (Kiev, 1957).

*Chervonoe kazachestvo, 1918—1923: Sbornik materialov* (Kharkov, 1924).

Dmytrienko, M. *Bil'shovyts'ka presa Ukraïny 1917—1918 rr. iâk istorychne dzherelo* (Kiev, 1967).

Karpenko, O. *Imperiiâlistychna interventsiiâ na Ukraïni, 1918—1920* (L'viv, 1964).

Khmil', I. *Z praporom myru kriz' polumiâ viïny: Dyplomatychna diiâl'nist' Ukraïns'koï RSR, 1917—1920* (Kiev, 1962).

Likholat, A. *Razgrom burzhuazno-natsionalisticheskoï direktorii na Ukraine* (Moscow, 1949).

Likholat, A. *Razgrom natsionalisticheskoï kontrrevoliûtsii na Ukraine, 1917—1922 gg.* (Moscow, 1954).

Udovychenko, P. *Z istoriï zovnishn'oï polityky URSR, 1919—1922 rr.* (Kiev, 1957).

Ukraine. Laws, statutes, etc. *Sobrania uzakoneniĭ i rasporîazheniĭ raboche-krest' îanskago pravitel' stva Ukrainy, nos. 1–30, 15 îanv.–30 iîunîa 1919 g.* (Kiev, 1919).

## West Ukrainian Republic

The breakup of the Austro-Hungarian empire in the autumn of 1918 created the possibility of independent political activity in the Ukrainian regions of the empire. A Ukrainian National Rada was established in L'viv, the principal city of eastern Galicia, under the leadership of Dr. Eugene Petrushevich. This organization proclaimed a Ukrainian national state that included eastern Galicia, northwestern Bukovina, and Transcarpathia on October 19, 1918. The new state became known as the Western Ukrainian Republic. The sentiment for joining with the nationalists in former Russian Ukraine was strong. In January 1919 the two Ukrainian states were joined in a federation under the Central Rada in Kiev. The military forces of the Western Ukrainian state, however, were unable to withstand the pressure of the better armed and better equipped Polish armies, which pressed into eastern Galicia and occupied L'viv in late November 1918. Until 1923 the government of the Western Ukrainian Republic led a harassed existence in Stanislaviv and other towns near the former Austro-Russian frontier. Little by little the area was annexed into reconstituted Poland. Some Hoover holdings on this topic are:

Kuchabs'kyĭ, V. *Die Westukraine im Kampfe mit Polen und dem Bolsche-wismus in den Jahren 1918–1923* (Berlin, 1934).
Lozyns'kyĭ, M. *Décisions du Conseil suprême sur la Galicie orientale* (Paris, 1919).
——. *Halychyna v rr. 1918–1920* (Vienna, 1922).
——. *L'Ukraïne occidentale est crime contre le droit* (Paris, 1919).
Stakhiv, M. *Zakhidnîa Ukraïna: Narys istoriĭ derzhavnoho budivnytstva ta zbroĭnoĭ ĭ dyplomatychnoĭ oborony v 1918– 1923*, 6v. (Scranton, Pa. 1958–1961).
Ukraine. *Protest of the Ukrainian Republic to the United States Against the Delivery of Eastern Galicia to Polish Domination* (Washington, D.C., 1919).
West Ukrainian People's Republic. *Mémorandum présenté à monsieur le président des Etats-unis d'Amérique par la Comité exécutif du Comité national ukrainien à Léopol (Galicie), faisant fonction de gouverne-ment provisoire de l'état ukrainien de Halitch sur les territoires ukrainiens de l'ancienne monarchie austro-hongroise* (Lausanne, 1918).

## Relations and War with Poland

In addition to the bloodshed and chaos in the Ukraine caused by the First World War, the battles with the bolsheviks, and the struggle for independence, the Ukrainians had difficult relations with the Poles. After declaring independence from Russia, the Poles, under the leadership of Marshal Piłsudski, tried to push their borders as far east as possible. In doing so, they began to occupy land also claimed by the Ukrainians. This led to a brief war between the Poles and Ukrainians, which ended with the Poles annexing large parts of Ukraine following the Treaty of Riga in 1921.

The Hoover Institution possesses a fair number of titles dealing with Ukrainian relations and the war with Poland, including:

Deruga, A. *Polityka wschodnia Polski wobec ziem Litwy, Białorusi i Ukrainy, 1918–1919* (Warsaw, 1969).

Inter-Allied Commission for the Negotiation of an Armistice between Poland and the Ukraine. *Minutes of the Commission and the Drafting of the Sub-Commission* (Paris, 1919).

Omelǐanovych-Pavlenko, M. *Ukraïns'ko-pol's'ka viïna, 1918*–1919 (Prague, 1929).

Pidhaǐnyǐ, O. *Ukrainian-Polish Problem in the Dissolution of the Russian Empire, 1919–1917* (Toronto,, 1962).

Poland. Treaties, etc. 1919–1922 (Piłsudski). *Traktat pokoju między Polską a Rosją i Ukrainą, podpisany w Rydze dnia 18 marca 1921 roku* (Riga, 1921).

Wasilewski, L. *Ukrainska sprawa narodowa w jej rozwoju historycznym* (Warsaw, 1925).

## General Works on Soviet Ukrainian History

A preceding section dealt with works on Ukrainian history in general. The following list of titles concerns the Soviet Ukraine in general (1920 to present):

Akademiǐa Nauk URSR. Instytut Istoriï. *Istoriǐa Ukraïns'koï RSR*, 2v. (Kiev, 1953–1958).

———. ———. *Istoriohrafichni doslidzhennǐa v Ukraïns'kiï RSR*, 5v. (Kiev, 1968–1972).

Borys, ǏU. *The Russian Communist Party and the Sovietization of Ukraine* (Stockholm, 1960).

Dǐadychenko, V. A. *Istoriǐa Ukraïns'koï RSR* (Kiev, 1965).

———. *Razvitie istoricheskoǐ nauki v Ukrainskoǐ SSR* (Kiev, 1970).

Dubyna, K., ed. *Istoriǐa Ukraïns'koï RSR*, 2v. (Kiev, 1967).

## THE INTERWAR PERIOD, 1923–1939

Although the years of the First World War, the revolution, and the civil war were catastrophic for the Ukrainian people, the cessation of hostilities and the interwar period (1923–1939) brought scarcely any improvement in their situation. The consolidation of Soviet power brought with it forced collectivization, the destruction of large parts of the peasantry (kulaks), famine, and Stalin's purges.

Especially during the 1929–1939 period, force and terror were used in an all-out attempt to silence Ukrainian nationalist opposition. According to William Henry Chamberlin in his book, *The Ukraine: A Submerged Nation* (New York, 1944),

> The Communist Party in the Ukraine was subjected to more frequent and violent purges than the same organization in Russia, because the impulse to assert national independence frequently cropped up even among Ukrainian communists. Two representatives of this tendency in the twenties were Shumsky and Volubuyev. The former, who was for a time Commissar for Education, took advantage of the cultural ukrainianization of the country to defend, so far as possible, the nationalist position. Volubuyev persisted in exposing the colonization tendencies of Soviet economic policy, the tendency to exploit the Ukraine for the benefit of Russia.

Two prominent victims of this period were the popular communist writer Mykola Khvylovyĭ and the veteran Ukrainian communist activist Mykola Skrypnyk, both of whom committed suicide in 1933. The total number of victims of this time of famine, deportation, and purges will probably never be known, but it is undoubtedly in the neighborhood of two to three million persons.

Hoover Library coverage of this period is not exceedingly strong, due to difficulty in obtaining material at that time. The library is attempting to strengthen this area through purchase of items dealing with the period, but published in more recent times.

Examples of the library's present holdings in this field are:

Haliĭ, M. *Het' masku! Natsional'na polityka na Radiǎns'kiĭ Ukraïni v svitli dokumentiv* (L'viv, 1934).

Herasymovych, I. *Holod na Ukraïni* (Berlin, 1922).

Khvylovyĭ, Mykola. *Tvory*, 5v. projected (Baltimore, 1978– ).

Kiev. Instytut Istoriï Partiï. *Z dosvidu diǐal'nosty orhaniv partiĭnoderzhav-noho kontroliǔ Ukraïny po zaluchenniǔ mas do upravlinniǎ derzhavoiǔ, 1923–1934 rr: Zbirnyk dokumentiv i materialiv* (Kiev, 1965).

Koshelivets', Ivan. *Mykola Skrypnyk* (Munich, 1972).

Kostiuk, H. *Stalinist Rule in the Ukraine: A Study of the Decade of Mass Terror, 1929–1939* (Munich, 1961).

Lewandowski, K. *Sprawa ukraińska w polityce zagranicznej Czechosłowacji w latach 1918–1932* (Wrocław, 1974).

Luckyj, G. *Literary Politics in the Soviet Ukraine, 1917–1934* (New York, 1956).

Malitskiĭ, A. *Grazhdanskiĭ kodeks sovetskikh respublik: Tekst i prakticheskiĭ komplementariĭ* (Kharkov, 1927).

Martynets', V. *Ukraïns'ke pidpillîa, vid U.V.O. do O.U.N.: Spohady ĭ materiîaly do peredistoriĭ ta istoriĭ ukraïns'koho orhanizovanoho natsionalizmu* (Winnipeg, 1949).

Petrov, T. *Les Minorités nationales en Europe centrale et orientale* (Paris, 1935).

Shevchuk, H. M. *Kul'turne budivnytstvo na Ukraïni u 1921–1925 rokakh* (Kiev, 1963).

Soloveĭ, D. *The Golgotha of Ukraine: Eye-Witness Accounts of the Famine in Ukraine* (New York, 1953).

Stercho, P. *Diplomacy of Double Morality: Europe's Crossroads in Carpatho-Ukraine, 1919–1939* (New York, 1971).

Ukraine. Arkhivne Upravlinnîa. *Komitety nezamozhnykh selîan Ukraïny, 1920–1933: Zbirnyk dokumentiv i materiîaliv* (Kiev, 1968).

―――. Narodniĭ Komissariat po Prosveshcheniîu. *Na fronti kul'tury* (Kiev, 1935).

*Ukraïns'ki kul'turni diîachi URSR 1920–1940-zhertvy bol'shevyts'koho teroru* (New York, 1959).

Zabolotnyĭ, I. *Chervona Volyn': Narysy z istoriĭ revoliûtsiĭnoho rukhu trudîashchykh Volyni, 1917–1939* (Lutsk, 1958).

The approximately five million Ukrainians who, due to the 1921 Treaty of Riga, ended up in reconstituted Poland did not face such terror or perils of death, but for them, too, political independence or autonomy was impossible.

## World War II, 1939–1945

One of the strongest areas in the Hoover Institution Library is documentation on the Second World War. The Ukraine, which again became a battleground, this time for the Wehrmacht and the Red Army, is heavily treated in the library's German and Russian collections. For general material on military campaigns and battles, these collections should be consulted.

A few Soviet or procommunist sources specifically on the war in the Ukraine are:

Belko, J. *Zápisnik z východného frontu* (Bratislava, 1965).

Kiev. Instytut Istoriï Partiï. *Kommunisticheskaiâ partiiâ-organizator osvo-bozhdeniiâ Sovetskoĭ Ukrainy ot fashistskikh zakhvatchikov* (Kiev, 1975).

———. ———. *Nimets' ko-fashysts' kyĭ okupatsiĭnyĭ rezhym na Ukraïni* (Kiev, 1963).

Lokshin, B. S., comp. *V bol' shom nastuplenii: Vospominaniiâ, ocherki i dokumenty ob osvobozhdenii Ukrainy v 1943–1944 gg.* (Moscow, 1964).

Nazarenko, I. D., ed. *Ukraïns' ka RSR u Velykiĭ Vitchyznianiĭ viĭni Radiâns' koho Soĭuzu, 1941–1945 rr.*, 2v. (Kiev, 1967).

Torzecki, R. *Kwestja ukraińska w polityce III Rzeszy, 1933–1945* (Warsaw, 1972).

The Germans, knowing the general Ukrainian dissatisfaction with Soviet rule, attempted to influence the Ukrainians through propaganda and publishing to favor the Nazi side. Two representative works are:

Doroshenko, D. *Die Ukraine und das Reich: Neun Jahrhunderte deutsch-ukrainischer Beziehungen im Spiegel der deutschen Wissenschaft und Literatur* (Leipzig, 1942).

Germany. Reichsministerium für die Besetzten Ostgebiete. *Amtliches Material zum Massenmord von Winniza* (Berlin, 1944).

Many Ukrainians did turn against the Soviets, and some actually joined the Germans, as described in W. Heike's *Sie wollten die Freiheit: Die Geschichte der ukrainischen Division 1943–1945* (Dorheim, 1973) and R. Ilnytzkyj's *Deutschland und die Ukraine 1934–1945*, 2v. (Munich, 1955–1956).

Others became involved in the independent Ukraïns'ka Povstans'ka Armiiâ (Ukrainian Insurgent Army), which was the military arm of the Orhanizatsiiâ Ukraïns'kykh Natsionalistiv. The Hoover Library has many titles dealing with this subject, including:

Dmytryk, Ivan. *U lisakh Lemkivshchyny* (Munich, 1977).

Hordiênko, M. *Z volyns'kykh i polis'kykh reĭdiv: Iz diï UPA-Pivnich, 1943–1944* (Toronto, 1959).

Krokhmaliûk, ÎU. *Guerra y libertad: Historia de la División "Halychyna"* (Buenos Aires, 1961).

Lebed', M. *UPA, Ukraïns'ka Povstans'ka Armiïa* (Augsburg, 1946).
Orhanizatsiïa Ukraïns'kykh Natsionalistiv. *U borot'bi za volïu–pid boïovymy praporamy UPA* (Augsburg, 1949).
Rakhmannyĭ, Roman. *Krov i chornylo* (New York, 1960).
Shankovs'kyĭ, L. *Pokhidni hrupy OUN* (Munich, 1958).
United Committee of the Ukrainian-American Organizations of New York. *The Ukrainian Insurgent Army in Fight for Freedom* (New York, 1954).

Other general publications concerning World War II from the Ukrainian point of view are:

Fedorov, A. *Partisans d'Ukraïne* (Paris, 1966).
Hryhorijiv, N. *The War and Ukrainian Democracy* (Toronto, 1945).
Kamenetsky, I. *Hitler's Occupation of Ukraine, 1941–1944* (Milwaukee, 1956).
Nemec, F. *The Soviet Seizure of Subcarpathian Ruthenia* (Toronto, 1955).
Rudnyts'ka, M. *Zakhidna Ukraïna pid bol'shevykamy, IX. 1939–VI. 1941: Zbirnyk* (New York, 1948).
Weber, H. *Die Bukowina im zweiten Weltkrieg* (Hamburg, 1972).

## POST–WORLD WAR II PERIOD

In the years following World War II, the Ukrainian territories formerly within the Soviet Union have been totally reintegrated into the state. The area has become one of the most important areas in the USSR, both agriculturally and industrially.

The western Ukrainian ethnic lands formerly under Polish administration, the Carpatho-Ruthenian area formerly belonging to Czechoslovakia, and Bukovina were all integrated into the Ukrainian SSR.

The Hoover Library's collection on the Ukrainian SSR in the postwar period is fairly strong, including such titles as:

Akademiia Nauk URSR. Instytut Istoriï. *Istoriïa selïanstva Ukraïns'koï RSR*, 2v. (Kiev, 1967).
———. Sektor Derzhavy ï Prava. *Ukraïns'ka RSR u mizhnarodnykh vidnosynakh, 1945–1965*, 2v. (Kiev, 1959–1966).
———. *Ukraïna v period rozhornutoho budivnytstva komunizmu*, 5v. (Kiev, 1967).

Bilinsky, Y. *The Second Soviet Republic: The Ukraine After World War II* (Newark, N.J., 1964).

Konenko, I. P., ed. *Tsyvil'nyĭ protsesual'nyĭ kodeks Ukraïns'koï RSR: Naukovo-praktychnyĭ komentar* (Kiev, 1973).

Kuzovkin, G., comp. *Est' takoĭ front: Sbornik ocherkov* (L'vov, 1971).

Lewytzkyj, B. *Die Sowjetukraine, 1944–1963* (Cologne, 1964).

L'vov. Oblasnyĭ Derzhavnyĭ Arkhiv. *Pid praporom zhovtnîa: Vplyv Velykoï zhovtnevoï revolîutsiï na pidnesennîa revolîutsiĭnoho rukhu v Zakhidniĭ Ukraïni* (L'vov, 1964).

Mazlakh, S. *On the Current Situation in Ukraine* (Ann Arbor, Mich. 1970).

Santsevych, A. *Problemy istoriï Ukraïny pislîavoîennoho periodu v radîans'kiĭ istoriohrafiï* (Kiev, 1967).

———. *Dzhereloznavstvo z istoriï Ukraïns'koï RSR pislîavoîennoho periodu, 1945–1970* (Kiev, 1972).

Sosnovskyĭ, M. *Ukraïna na mizhnarodniĭ areni, 1945–1965: Problemy ĭ perspektyvy ukraïns'koï zovnishn'oï polityky* (Toronto, 1966).

Ukraine. Arkhivne Upravlinnîa. Tsentral'nyĭ Derzhavnyĭ Istorychnyĭ Arkhiv. *Uchrezhdeniîa Zapadnoĭ Ukrainy* (L'vov, 1955).

———. Constitution. *Konstitutsiîa Ukrainskoĭ Sovetskoĭ Sotsialistiche-skoĭ Respubliki* (Moscow, 1972).

———. Laws, statutes, etc. *Kodeks zakoniv pro pratsîu Ukraïns'koï RSR: Ofitsiîal'nyĭ tekst iz zminamy . . . ta z dodatkamy systematyzovanykh materiîaliv* (Kiev, 1965).

## THE NATIONALITY QUESTION

The nationality question has been a persistent problem in the Ukraine since prerevolutionary times and is still today a thorn in Moscow's side, perhaps sharper than ever. The Hoover Ukrainian Collection is strong in this field. A small selection of the many works on Ukrainian nationalism are:

Allworth, E. *Soviet Nationality Problems* (New York, 1971).

Bakalo, Ivan. *Natsional'na polityka Lenina* (Munich, 1974).

Dmytryshyn, B. *Moscow and Ukraine: A Study of Russian Bolshevik Nationality Policy* (New York, 1956).

Dzîuba, Ivan. *Internatsionalizm chy rusyfikatsiîa?* 2d ed. (Munich, 1978).

Kleĭner, Izraïl'. *Natsional'ni problemy ostann'oï imperiï* (Paris, 1978).

Kupchyns'kyĭ, Roman, ed. *Natsional'nyĭ vopros v SSSR: Dokumenty* (Munich, 1975).

Markus', Vasyl', and Pelens'kyĭ, ĬAroslav. *Pytanniâ natsional'noï poli-tyky SRSR* (New York, 1960).

*Molod' Dnipropetrovs'ka v borot'bi proty rusyfikatsiï* (Munich, 1971).

*Natsional'naiâ politika KPSS za 60 let perebyvaniiâ eë u vlasti* (Munich, 1978).

Naulko, V. *Razvitie mezhėtnicheskikh sviâzeĭ na Ukraine: Istoriko-etnograficheskiĭ ocherk* (Kiev, 1975).

Sil'nitskiĭ, Frantishek. *Natsional'naiâ politika Kommunisticheskoĭ Partii Sovetskogo Soiûza v period 1917–1922 g.* (Munich, 1978).

Skrypnyk, Mykola. *Statti ĭ promovy z natsional'noho pytanniâ* (Munich, 1974).

## CLANDESTINE MATERIAL

As with other peoples of the Soviet Union and Eastern Europe, the Hoover Institution is making a concerted effort to collect all material dealing with Ukrainian political, nationalist, and religious dissent. Already the library has a large number of items concerning these dissident movements and an ever increasing collection of the movements' "samvydav" (Ukrainian equivalent of the Russian samizdat) documents. Most of these documents are circulated illicitly in the Ukraine and later published in the West. As a depository for the *Sobranie dokumentov samizdata* and the *Materialy samizdata* collected and published by the Arkhiv Samizdata in Munich, the Hoover Institution receives all included Ukrainian documents; for example, volumes 18 and 19 of the *Sobranie*. Other examples of samvydav literature and studies of the phenomenon are:

Browne, M., comp. *Ferments in Ukraine: Documents by V. Chornovil and Others* (New York, 1971).

Chornovil, Viâcheslav. *The Chornovil Papers* (New York, 1968).

*Dissent in Ukraine: The Ukrainian Herald, Issue 6*, ed. and tr. by Lesya Jones and Bohdan Yasen (Baltimore, 1977).

*Ethnocide of Ukrainians in the USSR: The Ukrainian Herald, Issues 7 & 8*, ed. and tr. by Olena Saciuk and Bohdan Yasen (Baltimore, 1979).

Hryhorenko, Petro. *Nashi budni* (Munich, 1978).

*Informatsiĭnyi biûleten', Ch. 1–2* (Baltimore, 1978–1979).

*An Interview with Political Prisoners in a Soviet Perm Camp* (Baltimore, 1975).

*Khronika taborovykh budniv* (Munich, 1976).

Liber, George, and Mostovych, Anna. *Nonconformity and Dissent in the Ukrainian SSR, 1955–1975: An Annotated Bibliography* (Cambridge, Mass., 1978).

Lobaĭ, D. *Neperemozhna Ukraïna: Fakty z sovĩets'kykh vydan' pro borot'bu Moskvy z ukraïns'kym natsionalizmom na kul'turnomu fronti po Druhiĭ Svitoviĭ Viĭni* (Winnipeg, 1950).

Moroz, Valentyn. *Boomerang* (Baltimore, 1974).

――――. *Eseĭ, lysty, dokumenty* (Munich, 1975).

――――. *Moĭseĭ i Datan* (Baltimore, 1978).

*Russian Oppression in Ukraine: Reports and Documents* (London, 1962).

Tereliâ, ÎOsyp. *Notes from a Madhouse: A Firsthand Report from a Soviet Psychiatric Prison* (Washington, D.C., 1977).

*Ukraïns'ka inteligentsiiâ pid sudom KGB: Materiîaly z protsesiv V. Chornovola, M. Masiûtka, M. Ozernoho ta inshykh* (Munich, 1970).

*Women's Voices from Soviet Labor Camps* (Baltimore 1975).

Zinkevych, O., ed. *Ukraïns'kyĭ pravozakhysnyĭ rukh: Dokumenty i materiîaly kyïvs'koï Ukraïns'koï Hel'sins'koï Hrupy* (Baltimore, 1978).

*Zoshyty samvydavu: Zbirka Samvydavnykh dokumentiv* (Munich, 1978).


## THE UKRAINIAN ECONOMY

As a vital part of the general economy of the Russian empire and of the Soviet Union, much has been written concerning the Ukrainian economy. Many such items can be found in the Russian Collection and some in the Polish Collection. The following are a few of the many items in the Ukrainian Collection treating the region's economy before the revolution:

Akademiîa Nauk URSR. *Narysy z sotsial'no-ekonomichnoï istoriï Ukraïny dozhovtnevoho periodu* (Kiev, 1963).

Bureau Ukrainien de Presse, Paris. *L'Importance économique de l'Ukraïne: Recueil des matériaux et statistiques concernant les questions économiques et financières de l'Ukraïne* (Bruxelles, 1920).

Hurzhiĭ, I. *Ukraïna v systemi vserosiĭs'koho rynku 60–90kh rokiv XIX st.* (Kiev, 1968).

Kononenko, K. *Ukraine and Russia: A History of the Economic Relations Between Ukraine and Russia, 1654–1917* (Milwaukee, 1958).

Mazurenko, V. *Ekonomichna samostiĭnist' Ukraïny v chyslakh* (Vienna, 1921).

Timoshenko, V. *Relations économiques entre l'Ukraïne et la France* (Paris, 1919).

Ukrainian National Council of Eastern Galicia. *La Situation économique de la Galicie orientale et son importance pour la reconstruction de l'Europe* (Genoa, 1922).

The Ukrainian Collection also includes a large number of publications dealing with the Soviet Ukrainian economy, including:

Akademiía Nauk URSR. Instytut Ekonomiky. *Entsyklopediía narodnoho hospodarstva Ukraïns'koï RSR,* 4v. (Kiev, 1969–1972).

———. ———. *Narodne hospodarstvo Ukraïns'koï RSR u pislíavoíenni roky, 1946–1964* (Kiev, 1965).

———. ———. *Ocherki razvitiía narodnogo khozíaïastva Ukrainskoï SSR* (Moscow, 1954).

Derevíankin, T. *Ekonomichnyï rozvytok Radíans'koï Ukraïny, 1917–1970* (Kiev, 1970).

Fomin, P. *Ukraina: Ekonomicheskaía kharakteristika* (Kharkov, 1923).

Hurwicz, A., ed. *Aspects of Contemporary Ukraine* (Chicago, 1955).

Líalikov, N. *Sovetskaía Ukraina: Ocherk ekonomicheskoï geografii* (Moscow, 1954).

Peresypkin, V. F., ed. *Ukraïns'ka sil's'ko-hospodars'ka entsyklopediía,* 3v. (Kiev, 1970–1972).

Postyshev, P. *Soviet Ukraine Today: The Results of the Agricultural Year 1933 and the Immediate Tasks of the Communist Party of the Ukraine* (New York, 1934).

Ukraine. Tsentral'ne Statystychne Upravlinnía. *Dinamika narodnogo khozíaïstva Ukrainy 1921–1922, 1924–1925 gg.* (Kharkov, 1926).

Virnyk, D.F., ed. *Rozvytok narodnoho hospodarstva Ukraïns'koï RSR, 1917–1967,* 2v. (Kiev, 1970).

Wynar, B. *Ekonomichnyï koloniíalizm v Ukraïni* (Paris, 1958).

## SERIAL COLLECTION

The Ukrainian Collection includes a modest serial collection, consisting of some 230 periodical titles and files of more than 80 newspapers. Many of the runs are broken and incomplete, but still represent a source for research.

The following is a selection of the more important, longer, and more complete sets of periodicals:

*Do zbroï* (Hamburg, 1946–1955)
*Hromads'kyï holos* (New York, 1946–1973)
*Hurtuïmosía* (Prague, 1930–1938)
*Istorychnyï kalendar-al'manakh chervonoï kalyny* (Kiev, 1923–1930)
*Litopys revolíutsiï: Zhurnal istoriï KP(b)U ta zhovtnevoï revolíutsiï na Ukraïni* (Kharkov, 1923–1933 [scattered issues on microfilm])

*Nasha kul'tura* (L'viv, 1935–1937)
*Nova Ukraïna* (Berlin, 1923–1928)
*Rozbudova natsiï: Orhan Provodu ukraïns'kykh natsionalistiv* (Prague, 1928–1932)
*Students'kyĭ visnyk* (Prague, 1927–1931)
*Suchasnist'* (Munich, 1961–)
*Ukraïna* (Paris, 1949–1953)
*Ukrainian Commentary* (Winnipeg, 1952–1958)
*Ukrainian Observer* (London, 1949–1953)
*Ukrainian Quarterly* (New York, 1944–)
*Ukrainian Review* (London, 1954–)
*Ukraïns'kyĭ istorychnyĭ zhurnal* (Kiev, 1959–)
*Ukraïns'kyĭ visnyk: Zlĭavnyĭ zhurnal z Ukraïny* (Baltimore, 1971–1974)
*Ukraïns'kyĭ zbirnyk* (Munich, 1954–1960)
*Zhyttĭà* (Buenos Aires, 1948–1958)

The following relatively complete files of Ukrainian newspapers can be found within the collection:

*Ameryka* (Philadelphia, 1933–1934, 1945)
*Bat'kivshchyna: Orhan ukraïns'koï konservatyvnoï dumky* (Toronto, 1957–)
*Dilo* (L'viv, 1915–1934, 1939)
*Kanadiĭs'kyĭ Farmer* (Winnipeg, 1938–1952)
*Kanadiĭs'kyĭ Ukraïnets'* (Winnipeg, 1919–1922, 1931)
*Krakivs'ki visti* (Kraków, 1940–1943)
*Khrystiĭans'kyĭ holos* (Munich, 1949–)
*Narodna volĭà* (Scranton, Pa., 1931–1945, 1947)
*Nashe zhyttĭà* (Augsburg, 1945–1948)
*Nedilĭà* (Aschaffenburg, Ger., 1946–1951)
*Perelom* (Buenos Aires, 1943–1947)
*Radĭans'ka Ukraïna: Orhan Tsentral'noho Komitetu KP(b)U, Verkhovnoï rady i Rady narodnykh komisariv URSR* (Kiev, 1945–1958)
*Suchasna Ukraïna* (Munich, 1951–1960)
*Svitlo* (Toronto, 1945–1949)
*Svoboda* (Jersey City, N.J., 1916–1939)
*Ukrainische Nachrichten* (Vienna, 1914–1917)
*Ukraïns'ka hromads'ka pora* (Detroit, 1945–1949)
*Ukraïns'ka nyva* (Lutsk, 1933–1935)
*Ukraïns'ka trybuna* (Munich, 1947–1949)
*Ukraïns'ke slovo* (Paris, 1934, 1950–1951)

*Ukraïns'ki visti* (Ulm, Ger., 1947–1963)
*Ukraïns'kyĭ holos* (Winnipeg, 1923, 1933–1945)
*Ukraïns'kyĭ samostiĭnyk* (Munich, 1950–1957)

## ARCHIVAL MATERIALS

The Hoover Institution Archives has few manuscript collections specifically classified as Ukrainian collections. Great amounts of material concerning Ukrainian history, however, may be found within collections listed as Russian, Polish, or Czechoslovak. Any researcher interested in Ukrainian topics should consult such holdings.

# ( YUGOSLAVIA )

The Yugoslav Collection of the Hoover Institution, with more than 18,000 books, 350 periodicals, and 180 newspapers, originated with the material gathered early in 1921 by Prof. F. A. Golder from the recently formed Kingdom of Serbs, Croats, and Slovenes. Professor Golder was charged with collecting materials throughout Europe concerning the origins and course of World War I. Traveling through countries only beginning to recover physically from the Great War, dealing with governments in turmoil, and working with cultures and histories with which he was unfamiliar, Professor Golder initially collected only primary materials directly related to the outbreak and conduct of the European war. The intent of the Hoover War Collection, as it was then known, was to document events of international impact and significance, not to gather materials on the historical development of the individual countries involved.

As scholars have been drawn over the years to the documentary and archival collections of the Hoover Institution, the library has acquired an excellent collection of secondary works to support their research. The Yugoslav Collection is strongest in the areas of World Wars I and II, especially their internal political and social aspects, the evolution of the Yugoslav Communist Party, and the emergence of a socialist society in Yugoslavia after 1945. Other aspects of the development of the Yugoslav peoples since the nineteenth century are covered only insofar as it is necessary to establish the historical context. The Yugoslav Collection is supplemented not only by other Hoover Institution holdings, especially those dealing with the neighboring states or with international communism, but also by the holdings of the main Stanford Library in literature, philosophy, social science, and earlier history of the Yugoslav peoples.

In view of the scope of the Yugoslav Collection at the Hoover Institution, the listings of books and archival material in this chapter are illustrative rather than exhaustive.

## BACKGROUND SOURCES

The Yugoslav Collection includes most of the standard histories of the national and social movements in Serbia, among the Hapsburg South Slavs, and in Montenegro and Macedonia in the nineteenth and early twentieth centuries. Serbia, for example, is represented by the works of J. K. Jiřecek, Stojan Novaković, Mihailo Gavrilović, Stojan Protić, Grgur Jakšić, Živan Živanović, Stanoje Stanojević, Jovan Jovanović, Slobodan Jovanović, and Dragoslav Stranjaković, among others. The Alex Dragnich archival collection contains some invaluable and particularly rare background materials on Serbia in the nineteenth century. Among these are two protocols of sessions of the Serbian Skupština for the years 1859 and 1861 and an address to the Skupština by the minister of internal affairs, Nikola Hristić, in 1867. It also includes some fifteen political pamphlets (published in the second half of the nineteenth century), several by well-known Serbian leaders, that deal with Serbian domestic politics. Several pamphlets deal with foreign affairs and were written by men holding high offices in the nation: Jovan Ristić (four); Milan Piroćanac (one); Milan Hristić (one); Vladen Djordjević (one). Several published memoirs (exceedingly rare) are found in the Dragnich Collection:

> *Govori Jovana Dj. Avakumovića u opštini, sudovima, i Skupštini* (Belgrade, 1910).
> Milošević, Raša. *Timočka buna 1883 godine: Uspomene* (Belgrade, 1923).
> Ristić, Jovan. *Pisma Jovana Ristića Filipu Hristiću, od 1870 do 1873 i od 1877 do 1880* (Belgrade, 1931).
> Stranjaković, Dragoslav, ed. *Uspomene i doživljaji Dimitrija Marinkovića, 1846–1869* (Belgrade, 1939).
> Živanović, Živan, ed. *Memoari Stefana-Stevče-Mihailovića, 1813–1867* (Belgrade, 1928).

Historical material pertaining to Bosnia and Hercegovina in the second half of the nineteenth and the beginning of the twentieth centuries can be found in the works of Vladimir Ćorović and Vaso Čubrilović. The destiny of the Hapsburg South Slavs during the same period is described in works by the British historian R. W. Seton-Watson, Ferdinand Šišić, Vaso Bogdanov, and others. The collection has political writings of these prominent Croatian political personalities of the same period: Ante Starčević, Stjepan Radić, and Frano Supilo.

The socialist movement is treated in the works of Svetozar Marković, the founder of Serbian socialism, as well as in the writings of the socialist leader Dragiša Lapčević and the Marxist publicist Dimitrije Tucović. The history of the workers' movement in Croatia and Slavonia from its inception until 1922 was written by Vitomir Korać. The seven volumes of the *Istorijski arhiv komunističke partije Jugoslavije* (Belgrade, 1949–1951) contain, together with post-1918 material, valuable primary sources dealing with the beginnings of the socialist movement throughout Yugoslavia. The Hungarian Collection also has a section concerning ninteenth- and early twentiety-century workers' movements, embracing the South Slav components of the Hungarian monarchy.

The intellectual and political history of the "Yugoslav idea" is covered from within and without, in the correspondence of Bishop Strossmayer and Franjo Rački, *Politički spisi* (Zagreb, 1971); Ferdinand Šišić's *Jugoslovenska misao* (Belgrade, 1937); and Herman Wendel's *Der Kampf der Südslawen um Freiheit und Einheit* (Frankfurt am Main, 1925).

Some of the more significant books in the Yugoslav Collection dealing with this pre–World War I period are:

Djonović, Jovan. *Ustavne i političke borbe u Crnoj Gori, 1905–1910* (Belgrade, 1939).

Djordjević, Dimitrije. *Carinski rat Austro-Ugarske i Srbije, 1906–1911* (Belgrade, 1962).

Grujić, Jevrem. *Zapisi Jevrema Grujića*, 3v. (Belgrade, 1922–1923).

Lavrov, Petr A. *Aneksiiâ Bosnii i Gertsegoviny i otnoshenie k neĭ slaviânstva* (St. Petersburg, 1909).

Marjanović, Milan. *Savremena Hrvatska* (Belgrade, 1913).

Mitrinović, Čedomil, and Brašić, Miloš. *Jugoslovenske narodne skupštine i sabori* (Belgrade, 1937).

Priklmajer, Zorica. *Srpska social-demokratija u aneksionoj krizi, 1908* (Belgrade, 1953).

Prodanović, Jaša. *Ustavni razvitak i ustavne borbe u Srbiji, 1906–1911* (Belgrade, 1936).

Radev, Simeon. *Makedoniiâ i bŭlgarskoto vŭzrazhdane v XIX vek,* 3v. (Sofia, 1927–1928).

Šišić, Ferdinand. *Geschichte der Kroaten* (Zagreb, 1917).

The Hoover Institution holds complete runs of the publications of the Institut Slaviânovedeniiâ of the Soviet Academy of Sciences, which contain primary and secondary material on these years.

The relatively small amount of pre-1914 provincial parliamentary documents is most extensive for Croatia, Slovenia, and Dalmatia, including 50 volumes of *Stenografski zapisnici sabora Kraljevine Hrvatske, Slavonije i Dalmaciji* (1887–1892, 1913–1918). The shortages in provincial government documents are to some extent supplemented by the better coverage of Austrian and Hungarian parliamentary bodies (see the respective collection surveys). The Red Books of the Austrian Foreign Office are available in an unnumbered set that is virtually complete for the immediate pre—First World War period. The Red Books contain correspondence between ministers and other officers of the several dominions within the Austro-Hungarian empire.

Holdings of provincial journals and newspapers are sparse for the prewar years, but are quite numerous thereafter. For journals published in this period, the researcher should check Stanford's Green Library, especially for the publications of universities and scholarly institutes. As with government documents, the limited holdings of journals and newspapers are supplemented to an extent by holdings of Austrian, German, and Hungarian publications carrying news and articles on South Slav affairs.

## THE BALKAN WARS, WORLD WAR I, AND THE FORMATION OF THE KINGDOM OF SERBS, CROATS, AND SLOVENES

Material of Yugoslav origin on South Slav involvement in the Balkan Wars of 1912—1913 is limited. Researchers are advised to check the contents of the Romanian and Bulgarian collections for materials on this topic. The Yugoslav Collection holds the official newspaper of the Kingdom of Serbia, *Srpske novine,* for 1916 to 1919 and a nearly complete run of the Interior Ministry's *Policijski glasnik* for 1907 to 1910 and 1912. In 1914, the Carnegie Endowment published in French and English the report of its International Commission on the Balkans, and in 1922 the French Ministry of Foreign Affairs produced the three-volume *Documents diplomatiques: Les affaires balkaniques, 1912—1914.* For the First Balkan War, which terminated Turkey's rule in Europe, these are supplemented by *Prvi balkanski rat 1912—1913,* vol. 1 (Belgrade, 1959), published by the Yugoslav army's Military-Historical Institute. An early treatment is Jacob Gould Schurman's *The Balkan Wars, 1912—1913* (Princeton, N.J., 1914). The Balkan Wars are treated by many books in the collection that deal with World War I and the formation of Yugoslavia; for example, Henry Barby's *L'Epopée serbe: L'Agonie d'un peuple* (Paris, 1916).

The Hoover Library, in general, and its Yugoslav Collection, in particular, contain many books and government documents, in several languages, dealing with the causes and events leading to the outbreak of World War I. The archives has a copy of a translated manuscript (into English) written in the 1930s by a noted Serbian historian, Vladimir Ćorović, entitled "Relations between Serbia and Austria-Hungary in the XXth Century," which explores, among other topics, the problem of war responsibilities.

The collection contains two excellent sets of sources on the course of the First World War in the Yugoslav lands. The first is long runs of newspapers from

Belgrade (three), Sarajevo and Cetinje (two each), and Zagreb (one). (For titles and approximate runs, consult the newspaper list at the end of this survey.) These are supplemented by the previously mentioned newspaper *Srpske novine* and the *Reports and Bulletins of the Serbian Press Bureau in Geneva* (1915–1918). The official gazette of the Montenegrin court-in-exile, *Glas crnogorca*, holdings of which are virtually complete for 1917 to 1920, deals not only with the conduct of the war, but political developments after the war as well. Its opposition to the new Kingdom of the Serbs, Croats, and Slovenes was supported by a barrage of propaganda from Rome, of which the collection has a representative sample; for example, *Le Monténégro devant la société des nations* (Rome, 1920).

The second invaluable source for the course of the war in the Yugoslav lands are the collections of laws and decrees of the occupying forces. For Montenegrin territory under Austro-Hungarian occupation, these include:

> *Allgemeine Grundzüge für die k.u.k. Militärverwaltung in Montenegro* (Cetinje, 1916).
>
> *Kundmachungen und Verlautbarungen des k.u.k. Militär-General-Gouvernements in Montenegro in der Zeit vom 1. März bis 31. Oktober 1916* (Cetinje, 1916).
>
> *Sammlung montenegrinischer Verwaltungsgesetze in deutscher Übersetzung* (Cetinje, 1917).

Similar sources for occupied Serbia are *Bericht über die Verwaltung des Kreises Belgrad-Land in der Zeit vom 1. November 1915 bis 31. December 1916* (Belgrade, 1917) and *Verordnungsblatt der k.u.k. Militärverwaltung in Serbien* (Belgrade, 1916–1917).

Also useful are the unpublished papers of Lazar Marković, notably "Uspomene, 1914–1925" and "Nikolas Pachitch" (the latter in French), kept in the Institution's archives.

The establishment of the new state of Serbs, Croats, and Slovenes on December 1, 1918, is well covered in the collection, in English, German, French, and the Yugoslav languages. Important books on this topic include:

> Djordjević, Milan. *Srbija i Jugosloveni za vreme rata, 1914–1918* (Belgrade, 1922).
>
> Ekmečić, Milorad. *Ratni ciljevi Srbije 1914* (Belgrade, 1973).
>
> Haumant, Emile. *La Formation de la Yougoslavie* (Paris, 1930).
>
> Jovanović, Jovan M. *Stvaranje zajedničke države Srba, Hrvata i Slovenaca*, 3v. (Belgrade, 1930).
>
> Popović, Dimitrije. *Borba za narodno ujedinjenje, 1908–1914* (Belgrade, 1936).

Radović, Andrija. *Program Crnogorskog odbora za narodno ujedinjenje* (Geneva, 1917).

Šišić, Ferdinand. *Dokumenti o postanku Kraljevine Srba, Hrvata i Slovenaca, 1914–1919* (Zagreb, 1920).

U.S. Department of State. *Records Relating to Internal Affairs of Yugoslavia, 1910–1929*, 27 microfilm reels (Washington, D.C., 1973).

Wendel, Hermann. *Aus der Welt der Südslawen* (Berlin, 1926).

## PARIS PEACE CONFERENCE, 1919

The basic documents presented at the Paris Peace Conference in 1919 by the Yugoslav delegation are contained in twelve volumes: (1) general claims of the Kingdom, (2) frontiers with Italy, (3) on the territories of Goritza and Gradiška, (4) Istria, (5) the Dalmatian question, (6) Rijeka (Fiume), (7) Trieste, (8) the northern frontier, (9) Serbian-Romanian borders, (10) Serbo-Bulgarian boundaries, (11) Albania, and (12) Serbian, Croatian, and Slovenian military efforts in the world war. In addition, the William A. Drayton Collection (1913–1946) in the archives contains material regarding Serbo-Bulgarian territorial questions and demands for reparations. Drayton was an American volunteer for the Serbian army during the war and served as a member of the Serbian delegation to the Paris Peace Conference.

Materials in the following list are classified as "delegation propaganda" and constitute merely a sample of the Yugoslav output:

*Bulletin Yougoslave* (Geneva, 1918–1919). The Institution has nos. 1–3 and 5–27 of this journal.

*Le Mouvement yougo-slave en Autriche-Hongrie pendant la guerre* (Paris 1919; also English edition).

Plamenats, Yovan S. *Montenegro Before the Peace Conference*, 3v. (Paris, 1919).

*Revue Yougoslave: Direction. La Ligue des universitaires serbo-croato-slovènes*, (Paris, 1919). The Institution has nos. 3 and 4.

Vošnjak, Bogumil. *Les Origines du royaume des Serbes, Croates et Slovènes* (Paris, 1919).

Yugoslavia. Ministarstvo Finansija. *Predlog budžeta državnih prihoda i rashoda Kraljevstva Srba, Hrvata i Slovenaca za 1919–1920 godinu* (Belgrade, 1919).

Yugoslavia. Ministarstvo Inostranih Dela. *Rapport de la Commission interalliée sur les violations des conventions de la Haye et du droit international en général commises de 1915 à 1918, par les Bulgares en Serbie occupée* (Geneva, 1919).

The Yugoslav Collection has excellent holdings of secondary material, both contemporary and more recent, dealing with the myriad problems of border delineation and with the internal workings of the Yugoslav representation in Paris. In addition, the Charles Wellington Furlong Collection (1917–1963) in the archives, consisting of nine manuscript boxes, contains the reports made by Major Furlong on events in Fiume (Rijeka) and Yugoslavia, particularly Montenegro. Major Furlong was a military aide to President Wilson and later a military observer for the American Peace Mission and reported on political, economic, and psychological conditions in the Balkans, the Middle East, and North Africa.

## THE INTERWAR PERIOD

The parliamentary progress of the new Yugoslav government from the Provisional National Assembly through the Constitutent Assembly, with its basic lawmaking committee, to the National Assembly, from late 1919 to mid-1921, is covered in complete sets of stenographic records for the first two bodies. The National Assembly lasted until 1929, when it was dissolved and the constitution suspended, but the Yugoslav Collection contains the *Stenografski beleške* only through 1925. Holdings of official government documents, official gazettes, and publications are weak for the late 1920s and the 1930s. An adequate collection of secondary works compensates for this weakness and provides a context for a diverse and irregular collection of professional journals and the publications of various ministries. Best represented are the ministries of Agricultural Reform, Agriculture and Waters, Army and Navy, Education, Finance, Foreign Affairs, Naval Affairs, Post and Telegraph, Social Affairs, Trade and Industry, and Transportation.

The holdings from the Ministry of Finance, one of the best covered ministries, and the *Annual Report of the National Bank of Yugoslavia* (complete for 1914 through 1939) form an excellent basis for assessing the economic development of interwar Yugoslavia. These holdings are supplemented by the Finance Ministry's seven-volume *Zbirka devizno-valutnih propisa od 1919 do 1925 god.* (Belgrade, 1919–1925), issued by the Generalni Inspektorat, and by quarterly bulletins and other publications of the National Bank. The Yugoslav Collection contains the annuals (1929–1939) and certain other publications of the National Statistical Office, but the Stanford Library has more complete statistical holdings (consult the heading "Yugoslavia—Direkcija državne statistike" in the Stanford Library catalog).

The intense political life of interwar Yugoslavia is well covered in an excellent collection of secondary materials dealing with events from the struggle to shape a constitution to the Nazi invasion of April 1941. The surveys of political parties and developments between the wars include Charles Austin Beard's *The Balkan Pivot: Yugoslavia. A Study in Government and Administration* (New York, 1929); Ferdo Čulinović's *Jugoslavija izmedju dva rata*, 2v. (Zagreb, 1961), Branislav Gligorijević's *Demokratska stranka i politički odnosi u Kraljevini Srba, Hrvata i Slovenaca* (Belgrade, 1970), and Lazar Marković's *Jugoslovenska država i hrvatsko pitanje, 1914—1929* (Belgrade, 1935). The microfilm collection of the Hoover Institution has 27 reels of the U.S. Department of State's records relating to internal affairs of Yugoslavia, 1910—1929 (Washington, D.C., 1973).

Among the sources on the Croatian (Republican) Peasant party are the published speeches, *Vodja govori* (Zagreb, 1936), of the party leader Vladko Maček and his autobiography, *In the Struggle for Freedom* (New York, 1957), and Ljubo Boban's *Maček i politika H.S.S. 1928—1941*, 2v. (Zagreb, 1974). Josip Horvat's *Stranke kod Hrvata i njihova idelogija* (Belgrade, 1939) is an inclusive work. Also useful are Vaso Bogdanov's *Historija političkih stranaka u Hrvatskoj* (Zagreb, 1958), V. Čubrilović's *Politička prošlost Hrvata* (Belgrade, 1939), and Dinko Tomašić's *Politički razvitak Hrvata* (Zagreb, 1938).

Slovenian political life in the interwar period is covered in Anton Melik's *Slovenačka* (Belgrade, 1927), Vekoslav Bučar's *Politička istorija Slovenačke* (Belgrade, 1939) and *Spominski zbornik Slovenije* (Ljubljana, 1939), and John Arnez's *Slovenia in European Affairs: Reflections on Slovenian Political History* (New York, 1958).

On the Serbian side, Count Carlo Sforza's *Fifty Years of War and Diplomacy in the Balkans* (New York, 1940) concentrates on Nikola Pašić, prime minister of the Yugoslav kingdom (1921—1926) and leader of the dominant Serbian Radical party. Sforza was Italian envoy to Serbia and later his country's foreign minister. The most recent study of Pašić is Alex N. Dragnich's *Serbia, Nikola Pašić and Yugoslavia* (New Brunswick, N.J., 1974). For a detailed study of political parties, see Jaša Prodanović's *Istorija političkih stranaka i struja u Srbiji* (Belgrade, 1947).

The strong figure of King Alexander, assassinated in Marseilles in October 1934, is discussed in a number of works in the Yugoslav Collection including favorable works by Stephen Graham and Momčilo Vuković-Birčanin and critical volumes by Svetozar Pribićević and Louis Adamič.

For general coverage of Prince Paul's regency, Jacob Hoptner's *Yugoslavia in Crisis, 1934—1941* (New York, 1962) and Nikola Milovanović's *Od Marseljskog atentata do trojnog pakta* (Zagreb, 1963) are useful. On the premiership of Milan Stojadinović (1935—1939), see the third volume of Gilbert In der Maur's *Die Jugoslawien einst und jetzt* (Leipzig and Vienna, 1935—1938), and Stojadinović's *Ni rat ni pakt: Jugosklavija izmedju dva rata* (Buenos Aires, 1963). The period immediately following this is discussed in Ljubo Boban's *Sporazum Cvetković-Maček* (Belgrade, 1965), Maček's previously cited English-language autobiography, and in several issues of the collection, *Dokumenti o Jugoslaviji* (Paris, 1954–1958).

The archives has parts of the political papers of Dragiša Cvetković, prime minister of Yugoslavia between 1939 and 1941, covering both domestic and foreign events. There is also a manuscript by Cvetković entitled "Rat ili pakt: Unutarnja i spoljna politika namesništva," written in exile in 1965 (usage of this manuscript is restricted until July 1, 1980, and of the remaining papers until 1992).

Many library and some archival sources cover the events of March 1941, that is, Yugoslavia's adherence to the Tripartite Pact on March 25 and the coup d'etat of March 27. The previously mentioned book by Jacob Hoptner argues in favor of the Cvetković-Maček government's policy of accommodation with the Axis powers. Interpretations favorable to the coup may be found in the memoirs of Peter II, *A King's Heritage* (London, 1955) and in *Yugoslavia's Revolution of 1941* (Philadelphia, 1966) by Dragiša N. Ristić, a captain in the Yugoslav air force and an aide to the leader of the anti-Axis coup, Gen. Dušan Simović. Yugoslav communist interpretations of the March 1941 events may be found in books published in the 1950s and early 1960s by Ferdo Čulinović, Velimir Terzić, and Nikola Milovanović. The archives has the papers of Žarko Popović, Yugoslav military attaché to the Soviet Union, 1939–1941, which relate partly to the coup of March 27. (Usage of portions of these papers is restricted until November 18, 1984.) A manuscript by Dragoslav Djordjević, "Two Days in Yugoslav History, March 25 and 27," written in 1967, is also held in the archives.

Two open archival collections largely concern the interwar period. The Eliot G. Mears Collection (1920–1945) contains reports made for the U.S. Department of Commerce by Dr. Mears in his capacity as trade commissioner concerning economic and financial conditions in the postwar Balkans. The Friedrich Katz Collection (1880–1945) contains over 162 boxes of material on Croatia, the Jewish question, and world politics and economics from 1880 to 1945. A manuscript by Georges Desbons, the defense lawyer at the trial of the assassins of King Alexander I, entitled "Les Origines historiques et politiques de l'attentat de Marseilles et le procès de Aix-en-Provence," pertains to the historical and political background of the assassination.

The collection's coverage of the development of the Communist Party of Yugoslavia (CPY) is excellent, with abundant primary and secondary sources. Supplementary materials available in the Comintern and Russian collections are especially important for the early years.

The basic surveys of the Communist party for the interwar years are Ivan Avakumović's *History of the Communist Party of Yugoslavia,* (Aberdeen, 1964), Josip Broz Tito's *Borba i razvoj KPJ izmedju dva rata* (Belgrade, 1977), and *Kongresi i zemaljske konferencije KPJ, 1919–1937*, published in 1949 by the

Istoriski Arhiv KPJ. There are also surveys of regional communist parties, CPY conferences, and CPY attitudes on specific issues; for instance, Batrić Jovanović's *Komunistička partija Jugoslavije u Crnoj Gori, 1919–1941* (Belgrade, 1949), *Peta zemaljska konferencija KPJ* (October 1940), and *Zbornik radova* (Zagreb, 1972), and Kiril Miljovski's *Makedonskoto prašanje vo nacionalnata programa na KPJ, 1919–1937* (Skopje, 1962).

The collection also contains writings of individual communist leaders and party militants during the interwar period. They include two volumes of selected works of the first CPY secretary, Filip Filipović (Belgrade, 1962); studies of another party secretary, Sima Marković, *Der Kommunismus in Jugoslawien* (Hamburg, 1922); *Ustavno pitanje i radnička klasa Jugoslavije* (Belgrade, 192? microfilm); and personal recollections of a party leader, Božidar Maslarić, *Moskva Madrid Moskva* (Zagreb, 1952); as well as several volumes of reminiscences of party activists published under the title *Četrdeset godina*, beginning in 1917. Holdings include collections of documents from the early party conferences published on the thirtieth, fortieth, and fiftieth anniversaries of the founding of the CPY in 1949, 1959, and 1969, respectively.

## WORLD WAR II: OCCUPATION AND RESISTANCE

The short April 1941 war of the Axis powers against Yugoslavia, as well as the dismemberment of the country by different occupying forces, is covered by many general histories of World War II, in various languages. Two valuable and interesting volumes concerning the war are *Aprilski rat 1941: Zbornik dokumenata* (Belgrade, 1969) and *A Nation's Fight for Survival: The 1941 Revolution and War in Yugoslavia as Reported by the American Press* (n.p., 1944).

Hoover Library holdings have ample documentation concerning the establishment and functioning of the so-called Croatian Independent State, created on April 10, 1941, by the Axis powers. Some of the most important sources are:

Basta, Milan. *Agonija i slom NDH* (Belgrade, 1971).
Bzik, Mijo. *Ustaška borba* (Zagreb, 1942).
Croatia (Kingdom and Republic, 1941–1945). *Zakoni, zakonske odredbe, naredbe, itd., proglašeni od 11. travnja 1941 do 5. prosinca 1944* (Zagreb, 1945).
———. *Medjunarodni ugovori, 1941–1943* (Zagreb, 1944).
Fricke, Gert. *Kroatien 1941–1944: Der "Unabhängige Staat" in der Sicht des deutschen Bevollmachtigen Generals in Agram, Glaise v. Horstenau* (Freiburg, Switz., 1972).
Hory, Ladislaus, and Broszat, Martin. *Der kroatische Ustascha-Staat 1941–1945* (Stuttgart, 1964).

Jelić-Butić, Fikreta. *Ustaše i NDH, 1941–1945* (Zagreb, 1977).

Neue Ordnung. *Kroatien marschiert: Erste Jahreslese in Wort und Bild aus der Wochenschrift "Neue Ordnung"* (Zagreb, 1942).

———. *Kroatien baut auf: Zweite Jahreslese in Wort und Bild aus der Wochenschrift "Neue Ordnung"* (Zagreb, 1943).

Pavelić, Ante. *Die kroatische Frage* (Berlin, 1941).

Simić, Sava. *Prekrštavanje Srba za vreme Drugog svetskog rata* (Titograd, 1958).

Sinovčić, Marko. *NDH u svetlu dokumenata* (Buenos Aires, 1950).

The occupation of Serbia, the functioning of the German-appointed administration under General Milan Nedić, and the activities of Serbian collaborationists are well documented in the collection. Stanislav Krakov's *General Milan Nedić,* 2v. (Munich, 1963–1968) is the most significant pro-Nedić biography, while Jovan P. Trišić offers a critical view of the Serbian "Pétain" in his *O Milanu Nediću* (Windsor, Ontario, 1960). Boško N. Kostić's *Za istoriju naših dana* (Lille, 1949) remains a major source for the study of Nedić's government. Followers of Dimitrije Ljotić, the leader of the Serbian proto-fascist movement Zbor, published a compendium entitled *Dimitrije Ljotić u revoluciji i ratu* (Munich, 1961). The archives has a folder containing letters from Trivun Jeftić, a Serb proponent of national socialism, to Adolf Hitler and Milan Nedić.

The Hoover collection on the London-based Yugoslav government-in-exile, especially the documentation on the two resistance movements led by Gen. Draža Mihailovich and Josip Broz Tito and the subsequent civil war between them, is particularly rich. The collection possesses the London government's official gazette, *Službene novine Kraljevine Jugoslavije,* in a set that is complete for August 19, 1941 to August 25, 1943. It holds an information bulletin, *Jugoslovenski glasnik* (Cairo, 1941–1942 [incomplete]), as well as *Yugoslav News Bulletin* and *Obaveštenja štampi* from Yugoslav information centers in New York and London. The library has books written after the war in Yugoslavia or abroad by former members of the government-in-exile or political figures who spent the war years in London (for example, Branko Čubrilović, Većeslav Vilder), and the archives is the repository for the papers of Milan Gavrilović, ambassador to the Soviet Union, 1940–1941, and member of the Yugoslav government-in-exile (this collection is closed until 1995).

The Mihailovich resistance movement, usually called the Chetniks, which was the main civil-war enemy of the CPY-led Partisans, is well represented by many publications in Serbo-Croatian, English, German, French, and Italian, which have appeared either in Yugoslavia or abroad. Yugoslav publications usually reflect the official view of Tito's regime—that General Mihailovich was a traitor and a collaborator with the enemy—although in recent years Yugoslav historiography is less categorical on this subject, with authors recognizing in the movement, especially in the earliest phases of the occupation, a pro-Western, resistance character. Library holdings on Mihailovich include:

Aćin-Kosta, Miloš. *Draža Mihailović i Ravna Gora*, 4v. (Zurich, 1976–1977).

Avakumović, Ivan. *Mihailović prema nemačkim dokumentima* (London, 1949).

*General Mihailovich: The World Verdict* (Gloucester, Eng. 1947). A collection of articles on the first resistance leader in Europe published in the world press.

Karchmar, L. "Draža Mihailović and the Rise of the Četnik Movement, 1941–1942" (Ph.D. dissertation in history, Stanford University, 1973).

Knežević, Radoje L., ed. *Knjiga o Draži*, 2v. (Windsor, Ontario, 1956).

Martin, David. *Ally Betrayed: The Uncensored Story of Tito and Mihailovich* (New York, 1946).

Milazzo, Matteo, J. *The Chetnik Movement and the Yugoslav Resistance* (Baltimore, 1975).

*Patriot or Traitor: The Case of General Mihailovich. Proceedings and Report of the Commission of Inquiry of the Committee for a Free Trial for Draja Mihailovich* (New York, May 1946). Reprinted with an introductory essay by David Martin (Stanford, 1978).

Roberts, Walter R. *Tito, Mihailović and the Allies, 1941–1945* (New Brunswick, N.J., 1973).

*Spomenica: Tridesetogodišnjica smrti Vožda Trećeg Srpskog Ustanka Draže Mihailovića* (Chicago, 1976).

Tomasevich, Jozo. *The Chetniks* (Stanford, 1975).

*The Trial of Dragoljub-Draža Mihailović: Stenographic Records and Documents* (Belgrade, 1946). This is an English translation of the original published in Serbo-Croatian in Belgrade in 1946.

Vukčević, Radoje. *Na strašnom sudu* (Chicago, 1968).

Yourichitich, Evguéniyé. *Le Procès Tito-Mihailovich* (Paris, 1950).

Živanović, Sergije. *Treći srpski ustanak*, 3v. (Chicago, 1962).

The archives contains valuable material on the Mihailovich movement. The papers of Mladen Žujović, former Belgrade attorney and a close adviser to General Mihailovich, and of Konstantin Fotitch, Yugoslav ambassador to the United States (1935–1944), contain a wealth of information. (Access to Žujović's papers requires written permission from his widow; usage of Fotitch's papers is restricted until 1989.) An open collection of Yugoslav materials, donated to the Institution by David Martin, includes reproductions of British war documents concerning Yugoslavia and many taped interviews with the U.S. and

British officers who spent some time during the war as members of various Allied military and intelligence missions with General Mihailovich and his units in occupied Yugoslavia. The archives contains one manuscript box of intelligence reports on the Chetnik movement from the Office of Strategic Services prepared during the war. Finally, the archives has an unpublished manuscript by Col. Robert H. McDowell, devoted largely to his war experiences in Yugoslavia as head of an American mission to General Mihailovich, as well as related intelligence documents on war events in Yugoslavia.

The CPY-led resistance movement, the Partisans, also called the "people's liberation struggle," is thoroughly documented in the Hoover Library holdings. The most massive collection covering all aspects of the Partisan struggle is *Zbornik dokumenata i podataka o narodnooslobodilačkom ratu jugoslovenskih naroda*. It was prepared by the Institute of Military History in Belgrade, starting in 1949, and is divided into thirteen tomes, each consisting of many separate books, totaling 144 volumes (as registered in the library's catalog). This collection covers Partisan military operations during the war in all parts of Yugoslavia, reproduces bulletins and documents both of the supreme Partisan headquarters and of the CPY's Central Committee, and includes selected German and Italian official documents. The collection is particularly valuable for its integration of military and political developments, although many documents are reproduced only in part.

Besides the Institute of Military History, two other institutes (for contemporary history and for social sciences) have, over the years, produced series of publications, in the form either of individual monographs or of symposia of specialized articles covering different aspects, domestic and foreign, of the Partisans' struggle and of the civil war under occupation. Other general works on the same subject are:

> Brajović, Peter, ed. *Oslobodilački rat naroda Jugoslavije, 1941–1945*, 4v. (Belgrade, 1965–1972).
>
> Cubelić, Tomo, and Milostić, Milovan. *Pregled historije narodnooslobodilačkog rata i revolucije naroda Jugoslavije* (Zagreb, 1959).
>
> Dedijer, Vladimir. *Dnevnik*, 3v. (Belgrade, 1945, 1946, and 1950).
>
> *Hronologija oslobodilačke borbe naroda Jugoslavije, 1941–1945* (Belgrade, 1964).
>
> Marjanović, Jovan. *Narodnooslobodilački rat i socijalistička revolucija, 1941–1945* (Belgrade, 1975).
>
> Terzić, Velimir, ed. *Oslobodilački rat naroda Jugoslavije, 1941–1945*, 2v. (Belgrade, 1957–1958).

The Yugoslav Collection contains a large number of memoirs and reminiscences of Partisan leaders, as well as monographs and volumes of documents dealing with Partisan warfare in different regions of the country or with the underground activities in the cities. In addition, there are books written by British and American officers who spent time during the war in Partisan headquarters or with the Partisan units; for example, Davidson, Basil. *Partisan Picture* (Bedford, 1946); Deakin, F. W. D. *The Embattled Mountain* (London, 1971); Maclean, Fitzroy. *Eastern Approaches* (London, 1949); and Huot, Louis. *Guns for Tito* (New York, 1945). Monographs by Yugoslav writers on Partisan relations with the major Allied powers include Moše Pijade's *About the Legend That the Yugoslav Uprising Owed Its Existence to Soviet Assistance* (London, 1950) and Dušan Plenča's *Medjunarodni odnosi Jugoslavije u toku Drugog svetskog rata* (Belgrade, 1962). In addition, volumes of essays and documents, especially British, discuss Allied war policies towards Yugoslavia; for example, Auty, Phyllis, and Clogg, Richard, eds. *British Policy Towards Wartime Resistance in Yugoslavia and Greece* (London, 1975).

The strictly political arm of the Partisan struggle, the so-called Antifascist Council of People's Liberation of Yugoslavia (Antifašističko Veće Narodnog Oslobodjenja Jugoslavije; AVNOJ), established on November 26, 1942, and transformed a year later into a supreme legislative and executive organ of the new "people's power," is well represented in the library's holdings. Basic works on AVNOJ are Leon Geršković's *Historija narodne vlasti* (Belgrade, 1955) and Vojislav Simović's *AVNOJ: Pravno-politička studija* (Belgrade, 1958). Essential official interpretation of the organization, purposes, and workings of AVNOJ may be found in Tito's political report to the CPY's Fifth Congress in 1948, as well as in reports to the same congress by such top party leaders as Edvard Kardelj, Aleksandar Ranković, and Milovan Djilas.

At its third session in August 1945, AVNOJ was renamed the Provisional People's Assembly (Privremena Narodna Skupština), which quickly dissolved itself after laying the constitutional groundwork for the national government that came into being in 1946. The proceedings of the provisional assembly are represented by:

> *Treće zasedanje Antifašističkog veća narodnog oslobodjenja Jugoslavije i zasedanje Privremene Narodne Skupštine 7—26 august, 1945: Stenografske beleške* (Belgrade, 1945).
>
> *Zakonodavni rad Pretsedništva Antifašističkog veća narodnog oslobodjenja Jugoslavije i Pretsedništva Privremene Narodne Skupštine DFJ, 19 nov. 1944—27 okt. 1945, po stenografskim beleškama i drugim izvorima* (Belgrade, 1951).
>
> *Rad zakonodavnih odbora Pretsedništva Antifašističkog veća narodnog oslobodjenja Jugoslavije i Privremene Narodne Skupštine DFJ 3 apr.—25 okt. 1945. Po stenografskim beleškama i drugim izvorima* (Belgrade, 1952).

## SOCIALIST YUGOSLAVIA

A substantial part of the Yugoslav Collection consists of primary and secondary sources covering events, developments, and the emergence of new institutions following the coming to power of the Communists at the end of World War II. Hundreds of books and thousands of articles, in all languages, have been written on "Tito's Yugoslavia," and the essential ones can be found in the collection. This section covers some general works on post-1945 Yugoslavia, as well as sources on the Communist Party of Yugoslavia (after 1952 officially called the League of Communists of Yugoslavia; LCY), the constitutional, governmental, and administrative structure of the country, its political life, and "social self-management"—the hallmark of Titoism after 1950.

Although the coverage of the following books is occasionally wider in scope, they offer a general picture of Yugoslavia under communist rule:

> Božić, Ivan, et al. *Istorija Jugoslavije* (Belgrade, 1973).
> Hoffman, George W., and Neal, F. W. *Yugoslavia and the New Communism* (New York, 1962).
> Institut za Savremenu Istoriju. *Istorija XX veka*, 13v. (Belgrade, 1959–1975).
> McVicker, Charles P. *Titoism, Pattern for International Communism* (New York, 1957).
> Pavlowitch, Stevan K. *Yugoslavia* (New York, 1971).
> Shoup, Paul. *Communism and the Yugoslav National Question* (New York, 1968).
> Valev, L. B. et al., eds. *Istoriiā Iugoslavii* (Moscow, 1963).
> Vucinich, Wayne, ed. *Contemporary Yugoslavia* (Berkeley, 1968).
> Zalar, Charles. *Yugoslav Communism* (Washington, D.C., 1961).

An archival collection particularly important for the study of Yugoslav political life before the outbreak of the war, during the occupation, and in the immediate postwar period is that containing the writings of Dr. Dragoljub Jovanović, university professor, agrarian expert, and leader of the left-wing People's Peasant party. The archives has a copy of his typewritten memoirs entitled "Političke uspomene" (volumes 1 and 2 cover the period between 1940 and 1945) and a printed pamphlet "Šta nas košta svadja sa Hrvatima?" Tapes of interviews with Jovanović in 1975 and 1976 by Prof. Alex Dragnich are also kept in the archives. Dr. Jovanović published, before his death in Belgrade in 1976, two volumes of political portraits entitled *Ljudi ljudi* (Belgrade, 1973–1975), which are held in the library.

In addition to the sources mentioned in the interwar section of this survey, literature on the CPY in general is abundant and can be divided into (1) party histories, surveys, and chronologies; (2) minutes of CPY congresses, conferences, and other meetings; (3) biographies and autobiographies, memoirs, and collected or selected works (articles, speeches, etc.) by party leaders.

The most comprehensive party history is the collection edited by Rodoljub Čolaković, *Pregled istorije Saveza Komunista Jugoslavije* (Belgrade, 1963). It has, however, been criticized in detail by other experts on party history (see the publication of the Zagreb Institute for the History of the Workers' Movement, *Putovi revolucije*, 1964, nos. 3–4). The Institute for the Study of Workers' Movement in Belgrade has published over the years a series of symposia under the title *Istorija radničkog pokreta*, which includes studies and essays on specific aspects and problems of CPY history. Similar material is published in the series *Tokovi revolucije: Zbornik istoriskih radova*, 13v. (Belgrade, 1967–1975). A more recent and shorter party history is Maraca, Pero, et al., eds. *Istorija Saveza komunista Jugoslavije, Kratak pregled* (Belgrade, 1976). See also M. Sentić, S. Sigetlija, and M. Potočki's *Kronologija SKJ, 1919–1969* (Zagreb, 1970). A detailed study of the role of the Communist party in Serbia (and elsewhere) during the war is Venceslav Glisić's *Komunistička partija Jugoslavije u Srbiji, 1941–1945*, 2v. (Belgrade, 1974–1975). Consult the library's catalog for other historical works on CPY/LCY in Yugoslavia in general and in its constituent republics and regions.

The library has the stenographic minutes of all CPY/LCY congresses from the fifth (1948) to the eleventh (1978) and for many republican party congresses and conferences and meetings of the Central Committee. The collection includes books on individual party congresses (for example, Marjanović, Jovan. *O šestom kongresu KPJ* [Belgrade, 1952]) and a large number of pamphlets reproducing reports by the party leaders to individual congresses.

Of the party leaders, books by Tito and on Tito are by far the most numerous. There are, to begin with, his collected works, *Govori i članci* (Zagreb, 1959–). The Hoover catalog lists 21 volumes of these speeches and articles, the latest published in 1972. Obviously more volumes will be added. Four volumes of the military works of Tito, *Vojna djela*, were published in Belgrade between 1961 and 1972. Large numbers of Tito's reports, addresses, essays, and lectures have been printed both in Serbo-Croatian and in other languages. Consult the library catalog for a complete list of holdings.

Biographical works on Tito include:

Armstrong, Hamilton F. *Tito and Goliath* (New York, 1951).
Auty, Phyllis. *Tito, a Biography* (London, 1970).
Begović, Vlajko. *Tito, biografske beleške* (Belgrade, 1972).
Clissold, Stephen. *Whirlwind: An Account of Marshal Tito's Rise to Power* (London, 1949).
Damjanović, Pero. *Tito pred temama istorije* (Belgrade, 1972).

Dedijer, Vladimir. *Tito* (New York, 1952).

―――. *Josip Broz Tito, prilozi za biografiju* (Belgrade, 1972).

Halperin, Ernst. *The Triumphant Heretic* (London, 1958).

Maclean, Fitzroy. *The Heretic: The Life and Times of Josip Broz-Tito* (New York, 1957).

Staubinger, Zvonko. *Tito gradjanin sveta* (Beograd, 1974).

Vinterhalter, Vinko. *Zivotnom stazom Josipa Broza* (Belgrade, 1968).

The collection also holds pictorial albums and compilations of foreign press articles on Tito, as well as pamphlets on different aspects of his life, policies, and travels, both in Serbo-Croatian and in foreign languages.

Other major CPY-LCY leaders whose writings are represented in the collection are:

Kardelj, Edvard. *Problemi naše socijalističke izgradnje*, 9v. (Belgrade, 1960 – 1974).

―――. *Socialism and War, a Survey of Chinese Criticism of the Policy of Coexistence* (London, 1961).

―――. *Pravci razvoja političkog sistema socijalističkog samoupravljanja* (Belgrade, 1977).

Kidrič, Boris. *Sabrana dela*, 4v. (Belgrade, 1960).

Pijade, Moše. *Izabrani spisi*, 2v. (Belgrade, 1964 – 1965).

Čolaković, Rodoljub. *Izabrani govori i članci,* 2v. (Sarajevo, 1960).

―――. *Zapisi iz oslobodilačkog rata*, 3v. (Zagreb, 1961).

―――. *Kazivanje o jednom pokoljenju*, 2v. (Sarajevo, 1968).

Vukmanović, Svetozar. *Revolucija koja teče*, 2v. (Belgrade, 1971).

Ziherl, Boris. *Članci i rasprave* (Belgrade, 1948).

The collection has the writings of former party leader Milovan Djilas while he was in power (for example, *Članci 1941 – 1946* [Belgrade, 1947]), as well as those which were published abroad after his downfall:

*The New Class: An Analysis of the Communist System* (New York, 1957).

*Anatomy of a Moral* (New York, 1959).

*Conversations with Stalin* (New York, 1962).

*The Unperfect Society* (New York, 1969).

*Land Without Justice*, 3v. (New York, 1958).

*Memoir of a Revolutionary* (New York, 1973).

*Wartime* (New York, 1977).

Besides the books already mentioned, the library has the autobiography of Vladimir Dedijer, *The Beloved Land* (London, 1962), and a very rare book by

Cyrus Sulzberger, *The Resistentialists* (New York, 1962), which has a long chapter on Dedijer.

Hoover holdings on the constitutions and governmental and administrative structure of Yugoslavia are extensive. For a complete listing, consult the library catalog under the relevant headings. The collection contains texts of all postwar Yugoslav constitutions (1946, 1963, 1974), constitutional laws (that is, the unofficial constitution of 1953), and the constitutional amendments of 1967, 1968, and 1971. The Institution possesses stenographic records (*Stenografske beleške*) for all post-1945 parliamentary bodies, beginning with the Constituent Assembly and followed first by the conventional federal bicameral assembly system and continuing with the present system of delegation. Deputies to the chambers of commons, provinces, republics, and the two chambers of the Federal Assembly are presently elected not by direct popular vote but by sociopolitical organizations. The Hoover collection has the official gazettes (*Službeni list*) of Yugoslavia since 1945, of Croatia, Montenegro, and Bosnia-Hercegovina since 1968, and of Slovenia and Macedonia since 1969. There are scattered documentary and stenographic records of the legislatures of the six republics of Yugoslavia and of Vojvodina and Kosovo, the two autonomous regions within Serbia. Under "Laws, statutes, etc.," the library catalog lists holdings in the fields of economic planning, judicial, financial, criminal, press, educational, family, housing, civil, agricultural, military, and commercial (domestic and foreign) laws and regulations. In addition, the catalog lists periodical publications concerning legislative, administrative, communal, municipal, militia, social security, economic, banking, commercial, trade union, educational, cultural, public health, artisan, and railway bodies and institutions. The official bulletins of individual government departments are an additional source of documentation. Typically, they contain rules, regulations, orders, instructions, ordinances, and proceedings of meetings. Hoover holdings of these publications are generally spotty until 1967, but much more complete thereafter. Works by experts on constitutional and administrative law (for example, Edvard Kardelj, Jovan Djordjević, Leo Geršković) complete the collection in these fields.

The evolution of political life in post-1945 Yugoslavia is reflected in the previously mentioned publications of the CPY/LCY leaders, congresses, and various research institutes. To this should be added the reports of the American Universities Field Staff (stored in the Green Library), Radio Free Europe research reports, and the publications of the Institute of Political Studies in Belgrade. The following books are particularly useful for studying the establishment of Tito's Yugoslavia and the early postwar phase of Yugoslav politics:

Čulinović, Ferdo. *Stvaranje nove jugoslavenske države* (Zagreb, 1959).
Dragnich, Alex N. *Tito's Promised Land, Yugoslavia* (New Brunswick, N.J., 1954).

Korbel, Joseph. *Tito's Communism* (Denver, 1951).

Tudjman, Franjo. *Stvaranje socijalističke Jugoslavije* (Zagreb, 1960)

For later phases of political development, see:

Bakarić, Vladimir. *Aktuelni problemi sadašnje etape revolucije* (Zagreb, 1967).

Dolanc, Stane, et al. *Ideological and Political Offensive of the League of Communists of Yugoslavia* (Belgrade, 1972).

Johnson, A. Ross. *The Transformation of Yugoslav Ideology, 1945–1953* (Cambridge, Mass., 1972).

*SKJ u uslovima samoupravljanja* (Belgrade, 1969).

A particularly penetrating and useful survey of recent characteristics of Yugoslavia's political life is *The Yugoslavs* (New York, 1978) by Duško Doder, an American correspondent of Yugoslav origin. Also useful are K. Robert Furtak's *Jugoslawien, Politik-Gesellschaft-Wirtschaft* (Hamburg, 1975) and Carl Gustaf Strohm's *Ohne Tito, kann Jugoslawien überleben?* (Cologne, 1976). The surveys of Yugoslav developments contained in the *Yearbook on International Communist Affairs* (Stanford: Hoover Institution, 1966–) are a useful research tool.

The Yugoslav Collection has ample documentation in various languages on the CPY conflict with the Cominform (1948–1955). A nearly complete run of the official organ of the Information Bureau of Communist and Workers' Parties, *For a Lasting Peace, for a People's Democracy* (1947–1956), published first in Belgrade and then in Bucharest, may be found in the Romanian newspapers collection. Some of the most useful books and documents on the origins and the different aspects of the conflict are:

Adamic, Louis. *The Eagle and the Roots* (New York, 1952).

Bass, Robert H., and Marbury, Elizabeth, eds. *The Soviet-Yugoslav Controversy, 1948–1958: A Documentary Record* (New York, 1959).

Dedijer, Vladimir. *The Battle Stalin Lost* (New York, 1959).

Gribanov, B. *Banda Tito: Orudie amerikano-angliĭskih podzhigateleĭ voĭny* (Moscow, 1951).

Radonjić, Radovan. *Sukob KPJ s Kominformom, 1943–1950* (Zagreb, 1975).

Sofokli, Lazri, and Javer, Malo. *Dans les prisons et les camps de concentration de la Yougoslavie* (Tirana, 1960). A very rare pamphlet.

Ulam, Adam. *Titoism and the Cominform* (Cambridge, Mass., 1952).

Yugoslavia. Ministry of Foreign Affairs. *White Book on Aggressive Activities by the Governments of the USSR, Poland, Czechoslovakia,*

*Hungary, Rumania, Bulgaria, and Albania Towards Yugoslavia* (Belgrade, 1951).

The Hoover collection has significant documentation concerning opposition currents of different orientations and at various times within Tito's Yugoslavia. The phenomenon of Croatian nationalism (real or alleged) is well covered in many publications, both from within Yugoslavia and from abroad. Many of these cover the cases of the CPY Central Committee member Andrija Hebrang during and after the war (for example, Milatović, Mile. *Slučaj Andrije Hebranga* [Belgrade, 1952]) and the purge of the Croatian party leadership in December 1971 (Ciliga, Ante. *Crise d'état dans la Yougoslavie de Tito* [Paris, 1972]; and Omrčanin, Ivo. *Croatian Spring* [Philadelphia, 1976]). The purge of the Serbian "liberal" party leaders in 1972 and its background is well documented in the book by Dragan Marković and Savo Kržavac. *Liberalizam od Djilasa do danas*, 2v. (Belgrade, 1978). The student rebellion at the University of Belgrade in June 1968, which had ramifications at universities throughout the country, is thoroughly documented in a special, sizable, and very rare issue of the journal *Praxis: Jun-Lipanj 1968, Dokumenti* (Zagreb, 1969). The library has books, in Serbo-Croatian and English, of the most important Marxist critics of Tito's regime, all of whom are members of the editorial or the advisory boards of the review *Praxis*: Mihailo Marković, Gajo Petrović, Svetozar Stojanović, Rudi Supek, Ljubo Tadić, and Predrag Vranicki. In the same context, see Mihailo Marković and Robert S. Cohen's *Yugoslavia: The Rise and the Fall of Socialist Humanism: A History of the Praxis Group* (Nottingham, Eng., 1975) and Gerson S. Sher's *Praxis: Marxist Criticism and Dissent in Socialist Yugoslavia* (Bloomington, Ind., 1977). At the other end of the political spectrum, the archives has a typewritten copy of an unpublished document entitled "Program i statut Komunističke partije Jugoslavije," issued in 1976 by the illegal, anti-Titoist group called the Cominformists.

Another large section of the Yugoslav Collection is devoted to documentation of the Yugoslav economy, more specifically to the system of workers' self-management and its subsequent evolution and modifications. Besides a wealth of books (some of which are listed below), the library has many official documents issued by the Federal Assembly, the Federal Institute of Statistics, the Federal Planning Institute, and the Organization for Economic Cooperation and Development in Paris. Different specialized institutes, such as Institut za Društvena Istraživanja (Zagreb), Institut Društvenih Nauka, Institut za Političke Studije, and Institut Ekonomskih Nauka (all in Belgrade) publish studies and monographs on the Yugoslav economy, social change, and self-managing socialism, many of which are in the Hoover Library. Articles in the following periodicals, to which the Institution subscribes, are indispensable for study of the Yugoslav socio-economic system: *Gledišta* (Belgrade), *Naše teme* (Zagreb), *Politička misao*

(Zagreb), *Problems of Communism* (Washington, D.C.), *Review of International Affairs* (Belgrade), *Slavic Review* (Columbus, Ohio), *Socijalizam* (Belgrade), *Yugoslav Life* (Belgrade), *Yugoslav Survey* (Belgrade [in Stanford's Green Library]), and *Yugoslav Trade Unions* (Belgrade). A list of economic reviews is given at the end of this survey.

Since the Yugoslav economic system has been reformed several times, especially in 1950 and 1965, the following books are especially useful for their descriptions and analyses of the system itself and of changes in it:

Bićanić, Rudolf. *Economic Policy in Socialist Yugoslavia* (Cambridge, Mass., 1973).

Bilandžić, Dušan. *Management of the Yugoslav Economy, 1945–1966* (Belgrade, 1967).

Bombelles, Joseph T. *Economic Development in Communist Yugoslavia* (Stanford, 1968).

Bošković, B., et al. *Privredni sistem SFRJ* (Belgrade, 1973).

Čobeljić, Nikola. *Privreda Jugoslavije (rast, struktura i funkcionisanje),* 2v. (Belgrade, 1974).

Džeba, K., and Beslać, M. *Privredna reforma: Šta i zašto se mijenja* (Zagreb, 1965).

Hamilton, F. E. I. *Yugoslavia: Patterns of Economic Activity* (London, 1968).

Horvat, Branko. *An Essay on Yugoslav Society* (White Plains, N.Y., 1969).

———. *Privredni sistem i ekonomska politika Jugoslavije* (Belgrade, 1969).

———. *The Yugoslav Economic System* (White Plains, N.Y., 1976).

Jelić, Borivoj. *Sistem planiranja u jugoslovenskoj privredi* (Belgrade, 1962).

Meier, Victor. *Das neue Jugoslawische Wirtschaftssystem* (Zurich, 1968).

Milenkovitch, Deborah D. *Plan and Market in Yugoslav Economic Thought* (New Haven, Conn., 1971 [in Stanford's Green Library]).

Pejovich, Svetozar. *The Market-Planned Economy of Yugoslavia* (Minneapolis, 1966).

Šefer, Berislav. *Ekonomski razvoj Jugoslavije i privredna reforma* (Belgrade, 1969).

The fundamental principles of what is usually called "the Yugoslav way to socialism" are enunciated in *The Program of the LCY* (New York, 1958), and the most comprehensive book in English tracing the evolution of the system is Dennison Rusinow's *The Yugoslav Experiment, 1948–1974* (Berkeley, 1977). For the text of the Law on Associated Labor, adopted in November 1976 and considered the second most important state document after the constitution, see *Zakon o udruženom radu* (Belgrade, 1976). Other useful books on the theory and practice of self-management are:

Aćimović, J. *Bibliografija o radničkom samoupravljanju* (Belgrade, 1968).

Bilandžić, Dušan. *Borba za samoupravni socijalizam u Jugoslaviji, 1945– 1969* (Zagreb, 1969).

———. *Ideje i praksa društvenog razvoja Jugoslavije, 1945–1973* (Belgrade, 1973).

Brockmeyer, M. J., ed. *Yugoslav Workers' Self-Management* (Dordrecht, Netherlands, 1970).

Djordjević, Jovan, et al., eds. *Teorija i praksa samoupravljanja u Jugoslaviji* (Belgrade, 1972).

Gorupić, Drago, and Paj, Ivan. *Workers' Self-Management in Yugoslav Undertakings* (Zagreb, 1970).

Hamel, H., ed. *Arbeiter Selbstverwaltung in Jugoslawien* (Munich, 1974).

Meister, Albert. *Socialisme et autogestion: L'Expérience yougoslave* (Paris, 1964).

Sirotković, J. *Planiranje u sistemu samoupravljanja* (Zagreb, 1966).

Šuvar, Stipe. *Samoupravljanje i druge alternative* (Zagreb, 1972).

Zukin, Sharon. *Beyond Marx and Tito: Theory and Practice in Yugoslav Socialism* (New York, 1975).

Two U.S. government publications are indispensable for researchers who cannot use Yugoslav materials in their original languages. The Foreign Broadcast Information Service (FBIS) in its section on Eastern Europe offers daily translations of current news and commentary monitored from Yugoslav broadcasts, news agency transmissions, newspapers, and periodicals. The Joint Publications Research Service (JPRS) publishes translations dealing with political, sociological, and military affairs. The Hoover catalog should be consulted regarding the availability of these sources.

## EMIGRATION

Another group of materials that gives the scholar a different perspective on Yugoslav affairs is the varied collection of émigré publications and newspapers that represent permanent or temporary settlements of Yugoslav peoples around the world from the late nineteenth century to the present. The collection includes over a dozen newspapers with runs of several years and scattered issues of dozens more. In addition, the holdings include collections of pamphlets and infrequent bulletins and statements from émigé organizations and societies of Yugoslavs abroad. The collection is particularly rich in material representing the Serbs and Croats in North America, and the catalog lists no fewer than 22 publications from Yugoslav societies, many now defunct, in the United States.

Political writers and historians from the post-1945 Yugoslav emigration, or more precisely from its Serbian and Croatian components, are well represented in the Hoover Library holdings, which also include a number of émigré periodicals published both in the United States and abroad. Serbian authors, with books and pamphlets in both the native and Western languages (mainly English), include Slobodan M. Drašković, Borivoje Karapandžić, Lazo Kostić, Branko Lazić, Kosta St. Pavlović, and Živko Topalović. Works by émigré Croatians include those of Ante Ciliga, Ilija Jukić, Ivan Meštrović, Vinko Nikolić, Bogdan Radica, and Stanko Vujica. Two émigré publishing houses, Srpska Misao (Melbourne, Australia) and Hrvatska Revija (Munich) have published a large number of books, in Serbian and Croatian respectively, many of which can be found at the Hoover Library.

There are also (more on the Croatian than on the Serbian side) volumes of essays sharply critical of the Tito regime, and in the Croatian case resolutely in favor of Croatian independence; for example, Bonifačić, Ante. *The Croatian Nation in Its Struggle for Freedom and Independence: A Symposium by Seventeen Croatian Writers* (Chicago, 1955); and *Hrvatska danas i sutra: Simpozij hrvatskih intelektualaca u Evropi, kolovoz-rujan 1968* (Munich, 1969).

Holdings of émigré periodicals include, on the Serbian side, continuous and long runs of *Beli orao* (Munich); *Glasnik srpskog istorisko-kulturnog društva "Njegoš"* (Chicago); and *Naša reč, organ saveza "Oslobodjenje"* (Harrow, Eng.); and on the Croatian side, *Hrvatska revija* (Munich); *Na pragu sutrašnjice* (Rome); *Nova Hrvatska* (London); and *Review of the Study Centre for Yugoslav Affairs* (London).

## SERIALS

As mentioned at the beginning of this survey, the Yugoslav Collection contains hundreds of serials (periodicals; newspapers; annuals in the form of reports, yearbooks, etc.; journals, proceedings, memoirs, and transactions of societies; and numbered monographic series) published in Yugoslavia and abroad. Besides the catalog of the Hoover Library, researchers are advised to consult the microfiche containing all serial titles at the Stanford and University of California at Berkeley libraries.

The following is necessarily a highly selective (but representative) list of serials (essentially periodicals and newspapers) to be found in the Yugoslav Collection. The list is divided into two parts: those published before and those published after 1945. The dates indicated are the years of first and last issues held; missing issues are not indicated.

*Belgrader Nachrichten* (Belgrade, 1915–1918)
*Bilten: Jugoslovenski antimarksistički komitet* (Belgrade, 1937–1939)
*Bosnischer Post: Organ für Politik und Wirtschaft* (Sarajevo, 1916–1918)
*Branič: Organ advokatske komore u Beogradu* (Belgrade, 1925–1929)
*Cetinjer Zeitung* (Cetinje, 1916–1918)
*Deutscher Volksblatt* (Novi Sad, 1937–1939)
*Echo de Belgrade* (Belgrade, 1939–1941)
*Ilustrovani list* (Zagreb, 1914–1916)
*Jugoslovenski Američki glasnik* (San Francisco, 1937–1945)
*Jugoslovenski glasnik: Organ of the Yugoslav Government-in-Exile* (Cairo, 1941–1942)
*Narodno blagostanje* (Belgrade, 1929–1939)
*Neue Ordnung: Kroatische Wochenschrift* (Zagreb, 1943–1945)
*Nova Evropa* (Zagreb, 1920–1940)
*Obzor* (Zagreb, 1917–1919)
*Radničke novine:: Organ srpske socijalne demokratije* (Belgrade, 1903, 1905, 1913–1915)
*Slovenski jug* (Odessa, 1917)
*South Slav Herald* (Belgrade, 1932–1936)
*Srpski književni glasnik* (Belgrade, 1920–1939)
*Spremnost: Misao i volja ustaške Hrvatske* (Zagreb, 1942–1945); microfilm

Post-1945 Yugoslav serials include many periodicals and newspapers that have been discontinued or have ceased to appear. The following were being received at the time of writing of this survey.

CURRENT NEWSPAPERS (DAILIES AND WEEKLIES):

*Borba* (Belgrade)
*Delo* (Ljubljana)
*Književne novine* (Belgrade)
*Komunist* (Belgrade)
*Narodna armija* (Belgrade)
*Oslobodjenje* (Sarajevo)
*Politika* (Belgrade)
*Student* (Belgrade)
*Studentski list* (Zagreb)
*Tribuna* (Ljubljana)
*Vjesnik* (Zagreb)

CURRENT PERIODICALS (WEEKLIES, MONTHLIES, AND QUARTERLIES):

*Anali pravnog fakulteta* (Belgrade, 1967−)
*Arhiv za pravne i društvene nauke* (Belgrade, 1945−)
*Bibliografija Jugoslavije* (Belgrade, 1950−)
*Borec* (Ljubljana, 1968−)
*Časopis za suvremenu povijest* (Zagreb, 1970−)
*Ekonomist* (Zagreb, 1948−)
*Ekonomska misao* (Belgrade, 1968−)
*Ekonomska politika* (Belgrade, 1952−)
*Ekonomska revija* (Ljubljana, 1952−)
*Ekonomski anali* (Belgrade, 1955−1958, 1967−)
*Ekonomski pregled* (Zagreb, 1967−)
*Finansije* (Belgrade, 1948−)
*Front* (Belgrade, 1977−)
*Glas koncila* (Zagreb, 1975−)
*Glasnik: Službeni list srpske pravoslavne patrijaršije* (Belgrade, 1958−)
*Glasnik vrhovnog islamskog starješinstva u SFRJ* (Sarajevo, 1970−)
*Gledišta* (Belgrade, 1960−)
*Ideja: Jugoslavenski studentski časopis* (Belgrade; 1970−)
*Jež* (Belgrade, 1973−)
*Jugoslovenska revija za medjunarodno pravo* (Belgrade, 1954−)
*Jugoslovenski istorijski časopis* (Belgrade, 1967−)
*Komuna* (Belgrade, 1960−)
*Medjunarodna politika* (Belgrade, 1968−)
*Medjunarodni problemi* (Belgrade, 1967−)
*Medjunarodni radnički pokret* (Belgrade, 1967−)
*Medjunarodni ugovori i drugi sporazumi* (Belgrade, 1972−)
*Mladost* (Belgrade, 1975−)
*Naše Teme* (Zagreb, 1967−)
*Nedeljne ilustrovane novine (NIN)* (Belgrade, 1970−)
*Politička misao* (Zagreb, 1967−)
*Pravoslavlje: Novine srpske patrijaršije* (Belgrade, 1967−)
*Pregled* (Sarajevo, 1960−)
*Privreda i pravo* (Zagreb, 1968−)
*Radni odnosi i samoupravljanje* (Belgrade, 1973−)
*Samoupravno pravo* (Belgrade, 1975−)
*Socijalizam: Organ Centralnog komiteta Saveza komunista jugoslavije*
    (Belgrade, 1960−)
*Vesnik: Organ Glavnog saveza udruženog pravoslavnog sveštenstva SFR*
    (Belgrade, 1953−)
*Vojnoistoriski glasnik* (Belgrade, 1967−)